D1605997

People Are No Damn Good

A Pastor's Struggle with Ethics and Morality

Jimmy R. Watson

RESOURCE *Publications* · Eugene, Oregon

PEOPLE ARE NO DAMN GOOD
A Pastor's Struggle with Ethics and Morality

Resource Publications
An Imprint of Wipf and Stock Publishers
199 W. 8th Ave., Suite 3
Eugene, OR 97401

www.wipfandstock.com

PAPERBACK ISBN: 978-1-6667-3715-8
HARDCOVER ISBN: 978-1-6667-9628-5
EBOOK ISBN: 978-1-6667-9629-2

APRIL 4, 2022 11:45 AM

I dedicate this book to:
Our dog, Leto, who growls at me when he senses who I really am
My wife, Annie, who calls me the "ethical pastor" in an unironic way
My mom, Pat, who, without much to work with on my end, did her best to raise me

Contents

Preface

I RECOMMEND that you begin reading this book here in the "pre-face," which is the act of reading (or any other activity) before shaving or applying makeup to one's face.[1] At the same time, I recommend proper caffeination levels in your body before you rummage through the pages of this book.

This book had been forming in my head and heart for many years, ever since I was a student of Christian Ethics in the early to mid-1990s. At the time, I had no idea where my educational odyssey would lead me. I had already begun as a pastor in the United Church of Christ, so that was a likely vocation. My fallback option was moving back home to my one-horse hometown to run my folks' grocery business, although that would have felt like a waste of my education.[2] I could also pursue teaching in an institution of higher learning, but those doors always seemed to shut fast and hard enough to use the word "slam." Option number one became my fate.

My foray into ethics began in a Southern Baptist context, at least in terms of the names of the institutions of higher learning in whose hallways I lurked back in the mid-1980s to mid-1990s. I loved studying Christian Ethics. I was introduced to such things as biblical ethics, wisdom literature, ethical norms, descriptive versus prescriptive norms, the relationship between religion and morality, the differences between Catholic and Protestant ethics, a focus on anthropology, human nature, sin, and how various theological categories connected with ethics, theism,

---

1. This is meant to be a gender-neutral comment because let's *face* it, some women shave, and some men wear makeup. This "struggle" to use the most inoffensive language possible while writing a book that is primarily a non-academically oriented introduction to ethics book, is noted in the title.

2. Is an education ever truly "wasted"? I think not.

God's judgment and grace, virtues, the connection between love and social justice, and a host of ethical issues that Christians love to discuss and debate, such as sexuality, birth and end of life issues, race, gender, economics, ecology, politics, war and peace, etc.

In 1996 I finished my dissertation titled, *The Emerging Concept of Just Peace Theory*, which was a summary of the previous decade and a half of literature on war and peace studies from a so-called Christian perspective. Before that I wrote papers about school choice, animal sacrificial systems, the nuclear arms race, Greenpeace, the power of government, enemies, democracy, the U.S. response to Haitian boat people, character ethics, truth-telling for terminally ill patients, ordination of homosexuals, abortion, cloning, and gun control, all from "a" Christian perspective, which basically means that the Bible was used as a secondary source for my papers. I could throw in a Bible verse here and there.[3]

Although the subject matter of this book corresponds to my graduate degree in ethics, I waited until now to put pen to paper. Like a banana, I wanted my experiences and knowledge to be ripe enough to be palatable for most people. I didn't want to write while I was still green, and I didn't want to wait until my mind turned to mush. So, there you go. That is the reason for my timing.

There is also something to be said for timing in terms of the fact that as the years have gone by, I have become more pessimistic about the goodness of humanity. Like the apple, or whatever was the featured fruit in the Garden of Eden story, I wake up most mornings, turn on the news, and conclude that there is more than a barrel full of rotten apples out there spoiling our human experience. I yearn for the day when my fellow Americans and beyond will convince me that we are redeemable. For now, all I can say is, "Change my mind." While writing this book, I had three goals in mind:

1. To be informative in a way that is accessible to an average reader. After all, I am an average writer with slightly above average knowledge of the discipline of ethics. I envision folks picking up this book, reading the words (because pictures are not available), and saying to themselves something like, "Whoa! I never knew that!"

2. To be humorous, and by humorous, I mean snarky because that's about the only way I know to be humorous. Not everyone will like

3. Interestingly (perhaps ironically), the Bible could not be used as a primary source, even in those Baptist institutions.

or appreciate my humor. And that's okay. When the movie comes out, the main character will be a comedian with impeccable timing and the ability to translate lame humor into an Oscar nomination.

3. To be personal because one day I will only be alive through what I might leave behind, such as my sermons, books like this one, my R.E.M. and Sinclair Lewis collections, and my Facebook page. Narcissistically, I want my offspring's descendants to name their rocket cars after me. And there will be many descendants because my family breeds early and often.

Other than that, I sincerely want all of you to become the best damn people you can be, to be the kind of person your dog thinks you are. If you have cats, just wing it.

Introduction

The Long View

I N 1996 I was promised the moon. I answered the landline phone that hung above the kitchen counter in the parsonage of a little country church in Eastern Missouri near the mighty Mississippi. I heard a man's deep voice with a pronounced drawl, more southern than West Texan. The voice said, "Are you Rev. Jimmy Watson?" "Yes," I answered, "To whom am I speaking?"[4] He told me his name and then proceeded to spell out the reason for his call. He was the chairperson of a pulpit search committee at a relatively new United Church of Christ congregation in Northeast Texas. They were in a hyper search mode for a new pastor.

Their newly retired pastor, Bill, was an acquaintance of mine. I had gotten to know Bill before I came to Missouri two years earlier as I was serving two congregations outside of Waco, Texas.[5] Apparently, the search committee was stuck, and because they were not in the hunt for an interim pastor, they were beginning to panic. I was told later that they were looking for a pastor from Texas, primarily because they were not exactly a progressive UCC congregation.[6] They wanted someone they could relate to, and the assumption in Texas is that folks that do not hale from "these parts" are like foreigners from another country. I am generalizing, of course, and yet I have known Texans who are reluctant to cross the Red River to the north, much less the Rio Grande to the south, for

4. I would not have said that. I would have said something like, "Yep, who's this?"

5. Pronounced "wacko" if one is referring to infamous events in Waco's history, including the Branch Davidian saga.

6. I am a fifth-generation Texan, yet much to their consternation as they got to know me better, I am more progressive than they bargained for.

fear that something might rub off on them that would eradicate their Lone Star State bona fides.

Bill got wind of the search committee's struggles and sent his wife to the next meeting with a slip of paper bearing my name and contact information. Hence, the phone call I received. I told the deep voice that I would think about his proposal to fly down there to speak with the committee. I do not remember the exact time of year it was, and yet it must have been either winter or not long afterwards, because I am almost certain that the promise of warmer weather factored into my decision. I had never shoveled snow before my time spent in Missouri and was not exactly enthusiastic about the next round of inclement weather. More money and being closer to Baylor University, from where I was still pursuing my PhD in Christian ethics, were also considered.

As a West Texan I had always considered East Texas to be an impos- ter—after all, most movies that feature "Texas scenes" are set in the west- ern part of the state (or New Mexico or Arizona).[7] Nevertheless, I took the bait. My family and I soon said our goodbyes to the Mississippi River folks and headed for the people of the pine woods in Longview, Texas.

My time in Longview was about as big a flop as one could envision for a young pastor who should have been eyeing a promising career in the pulpit. I was not expecting such abject failure. My first few years in ministry near Waco, followed by a brief stint in Missouri, were met with moderate enthusiasm from my congregations. Other than a minor hiccup in Missouri when my family's new puppy decided to spend his evenings chewing up the plastic flowers in the cemetery next to the church, most people enjoyed my preaching and efforts at ministry. I had no reason to think that a congregation back in my home state would be any different. In fact, I assumed things would get better because I was still on a learning curve. What I did not anticipate, however, was that following a long-term beloved pastor who sat in front of the pulpit on Sunday mornings, minis- tering to a white congregation in an area where memories of the Civil War are apparently still fresh, and the loss of that war not yet scabbed over, would create a cancerous ripple effect that led me to become what my colleagues labeled "an unintentional interim." I heard later that the next fellow that followed me lasted only one year. I lasted almost two.

My tenure in Longview was not a total bust, however. I did learn two things. First, I learned that when things start going badly do not get

---

7. Most recently, "Hell or High Water," starring Jeff Bridges, is set in West Texas, but the movie was filmed almost exclusively in Eastern New Mexico.

defensive. I had a tendency in those days to take criticism personally, possibly because I was not used to criticism. It was meted out sparingly in my young adulthood and first few years in ministry. In Longview, however, oftentimes the criticism was personal. At some point an effective pastor needs to grow thick skin and learn the art of a "non-anxious presence." There is a real benefit to learning how to let torrents of water roll off your back.

The second thing I learned in my Longview experience is something my (former) friend, Bill, repeated to me on several occasions when we would chat in his garage. Bill enjoyed giving me the insight scoop on some of his former parishioners to help me handle the above-mentioned criticism. His favorite line is something I have repeated on numerous occasions: "Jimmy, you know what the problem with the church is? Its full of people. And you know what the problem is with people? *They're no damn good.*" Ironically, the one place where this was most true, from my perspective, was the place where I learned this truth.[8]

As a pastor this was my wake-up call about human nature. Not that I could not learn about human nature just from following Socrates' admonition to examine my own life. There are enough examples of human shortcomings and sin in my autobiography that I really did not need to hear an experienced clergyman tell me about the no-damn-goodness of my species. And yet, this was the moment in my journey when I began asking the question in earnest that was at the core of all that book learning about ethics I had been receiving in school: *Exactly how bad are we?* For a multitude of reasons that will become apparent throughout this book, I believe I am uniquely qualified to answer that question.

Goat Roper Ethics

Many moons ago I met a girlfriend's grandfather for the first time. After eyeing me for only a few minutes, he referred to me as a "goat roper," i.e., a wannabe cowboy. I had heard that moniker before, having grown up in a small ranching community in West Texas. However, no one had ever used that label to describe *me*. In fact, I was probably the least goat roper-like young man in my nineteen-member high school graduating class of 1978. Most of the other non-Hispanic white boys in my class either lived on a ranch outside of town or, if they lived in town, willingly

8. Or, as the youngsters like to say, "This is *my* truth."

participated in agricultural institutions and activities such as FFA or rodeos. Almost all of them wore cowboy boots, oval-shaped belt buckles that looked extraordinarily uncomfortable (especially if one had to bend over), and cowboy hats. Most of them listened to country music, drove largish pickup trucks, and dipped snuff. I did none of that.

My folks owned and operated the town grocery store, meat market and all. Because there is always a certain amount of violent retribution against those who inhabit an alternative lifestyle or worldview, on occasion I would try to fit in by engaging in the cowboy subculture. One afternoon during my senior year I decided to see (or taste) what all the "snuff fuss" was about so I lifted a can of Copenhagen from behind the cash register and coolly walked out of my parents' store. I drove about a block, pulled over, opened the can, and put a pinch between my cheek and gum. I then drove away. Or tried to. For a moment I felt like I had crossed a cultural threshold and almost—almost—felt a *pinch* of pride. The feeling lasted about one block until I became so dizzy and nauseous that I had to pull over and engage in a minor act of heaving and hurling. My cowboy days were over for good.

For the sake of transparency, I confess that I now own a big old black Ford F-150 truck and a pair of boots that, from my experience, are *not* made for walking. The pickup comes in handy for hauling things around, which is almost certainly the best answer to the age-old question: What separates the human species from all other animal species. Think about it: You never see skunks and squirrels carry mattresses and scrap metal from one place to another in a pickup truck.

So, yes, I am decidedly one of the least likely West Texans to deserve the goat roper tag. And yet, if I may use the phrase "goat roper" as an analogy for another component of my life story, there is some validity to the notion that I was, or am, a *goat roper ethicist*. Although I have a PhD in ethics from an accredited university—something my family easily tires of hearing about while discussing such topics as guns, gays, and God—I am largely an ethicist wannabe or poser. I say this not because I sadistically enjoy the art of self-degradation, although I do. I say this for one simple reason: I am a pastor, not an academician. I say this with absolutely no shame or remorse because I thoroughly enjoy being a pastor. It affords me the opportunity to engage other human beings on a level above and below the student-teacher relationship: "above" in the sense that there is a spiritual component to our relationship, and "below" in the sense that I get to witness firsthand many of the foibles and frailties that accompany the human condition.

As I look back on my career one truth stands out above all others: As a pastor, I have learned more about the practical side of ethics and morality than I could have ever learned in the hallways of academia.[9] I do not mean that in the sense of accumulated knowledge, of course. For God's sake, I am not anti-intellectual! If I had traveled the path of an academician, I would without question have a greater knowledge of my chosen field of study. Certainly, I have read my fair share of books on the subject over the years—post-graduation—and yet my reading interests have broadened to the point that I cannot claim, with a straight face, that I am a professional ethicist. At best I am a generalist, not only about ethics, but about any number of topics related to my career as a pastor and as just a human being with varied interests. In fact, these days I do not read many books about religion or ethics. Instead, I have decided to spend the final chapters of my life and career (pardon the pun) reading whatever the hell interests me. Life is too short to waste it on being an expert on any one subject.

As a pastor it would have been impractical for me to spend all my time reading about ethics, and yet, at the same time, I have been fortunate enough to have a front row seat in the drama of human life that has unfurled in front of me. I have seen first-hand the practical side of ethical dilemmas as I continue to witness the struggles of my parishioners in their quest to do the right thing. It is not always easy. Nor do they always come to me for advice. As a pastor in small congregations, however, if I do not hear about their struggles directly, I learn about them indirectly through gossip, confidential remarks, or old-fashioned observation. If we were honest and transparent, every congregation should carry the words "Peyton Place" in the title of their church because, yes, people are no damn good.

The Original Sin

On occasion the dramas and struggles are so real I feel like God has transported me to the Garden of Eden with a handwritten note, which

9. I often use the terms "ethics" and "morality" synonymously, however, I also like to distinguish "ethics," the study of the issues, from "morality," the behavior of human beings in relation to the issues.

says, "Don't eat from the fruit of the tree of knowledge of good and evil." Wouldn't it be interesting to see what God's handwriting looks like? Seriously, I have never understood why God would want to keep the first folks in a state of ignorant bliss. Was bliss the original goal? If so, that did not last long.

Of course, I do not believe the Adam and Eve story is a literal-historical account of the first human beings. I concur with the scientific theory of evolution that suggests the first humans were just one or two hairs short of a chimp-like species. Nevertheless, the Garden of Eden myth does imply a provocative question. Were we meant to differ from the rest of the animals in terms of a developed conscience and a working knowledge of right and wrong, or good and evil? Ironically, why does the writer of Genesis suggest that the first sin was the act of becoming aware of sin? Thinking about this makes my head hurt.

True story: Back in the early 2000s I taught a few classes at Howard College in Big Spring, Texas. This Junior College caters to young West Texas women and men who often have no idea what they want to do with their lives. Most of them come from conservative rural homes. If they are religious, they are typically evangelical if not fundamentalist. I had a great time beginning each semester teaching Intro to Ethics telling the students that they were about to commit "the original sin." After soaking in the bewildered looks on their faces, I would tell the stunned students that they were about to follow in the footsteps of the parents of humanity and eat from the tree of knowledge of good and evil. I could tell from their reactions that many of these students began to worry about the eternal fate of their souls. More than one student questioned out loud in class, or to me privately, whether they should continue in the class. Fortunately, I never lost a student for this reason, and yet I suspect that more than a few of my students made darn sure they did not learn too much.[10]

My favorite experience teaching Intro to Ethics, however, did not occur on the campus of Howard College. Instead, it occurred several times at the local prisons through a Howard College program. Yes, I taught Intro to Ethics to *prison inmates*. I taught in the Federal prison and a privately-owned prison in Big Spring, as well as a Texas state prison in nearby Snyder, Texas. These classes were offered for college credit through Howard College. The federal prison was the swankiest, but it was still prison. No amount of swankiness could nullify the reality of the

10. I have the grades as evidence.

loss of one's freedom. The state prison was more akin to a $39 motel room on a rural highway. The privately-owned prison was relatively nice (and new) and full of brown people who had crossed the Texas border without proper paperwork. There was always a slight possibility of a lockdown, which meant that I could not get out until the lockdown was over. The most interesting, and harrowing, thing about walking into a prison is that you stroll past a sign that says something like "there are no hostage negotiations beyond this point." Nevertheless, after a few trips inside each of these prisons I began to feel comfortable about the prospect of spending the evening watching my back and listening to inmates explain how they were framed.[11]

After a couple of semesters teaching college courses in the prison system, the local newspaper decided to run a story about my experiences. The headline read (unironically, I think), "Ethics Behind Bars." One class that stands out in my memory was a class that consisted primarily of those who had committed "white collar" crimes. The lecture and discussion on "Business Ethics" proved to be especially exciting for a goat roping small church pastor from West Texas whose parents owned and operated a "mom and pop" grocery business.[12] My time spent in that prison classroom was about as eye-opening as eating an unspecified fruit from an unspecified tree in an ancient mythical garden.

Evilology

Why am I writing this book? Well, aside from my earlier training in ethics, as a pastor and teacher I feel I have garnered invaluable insight into the human ethical struggle. I have studied ethics from the underbelly. I am constantly trying to understand why people—including myself—come to certain perspectives about some of the most important issues of our day and why we do some of the things that we do. By the way, as proud as I am for working hard to earn a PhD in Ethics, I have concluded that a pastor with a PhD is sort of like a mechanic with a degree in automotive history. It is a little overkill. Nevertheless, it is just what I needed to get over the

---

11. According to many of the inmates I talked to, they were convicted for *conspiring* to commit a crime rather than committing the actual crime. In their minds, they did not do anything wrong (yet), so they should not have been convicted. I obviously agreed with them because, well, I like being alive.

12. When I tell folks that I grew up in a "mom and pop" grocery story, I need to clarify that it was *my* mom and pop.

hump and offer my own tiny contribution to the ongoing human struggle of discernment between good and evil.[13]

Because of my education and occupation, I consider myself to be an amateur "evilologist"—someone who analyzes evil. As a self-proclaimed evilologist it is my task to explain the presence of human evil in the world. The answers come from such luminaries as theologians, philosophers, social scientists, and crotchety old men (and women) that occupy the "wisdom tables" at the local Dairy Queen on Monday mornings, and yet the reason why human beings are no damn good remains a mystery. What is perhaps even more mysterious is the question of why people are *good* rather than evil, however, I do not have the credentials to be a "goodologist." I think we can all agree that as a species we are bad to the bone. The world needs us to fight against our evil tendencies and try to be a force for good. This is the ultimate human task: to prove to God and to one another that we are slightly better than no damn good.

Perhaps the only question I can answer with any certainty is the question, "*When* did we become aware of evil?" When did we as a species develop a conscience or moral compass? I think the answer to that question is obvious. The awareness of evil occurred one hot summer day when an unnamed caveman was sweating profusely in his fur coat and feeling the pangs of hunger due to an unsuccessful hunting and gathering excursion the day before. A cavewoman walked by and grunted at him using hand gestures signifying he was a loser. Because he had never been trained to control his violent impulses, he picked up a club and knocked her upside the head. It was at that very moment, as he heard the screams and saw the blood gushing from her ears, that a strange emotion that would later be identified by his talking descendants as "guilt" surged through his body. For the first time in his life, he felt bad. From that pivotal day forward, we have been trying to understand why we do such rotten things.[14]

My Longview, Texas experience gave me a foundation, a starting point, for, well, *the long view*. Coincidentally, just as I was learning first-hand about the underbelly of human nature in my new role as a pastor, I

---

13. Like Solomon, I could have just asked for this gift of discernment, but that would have been too easy.

14. Presumably, the person doing the clubbing could have been a cave*woman*, yet I surmise that when a cavewoman hit a caveman with a club, he likely deserved it and thus guilt would never have entered the psychological makeup of these early humans.

was writing my dissertation on war and peace.[15] I have come to realize that life has a funny way of preparing one for future assignments without one's awareness. All my experiences, from growing up in a rural West Texas community, to working at my mom and pop's "mom and pop" store, to "finding Jesus" in an evangelical context, to receiving an education with an emphasis on Christian ethics, to becoming a minister in a progressive denomination and pastoring for over thirty years, to landing in Ferguson, Missouri, where the Black Lives Matter movement took off in earnest[16] has helped me to find clarity in my quest to discover the extent of the goodness or badness of human nature. This book is a result of that quest. It is a personal, humorous, and informative attempt to ascertain just how no damn good we really are and how we might get gooder.[17]

15. As I was writing my dissertation on war and peace (titled, *An Emerging Concept of Just Peace Theory*), a television commercial featuring a student writing his dissertation on war and peace was on the air. It wasn't me.

16. Yes, *that* Ferguson.

17. Like "evilologist" and "goodologist," "gooder" is not a word; but let's be honest: The English language is as fluid as the Mighty Mississippi, and I aim to take advantage of that.

1

Exorcisms to Ethics

A RE we no damn good? From Cain's pre-historic murder of Abel to the attempted insurrection of the U.S. Capital on January 6, 2021, the evidence is overwhelming. We obviously suck as a species. We could be and do better.[1] To those who, in response to January 6, like to say, "This is not who we are," I suggest this is exactly who we are. The proof is in the pudding, and the fact that pudding is, and always will be, associated with Bill Cosby, further drives home the thesis of this book.

Ground Zero

Some folks will read this book and suggest that my general approach to the art of manuscript organization is best described as a "scattershot approach." As a youngster, I fired a few shotguns in my day. I once downed two turkeys with one pull of the trigger because—let's be frank—with a shotgun you just need to aim in the general direction.[2] A scattershot approach in book writing suggests that one's topic is "broad but random and haphazard in its range." I have organized my chapters, however, into valid, and sporadically at least, decipherable, categories. In this chapter I will attempt to answer, with some clarity the question: *Are* we no damn good?

1. We can even "Be Best" as one of our philosophers once said.
2. The reader will discover that I am not exactly what the pundits call "pro-gun," mainly because guns are dangerous in the hands of bad guys who are posing as good guys.

If nothing else, our experiences tell us that people are no damn good. Do you remember where you were when you heard the news that the World Trade Center and the Pentagon had been attacked and another plane crashed in rural Pennsylvania on September 11, 2001? I happened to catch the news at home when the first plane flew into the building. At that moment, most of us thought it was some sort of weird accident—mechanical or human failure on the part of the pilots. I hurriedly rushed to my office. Shortly after I arrived and turned on the television at work, we saw the second plane crash into the World Trade Center. The rest of the day, if not the rest of the year, was a blur. In some ways we have been trying to rebuild our national lives from the rubble of "Ground Zero" ever since.[3]

If that day taught us anything at all, it is that evil exists in this world. But how and why? Some people like to explain evil in mystical or spiritual terms, even going so far as to personify evil in a character known as Satan or the devil. Others prefer to talk about the "Fall" of humanity, original sin, and the corruption of human nature. Still others prefer to talk about evil solely in natural terms—we are nothing more than advanced animals and therefore we are inherently violent.[4] Whatever your favorite explanation for the presence of evil in the world is, the bottom line is that it is real. It exists. Evil, and its sidekick, suffering, dominate the news around the world every day.

Human experience also informs us that there are two kinds of evil in the world. There is *natural* evil, which includes things like hurricanes, pandemics, and accidents, and there is *moral* evil, which is what people do to one another, to other creatures, and to the environment. Both kinds of evil cause suffering. The difference between natural and moral evil is the absence of motive in the former and the presence of motive in the latter. Unless we want to make the asinine argument that a personal God is responsible for natural evil, motivated by retribution or a divine mean streak, then natural evil *just is*. There is no *intention* behind the act. We therefore do not need to spend much time on the causes of natural evil.

---

3. "Ground Zero" of 9/11 is, in many ways, a contemporary manifestation of the Garden of Eden myth. It is where this generation "lost its innocence."

4. Maybe what we think is "advanced" is really that part of us that will inevitably lead to the destruction of all creation. If I were not so inebriated right now that would be a sobering thought.

Moral evil, on the other hand, often occurs because someone *intends* to do harm to someone or something else. This is the kind of evil that I will be observing, with the keen eye of an evilologist, in this book.

Evil is ever-present. It is not going away any time soon. Every day is an ethical Ground Zero. Every day we are forced to go back to square one, or the forbidden fruit, and wonder why. In this chapter I will make the argument that yes, we are no damn good, which is a very simple argument to make.

There is no One Who Does Good

Perhaps the loudest voices in our tradition that tried to tell us how evil, sinful, and bad we really are, are the prophets of the Hebrew scriptures. The prophet Jeremiah is a good example for us to consider. Jeremiah knew a thing or two about evil and suffering. His book was written in the context of violence (a particularly nasty form of evil) and suffering. It is the sixth century BCE and Babylon has invaded the nation of Judah and its capital city Jerusalem. If I did not know any better, I would think Jeremiah was foreshadowing the events of September 11, 2001.[5] He was not, of course, and yet his words sound much like a description of 9/11.

In the fourth chapter of his book, beginning in verse 11, Jeremiah channels his inner-God-voice and writes, "At that time it will be said to this people and to Jerusalem: A hot wind comes from me out of the bare heights in the *desert* toward my . . . people." (Note that the people who attacked us on 9/11 were people from the desert in the Middle East.) From Jeremiah's perspective, God was using the Babylonians to punish the Israelites. The Israelites are called "foolish," "stupid children" and "skilled in doing evil." And then it gets very interesting. Listen to the angry voice of Jeremiah's God with a little inappropriate commentary:[6]

> I looked on the earth, and lo, it was waste and void (like Ground Zero in New York City); and to the heavens, and they had no light. I looked on the mountains, and lo, they were quaking, and all the hills moved to and fro (think of the mountains and hills as metaphors for the Twin Towers). I looked, and lo, there was no one at all, and all the birds of the air had fled (think of people

5. I do not really know any better but let us pretend I do.

6. The following is inappropriate because I use the time-dishonored method of "eisegesis," which is the process of incorporating one's own agenda into an interpretation of the text.

jumping to their deaths from the fiery buildings). I looked, and lo, the fruitful land was a desert, and all its cities were laid in ruins (no explanation needed) . . . For thus says the Lord: The whole land shall be a desolation . . . Because of this the earth shall mourn, and the heavens above grow black (think of the black smoke from the burning towers and the Pentagon).[7]

That is sort of eerie, is it not? Jeremiah is not predicting 9/11, of course, yet the lessons of the past continue as lessons of the present: evil is real, there are people who want to harm us, and most importantly we need to be aware of how our own decisions and actions can lead to hatred and violence—evil and suffering—in the world.

Jeremiah's theological view that God was punishing the Israelites through the Babylonians may seem archaic to us, and yet it is interesting that he was willing to assign at least some of the blame for the Babylonian invasion to the Israelites themselves. If we as a nation are wise, we will look at how our own policies can foment violence in a world that is always on a short fuse.

Evil is real, yet complicated. Psalm 14 does not mince words by claiming that there is a wide swath of "evildoers": "There is no one who does good . . . they have all gone astray, they are all alike perverse; there is no one who does good, no, not one" (vss. 1–3).[8] That is a harsh view of humanity, and yet we can only imagine what the psalmist was living through as he or she wrote those words.

The Exorcist

There are folks that are so "no damn good" that they think they might be *possessed*.[9] When family and friends came to see us for the first time in St. Louis, my wife and I liked to take them on the neighborhood tour, which consists of the home Mickey Carrol of *The Wizard of Oz* munchkin fame lived in until his passing a few years ago, and the home where an event occurred in 1949 that inspired the 1973 movie *The Exorcist*.[10] The latter house is directly two blocks behind our home. We often walk past it and

7. Jeremiah 11:23–28a.

8. I knew a lady once who did no wrong. Her name was Ann Beckemeyer. You can look it up.

9. If you have a weak stomach, please do not read this section.

10. Spoiler alert: the movie is not very accurate, and yet green pea vomit and Linda Blair's head twisting 360 degrees is totally worth it.

take selfies, hoping that the current occupants do not get perturbed with passersby acting foolish.[11]

I do not mean to make light of such a potentially serious subject as exorcisms, but I cannot help myself. I have even been thinking about getting an exorcism for myself because I have a little mischievous side in me, which I assume is the result of supernatural foul play. There is no other plausible explanation. Before I make my final decision, however, I have a couple of questions to ask: First, are exorcisms covered by my insurance company? Second, if I do not pay my exorcist, will I get repossessed? These are questions I need to have answered before I call the Vatican. I am teasing, of course. I do not really need an exorcism, although I do wonder: Would a person who needs an exorcism be aware of their need for an exorcism, or would the demonic spirits operate in such a subtle way that one is totally oblivious to the level of evil that inhabits an unsuspecting person?[12]

In case you are so religiously illiterate you could not provide the question for the lowly $100 answer in the category of religion on *Jeopardy*, an exorcism is the act of expelling an evil spirit (or spirits) from a person. I do not for one minute believe that exorcisms are real. However, *if* exorcisms happen to be real supernatural events, another question I need answering is, "Where do the evil or unclean spirits go?" May we assume they either go back to where they came from, jump into the nearest person (such as an unfortunate priest), or inhabit a herd of pigs that disturbs them so much they run down a slope headfirst into a lake below?[13]

Are exorcisms a real thing? There are at least three possible answers to that question. First, exorcisms are real, and yet they seem to occur primarily in Roman Catholic or Pentecostal settings in Third World countries. Does the fact that most exorcisms are reported among poor and uneducated folks discredit the reality of demon possession and exorcisms? Probably.

---

11. Every time I walk or ride my bike past this house, I am reminded of the time I went to see *The Exorcist* in the theater with my cousin and roommate. My roommate thought it was a good idea to have a few tokes before entering the theater. About halfway through the movie he began to hyperventilate so we took him outside, stuffed him in the car, and went back inside. We were not going to miss the movie on his account.

12. Sort of like being unaware of an open fly or visible booger.

13. Mark 5:1–20.

The second possible answer is that exorcisms did occur in the past *but not any longer*. This is called the "cessationist" view. Cessationists believe that miracles, including exorcisms, used to happen in biblical times, but no longer happen. Proponents of this view argue that this explains why we read about miracles in the Bible and yet no longer see or experience such miracles today. This view is a little too convenient for my tastes. In fact, let's just call it what it is: BS!

The third possible answer is that exorcisms are not real things and that the stories we hear about, both ancient and modern, are about *psychological trauma* rather than spiritual events. In other words, a "possessed" person is probably a mentally ill person. I think we need to seriously consider this as the correct answer.

Nevertheless, there are folks out there who claim to perform actual exorcisms. One of my favorites is the Vatican-trained exorcist, Father Vincent Lampert, a priest in the archdiocese of Indianapolis, one of fifty such trained Catholic exorcists in the United States. He says it helps to have a sense of humor when one is staring down evil.[14] For example, when he gives talks about exorcisms, he introduces his assistant, Mary, by telling his audience, "She's my exorcistant." He also claims that he never does an exorcism in a scary place, like an abandoned house or a dead-end street at midnight. And finally, he says that after a particularly difficult exorcism he likes to stop by the local Dairy Queen for a chocolate shake.[15]

From Exorcist to Ethicist

All kidding aside, there is real evil in the world, although I am just not sure it can be expelled from a person's body with a little holy water and anointing with oil. But we do encounter evil—real evil—in this world. It is a cliché to say that all you need to do to encounter evil is turn on the news. Certainly, the news constantly draws our attention to the weaknesses, shortcomings, sinful nature, and downright depravity of humanity in all its ugly forms. And yet sometimes it seems to go deeper than that, to a place that can only be described as pure evil.

The story of David and Louise Turpin, the California couple who kept their thirteen children hidden from the public, chained them to their

---

14. A sense of humor is a good idea. Getting the hell out of Dodge is an even better idea.

15. https://en.wikipedia.org/wiki/Vincent_Lampert.

bedposts and malnourished them, is a case in point.[16] If that is not evil, I do not know what is. I am sure some folks are saying that the Turpin's are possessed by unclean spirits. Ironically, they are religious extremists, and my guess is that they have undergone psychological testing to see what made them do that to their own children. I am convinced there is something other than a vulgar speaking, green pea soup puking demon making them abuse their children like that.

You and I will encounter evil from time to time in our lives, although maybe not to the extent we saw in the Turpin's. When we do, what do we do? As a pastor, I often approach this "What do we do?" question either directly or indirectly, if not subtly. Some of the stories from the Bible highlight how evil was encountered, at least according to the imaginations of the biblical writers. A good example is Jesus' encounter with a man in the synagogue in Capernaum recorded in Mark 1:21–28. Evil is not always apparent, and yet in this case it was (or at least that is implied in the story). The Gospel writer tells us that one day Jesus is teaching in the synagogue. His audience is in awe because there is something special about the way he taught. In the audience that day is a man who does not exactly appreciate what Jesus is saying. Mark says he has an unclean spirit, that is, he is possessed. He gets in Jesus' face and screams at him, "What have you to do with us, Jesus of Nazareth? Have you come to destroy us? I know who you are, the Holy One of God."

I can relate to Jesus here, minus the "Holy One of God" claim. Years ago, when I was a pastor in Terre Haute, Indiana, I would occasionally do guest lectures or serve on debate panels at Indiana State University. The topics were always about controversial and important ethical issues. One day I was lecturing about human sexuality, talking specifically about gay marriage (long before it became the law of the land), when a student stood up from her desk and started "preaching" at me. Interspersed with her Bible quotes she was yelling and cursing at me and continued to do so as she walked out of the room. She obviously had not yet accepted the spirit of detached, unemotional classroom discussions in the context of higher education. But she did seem to have another spirit. If I had been an exorcist rather than an ethicist, I might have done something different that day.[17]

---

16. https://en.wikipedia.org/wiki/Turpin_case.

17. No, I would not have used a caveman's club.

Similarly, in Mark's story, as the man with an unclean spirit is standing in front of Jesus and screaming at him, Jesus' response is clear and simple: "Be silent, and come out of him!" Sounds easy enough, does it not? Apparently, in Mark's memory or imagination, it works. The unclean spirit leaves the man.

Jesus' tactic probably would not work for us when we encounter what we suspect might be some manifestation of evil. And yet it is not his tactic that instructs us. None of us are ever going to get into the exorcism business. What instructs us is the fact that he did not ignore the man in the first place, which is our natural response. We do not like to confront evil. If we do, we do not have as much compassion and understanding as Jesus did. Instead, we like to fight fire with fire. We like to meet force with more force. We assume the evil in front of us is our enemy and so we treat it as such, if we pay any attention to it in the first place.

And yet we can learn two things from Jesus' encounter with this man with an unclean spirit. First, so long as we are not in physical danger, we should not ignore those who seem to have evil intentions. We should pay attention to them, even focus on them. Second, we should do so with compassion. We should acknowledge that the evil we see in a person likely has roots elsewhere. We are told that it takes a village to raise a child. It also takes a village to raise a villain. We are not just no damn good as individuals; we are no damn good *as a people*.

The Powers That Be

As we think about the source of evil in the world and the motivations behind it, we do not need a supernatural explanation. There are enough "earthly" culprits to keep us busy in our attempts to exterminate our no-damn-goodness like roaches in a dirty kitchen. Furthermore, we will never understand the depths of our problems until we inch away from an individualistic to a collective approach, that is, a "village" or social approach. This is simply a matter of enlarging our screen, our viewpoint, perhaps moving from "portrait" to "landscape" in our efforts to see the "wider picture."

On March 20, 1925, in London's Westminster Abbey, Frederick Lewis Donaldson delivered a sermon about the "seven social sins." His list includes wealth without work, pleasure without conscience, knowledge without character, commerce without morality, science without humanity, worship without sacrifice, and politics without principle. For any of these categories to be truly harmful, he suggests, there needs to be a social or systemic manifestation rather than just an individual manifestation. And there is. From a specifically Christian ethical perspective, scripture, tradition, reason, and Christian experience, i.e., the Wesleyan Quadrilateral, inform us that what we call "sin" is a bigger problem collectively than it is individually. And the main culprits, according to many of our finest thinkers, is the pursuit of power and its eager/evil sidekick, greed.

Reinhold Niebuhr was perhaps the preeminent American theologian of the twentieth century, born and raised in Wright City and St. Charles, Missouri, and was from the Evangelical and Reformed tradition of my denomination, the United Church of Christ. Much of Niebuhr's writings are about power. He said things like: "Goodness, armed with power, is corrupted; and pure love without power is destroyed." He had a way with words.[18]

At the end of Reinhold Niebuhr's teaching career at Union Seminary in New York City, he had a colleague named Walter Wink. Wink, who died in 2012, is, in my mind, one of the greatest American biblical scholars and theologians of our era. For some reason he was denied tenure at Union Seminary and ended up teaching for many years at Auburn Theological Seminary, also in New York City. Walter Wink was surely influenced by Reinhold Niebuhr, although they had their differences. Both, however, studied, understood, and wrote about *power*. Listen to the titles of Wink's most popular books: *Naming the Powers* (1984), *Unmasking the Powers* (1986), *Engaging the Powers* (1992), *When the Powers Fall* (1998), and *The Powers that Be* (1999).[19]

Wink describes "the powers that be" in every era in history as "domination systems." Like Niebuhr, he saw the ugly side of power exercised more in *systems* or institutions than in individuals. Power-hungry individuals are usually supported and propped up by systems—a nation, an institution, an organization, a corporation, a church, a family etc. Individual people do not have much power outside of a system that supports them. According to Walter Wink, our task is to name, unmask, engage, and help befall the oppressive powers of the world—the domination

18. I refer to Niebuhr as a "Word Architect" rather than a "Wordsmith" because he was *that good*.

19. He wanted to write a book titled, *Screw the Powers*, but thought better of it.

systems. Sounds like fun, right?[20] If Niebuhr or Wink could respond to this book, they would say, rightly so, that systems are inherently no damn good because systems are run by people and people are, well, you know.

A Bad Joke

We do not have to experience a terrorist attack or anything so dramatic to know that people are no damn good. Evil is often present in more subtle ways, such as one of the most insidious ways human beings harm one another: acts of greed. A first century evilologist named Jesus of Nazareth, tells a parable that seems particularly informative, if one can understand the punch line correctly:

> For it is as if a man, going on a journey, summoned his slaves and entrusted his property to them; to one he gave five talents, to another two, to another one, to each according to his ability. Then he went away. The one who had received the five talents went off at once and traded with them, and made five more talents. In the same way, the one who had the two talents made two more talents. But the one who had received the one talent went off and dug a hole in the ground and hid his master's money. After a long time the master of those slaves came and settled accounts with them. Then the one who had received the five talents came forward, bringing five more talents, saying, 'Master, you handed over to me five talents; see, I have made five more talents.' His master said to him, 'Well done, good and trustworthy slave; you have been trustworthy in a few things, I will put you in charge of many things; enter into the joy of your master.' And the one with the two talents also came forward, saying, 'Master, you handed over to me two talents; see, I have made two more talents.' His master said to him, 'Well done, good and trustworthy slave; you have been trustworthy in a few things, I will put you in charge of many things; enter into the joy of your master.' Then the one who had received the one talent also came forward, saying, 'Master, I knew that you were a harsh man, reaping where you did not sow, and gathering where you did not scatter seed; so I was afraid, and I went and hid your talent in the ground. Here you have what is yours.' But his master replied, 'You wicked and lazy slave! You knew, did you, that I reap where I did not sow, and gather where I did not

20. And rather dangerous. Just ask Jesus, MLK, Jr., Oscar Romero, Harvey Milk, and a handful of Kennedys, etc.

scatter? Then you ought to have invested my money with the bankers, and on my return I would have received what was my own with interest. So take the talent from him, and give it to the one with the ten talents. For to all those who have, more will be given, and they will have an abundance; but from those who have nothing, even what they have will be taken away. As for this worthless slave, throw him into the outer darkness, where there will be weeping and gnashing of teeth.'[21]

Sometimes Jesus' parables read like confusing riddles or bad jokes. Consider the above parable of the talents. This is not about talents that are related to our natural abilities or skills. This is about a unit of currency in the Roman Empire. One talent represented wages for approximately fifteen years, which means this parable is about an excessive amount of money. A man entrusts seventy-five years of wages to one servant, thirty years of wages to another, and fifteen years of wages to a third servant. This is not a gift, however. The money is given in trust. Perhaps the banks were not all that reliable in first century Palestine. Stock markets did not yet exist so there was no place to invest. Crypto currency was not even a twinkle in anyone's eye.[22]

While the rich man is gone, the first two servants put his money to work, doubling its initial value. The third servant, on the other hand, guards the man's fortune by burying it in the ground. When the man returns, the first two servants receive a handsome reward for their investment savvy—not so much the third servant. The parable takes a threatening turn. When the man learns that the third servant has hidden his money, he calls him out: "You wicked and lazy servant!" He confiscates the money and passes it along to the richest of the three servants. Adding insult to injury, he calls for the third servant to be cast into the outer darkness, where there is weeping and gnashing of teeth—a favorite line from the Gospel of Matthew.[23]

Here is Jesus, the champion of the poor and oppressed, offering a parable with the following "moral to the story": the rich get richer and the poor get poorer.[24] Is this a good riddle or a bad joke? Perhaps Jesus speaks

21. Matthew 25:14–30.

22. That twinkle I see in the eyes of the crypto-currency crowd is starting to freak me out, by the way.

23. When I die, I am taking a collection of mouth guards with me, so people will not have to gnash all day.

24. And go to the "bad place," which seems cruel to do to a person who never had

in parables so that his followers will be required to ponder that question on a deeper level.[25]

The Rich Get Richer, and the Poor Get Poorer

In 1968 two sociologists Robert Merton and Harriet Zuckerman, who were (conveniently) married, called this phenomenon "the Matthew effect of accumulated advantage."[26] The more you have the more you can acquire. I heard my daddy say it this way: "It takes money to make money."

The so-called Matthew Effect applies to other things as well, such as fame, status, or popularity. Matthew's Jesus seems to agree with this principle: "For to all those who have (fame or fortune), more will be given, and they will have an abundance; but from those who have nothing, even what they have will be taken away." The socialist, Karl Marx, called this "the Law of Increasing Poverty," which is why he believed capitalism would eventually fail. Marx also called this "the Law of Centralization of Capital." Small capitalists go bankrupt, he says, and their production means are absorbed by larger capitalists. The rich get richer, and the poor get poorer.

The Matthew Effect appears in the novel, *The Great Gatsby*, where someone says, "The rich get richer and the poor get—children!"[27] To give another example, the Matthew Effect is evident in the field of education. The psychologist Keith Stanovich used the Matthew Effect to explain how early success in learning to read leads to even greater success as the child gets older.[28] This is why it is important for children to learn to read well at an early age. If a child falls behind early in life, that child will read less, increasing the gap between them and their peers as the years go by. Imagine how this also applies to athletics and the arts.

Was Jesus a supporter of the so-called Matthew Effect? Was he okay with the rich getting richer and the poor getting poorer? Was he okay

---

a pot in which to piss.

25. Or Jesus was no damn good, which is not a theory I am yet willing to entertain because "outer darkness" seems like a spooky place.

26. https://en.wikipedia.org/wiki/Matthew_effect.

27. In my personal experience, there is a correlation between poverty and overly populated households. Observers have noted that in my family we breed early and often. If this book doesn't "pay off," my children will suffer.

28. https://www.readingrockets.org/articles/researchbytopic/4862.

with the powerful getting more powerful while the powerless became less powerful? This parable reads like a riddle because we need to decide if Jesus is *prescribing* the Matthew Effect or merely *describing* it. Does he agree with it, or is he trying to say this is simply a reality of life, that is, something to overcome?

Not a Prescription

Wait one moment as I put on my Captain Obvious superhero costume . . . Of course, Jesus is describing rather than prescribing! Many readers of this parable think Jesus is favoring the rich man and the first two servants in the parable because they are rewarded for their behavior. I want to make the case, however, that Jesus favors the third servant, the one who is punished. I know that sounds upside down but try to hang with me here.

This parable is a complex riddle because at first glance Jesus is favoring the rich man and the first two servants. After all, they invested wisely. The key to understanding this parable properly, however, lies in verse 26. The rich man says to the third servant: "You wicked and lazy slave! You knew, did you, that I reap where I did not sow, and gather where I did not scatter?" This is a clear indictment of the rich man. He achieved his wealth at the expense of others. There is no way this guy is the hero, much less the God-figure, in this parable. This should be a clue to us about how we should read this parable.

Therefore, here is my take on this parable: It reveals how challenging it is to remain ethical in a world that measures success by power and wealth. We tend to think Jesus is praising the first two servants for their economic savvy because we live in a culture that rewards economic savvy. This is our reality. And yet, Jesus' first century listeners would have understood that the first two servants are multiplying the dishonesty of the rich man, whereas the third servant is refusing to participate in a system where people reap what they do now sow and gather what they do not scatter. For this refusal he is abandoned and condemned to a place of suffering.

The same is true today. Those who either are not economically savvy or do not have the means to be economically savvy are more likely to suffer from a life of poverty and struggle. That is just the reality of the world in which we live. The Matthew Effect suggests that the gap between the savvy, privileged haves and the un-savvy unprivileged have nots will continue to get wider. This is the system, the village, in which we live. And it is no damn good.

The Search for a TOE

From a traditional Christian perspective, the word I should be using for both individual and collective no-damn-goodness is "sin." "People are inherently sinful" is a Christian way of saying, "People are no damn good." With that perspective firmly planted in my mind, I delivered the following sermon to my wife's congregation on March 26, 2017 (where she serves as a woman priest in an independent Catholic church named St. Stanislaus Catholic Church). From all accounts, I was the first Protestant to deliver a homily from their pulpit in the history of that 130-year-old congregation.[29] This homily confirms, yet minimizes, the notion that church tradition teaches that we are no damn good. It is a "yes, but" response to the question "Are we no damn good?"

> I want to thank this congregation for allowing me to come and speak to you today. I am confident that you have not had to listen to very many Protestant ministers over the years and so I promise to represent my tribe with as much grace as possible. Rest assured, however, that we have more in common than not. In the twenty-first century Catholics and Protestants are closer together than we have ever been. Our historical differences are not as pronounced or as important as they once were.
>
> Is there an issue that connects us in a way that makes us inseparable? If so, what would that be? There are obviously many points of intersection between Protestants and Catholics, and most of the things we have in common are worth celebrating and proclaiming to the world. However, there is one historic commonality that probably gets way too much attention. Both of our traditions call it "sin."
>
> Before I get to that, notice that in the political world, where the opposition and polarization these days reminds us of old Catholic-Protestant conflicts, peace-making folks are often asking what we all have in common. In 1992 the Bill Clinton campaign may have stumbled upon that commonality. Do you remember the slogan that likely got Clinton elected? "It's the

---

29. St. Stanislaus is (in)famous for its own battle for independence from the St. Louis Roman Catholic diocese in the early 2000s, led by their priest, Fr. Marek Bozek. The fact that they call their sermons "homilies" is the subject for another book.

economy, stupid!" This was coined by Clinton's favorite Cajun campaign strategist, James Carville. This slogan appealed to people on both sides of the political spectrum because everyone, it seems, wants to live in a country with a thriving economy. It is the one issue that serves as "common ground" for almost everyone.

Some people take that slogan, "It's the economy, stupid" even further than that. In the Freakonomics series of books, the authors, Steven Levitt and Stephen Dubner, argue that almost every human thought or action can be explained in purely economic terms.[30] They argue that economic forces exert the strongest influence on human thoughts and behaviors. In a sense, Levitt and Dubner are saying that economic theory can serve as our T.O.E. or "theory of everything." We usually talk about a theory of everything in terms of physics. By definition, a theory of everything is "a hypothetical single, all-encompassing, coherent theoretical framework of physics that fully explains and links together all physical aspects of the universe."[31] It will be interesting if either the social sciences (such as economic theory) or the physical sciences ever "stump their toes" on a "theory of everything." That will truly be a cause for celebration.

In the world of theology, however, long before there was economic theory or physics to help us explain things, long before we began looking for a "theory of everything," there was one thing we could all point to in our attempts to explain human thought and behavior: sin. We have been taught to believe that it is our sinful human nature that motivates us to think and do things even if we are totally unaware of its power over us. For many people in the ancient world and even in our world today, the doctrine of sin serves as our "theory of everything." "It's sin, stupid," could be the slogan that connects our shared religious tradition, Protestant and Catholic. From St. Augustine's doctrine of "original sin" to Karl Menninger's 1973 book, *Whatever Became of Sin?* to pulpit-pounding televangelists to Catholic confessionals to mainline Protestant unison prayers of confession, sin might be the common denominator among us all. It might be our "big toe."

But should it be? Is an emphasis on human sin the right message for the church in the twenty-first century? When folks look at your church, or mine, do we really want them to think that we are fixated on sin? I believe that if Jesus were standing

30. https://en.wikipedia.org/wiki/Freakonomics.

31. https://en.wikipedia.org/wiki/Theory_of_everything.

here and we asked him, "Lord, is there one theological issue or doctrine that we, as children of God, can use to explain our thoughts and behaviors?" I do not think Jesus would answer with the word "sin." I say that because he seems to have discredited it as a possible theory of everything.

In a story recorded in John 9:1–41, Jesus and his disciples were out for a stroll one day when they saw a blind man. Blindness was more common in the ancient world because there were no eye doctors, glasses, contacts, cataract surgeries, attachment of detached retinas, or laser surgeries. I assure you that if I had lived past the age of forty in that place and time, I would no longer be able to read.

Although blindness or the inability to see very well was such a common occurrence in the ancient world, Jesus' disciples felt the need to blame and explain. At the top of their list of explanations for physical ailments such as blindness and other adversities was sin: "Rabbi," they asked, who sinned, this man or his parents, that he was born blind?" Jesus's answer suggests that the man was born blind so that God could be glorified through his healing, but I do not really think that is the primary message the story is offering to us. The first part of Jesus's answer, in my opinion, is the crux of the matter: "Neither this man nor his parents sinned."

In other words, stop using sin as your go-to explanation for everything. Not every physical ailment or adversity is due to someone sinning. And especially stop this nonsense about God punishing people for the sins of their parents. Go back and read Jeremiah 31:29–30: "In those days they shall no longer say: 'The parents have eaten sour grapes, and the children's teeth are set on edge.' But all shall die for their own sins; the teeth of everyone who eats sour grapes shall be set on edge."

This gentleman was not born blind because he sinned. When could that sin have possibly taken place? While he was in his mother's womb? Did he kick his mother a little too strongly? Did he learn profanity in the uterus? Even today people use sin as an explanation for adversity, such as Hurricane Katrina, to use a famous example. It really is a ridiculous notion, theologically childish, and prone to encourage judgmental pronouncements from people who need to keep their thoughts to themselves.

Sin does not have to be our uber-explanation, it does not have to be our "theory of everything," and it does not have to be the one thing that connects us all as Christians. I think we can find other commonalities. How about God's love? Wouldn't the church universal benefit from a consistent theme of divine love? How about grace? Wouldn't the church send a better vibe throughout our society if grace became our "theory of everything"? My prayer is that in the future all of God's children will discover they have more positive things in common than not.

I cannot say that I received a standing ovation for this oratory exercise. They reserve enthusiastic clapping for my wife's occasional homilies. Still, I made my point, one that contrasts with the content of this book. Certainly, we are bad to the bone and no damn good—Catholics and Protestants are no worse or better than anyone else. And yet, this understanding of human nature should never become our "theory of everything." We also need to leave a little room for an overlooked concept called "grace," a doctrine that bleeds through much of the writings of scripture, hidden at times, playing peekaboo at other times, yet always in the picture.

A Caveat of Grace

Although Protestants and Catholics (and everyone else) might have more positive things in common, we are, according to our traditions, sinners. We are evil, i.e., no damn good. Human experience, scripture, reason, and church tradition all confirm this. The old man who yells at us and tells us to get off his grass confirms it. And yet, there are other voices in our circle of friends that we need to hear.

Jesus of Nazareth talked about those who have "gone astray" albeit with a little more nuance and perspective. In Luke 15, Jesus shares three parables about the "lost": the parables of the lost sheep, the lost coin, and the lost son (what we normally call the parable of the prodigal son because his money kept burning a hole in his pockets). Whereas the previously mentioned Jeremiah and Psalm 14 seem to give up on humanity, mainly due to the theological limitations of their place and time, Jesus portrays a much more evolved theology. He likens God to a shepherd who will drop everything and look for that one lost sheep, although there are still ninety-nine sheep in the fold, a woman who will sweep the entire house looking for one lost coin, although she still has nine coins at her disposal, and a father who will drop everything to meet his disobedient, yet repentant son, in the driveway, although he seems to be doing fine without him. Contemporary theologians call this a "theology of hope." As bad as things might seem there is always hope. For Jesus (as opposed to Jeremiah and the psalmist), God does not begin with judgment and punishment; God begins with hope and optimism, with grace serving as "true north" on the theological compass.

A few decades later, the Apostle Paul was able to move from Jeremiah and the psalmist's theological perspective of judgement and punishment to Jesus' theological perspective of hope and grace. It was not easy, however. He refers to his former self as a "blasphemer, a persecutor (of the early church), and a man of violence." "But I received mercy," he writes, "and the grace of our Lord overflowed for me with the faith and love that are in Christ Jesus" (1 Timothy 1:13–14).

The arc of scripture bends toward grace, much like the arc of the universe bends toward justice. Maybe life does as well. In the best-selling book, *Hillbilly Elegy*, J. D. Vance offers a sometimes poignant, but always hopeful, interpretation of his life story.[32] Vance came from what he calls a "hillbilly" family from Kentucky, by way of Ohio. In the book he repeatedly laments for deceased family members, in particular his grandparents that helped raise him. The theme of the book is that there seems to be very little hope for a large segment of that unique Scots Irish subculture in America, a subculture that is beset with drug and alcohol problems, lack of education and employment opportunities, and severe family dysfunctionality. According to statistics, Vance should have ended up either the victim of a violent crime, in prison, or in abject poverty. There seemed to be no hope for him or his family and friends. And yet, Vance overcomes all that through a four-year stint in the Marines and a successful college career and law school.[33] He should have been a lost sheep or a lost coin—and certainly a lost son—and yet his grandmother never let him give up.[34]

Such things as grace, hope, and mercy might serve as a caveat to the main thesis of this book, that we are no damn good. We can always hope that the caveat becomes the norm. In the meantime, if Jeremiah or the author of Psalm 14 were here today, they would probably laugh at any attempts to minimize the lack of consistent morality and ethics in *homo sapiens*. They would conclude that we are a graceless, hopeless, and useless waste of skin. We are, but why?

---

32. Vance, *Hillbilly Elegy: A Memoir of a Family and Culture in Crisis*. Harper publishers, 2016.

33. The former appeals to conservatives, and the latter appeals to liberals.

34. It did not hurt that he is a straight white male. More about that later.

2

Bad Bones to Malicious Marrow

T HE notion that we are no damn good is a given. No more evidence is
necessary. We can look no further than every family in our circle of
friends and relatives. All of them are dysfunctional, often more "fun" than
functional. Every system is vulnerable to the corrupting forces of power
and greed. Every individual is plagued with narcissistic tendencies. The
question is, "Why?" What is the root cause of our no-damn-goodness?
We are no damn good because . . .

Because We Have Malicious Marrow

Some days I wake up feeling a little extra evil. There is a good reason for
that. I am a human being, and you know what they say about human
beings.[1] I can understand why the Apostle Paul said, "For I do not do
the good I want, but the evil I do not want is what I do" (Romans 7:19).
To me, this is the most insightful statement ever made about humanity.
Kudos to Paul for being so smart. You and I may seem like good people
most of the time, yet we need to admit that humanity is often up to no
good. There is ample evidence that we are basically bad to the bone, that
we have *malicious marrow*. Again, why? Why do we often do what we
do not want to do? There has been no shortage of very important people
attempting to answer this "why" question. I thought it would be fun to
throw out a few of these answers for interested readers.

---

1. They're no damn good.

Original Sin

Let us begin with the most popular answer in my religious tradition. Original Sin is the doctrine that claims our evil nature is inherited from our parents at childbirth, and it goes all the way back to Adam and Eve.[2] Original Sin is implied in Romans 7:17, where Paul states, "But in fact it is no longer I that do it (that which I hate to do), but *sin that dwells within me.*" Personally, I do not take the doctrine of original sin literally, but I do take it seriously. As I observe human behavior, including my own, I am compelled to believe that there is indeed something rotten in the state of Denmark.[3] I am just not so sure we can always blame Adam and Eve for our bad behavior.[4]

The Devil (or whatever name other cultures ascribe to the personification of evil)

Flip Wilson thought he was being, well, flippant, years ago when he said in his comedy routine, "the devil made me do it." He was only echoing a theory that many people from many religious traditions claim, which is that there is a personal evil force out there that compels good people to do bad things. I do not subscribe to this theory either, yet when we observe the seemingly inexplicable cruelty of some people, it is understandable that people have attributed it to some metaphysical being that has taken over that person.

Years ago, I learned not to criticize this theory too much. I was teaching a Junior High Sunday school class one day when one of the young boys asked me what I thought of the devil. I was fresh off my graduate school experience at Baylor University, so I launched into a scholarly explanation of the origin of the concept of an evil deity.[5] The next day I received a phone call from a concerned parishioner, who said, "I heard

---

2. Some folks suggest it was Adam and Steve, not Adam and Eve. Could be. It makes perfect evolutionary sense that at a time in history when there were limited sex partner options, bisexuality (i.e., double the odds) would have been a practical orientation.

3. Which, by the way, has something to do with the mass production of bacon.

4. Yes, *obviously* Adam and Eve are purely fictional characters, although someone had to be the first Homo Sapiens, right?

5. I suggested, per the religion of Zoroastrianism, that the concept of an evil deity came out of Persia (and is therefore Iranian).

you don't believe in the devil." As I was sidestepping my response to this question, I realized that unless I came right out and said, "I believe in Satan" as strongly as I would say, "God bless Texas!" I was no longer going to be employed at that East Texas church. A few months later I was run off from that church in Longview, Texas. In hindsight, it seems obvious that the devil had something to do with it.

Genes

I am not talking about the jeans we wear.[6] I am talking about our genetic makeup. There is a big debate swirling around water cooler conversations pitting nature versus nurture—biology verses environment. Are we evil because we had rotten parents and our schools are cesspools of sin (nurture) or are we evil because we were born rotten (nature)? It is interesting how closely related the gene theory of human depravity is with the ancient doctrine of original sin—a doctrine that was formulated centuries before we knew anything at all about human genes. Perhaps human evil begins in the blue jeans after all, although I would not read too much into that.

Parents

If bad genes reflect the "nature" part of the nature/nurture debate, then our parents reflect the "nurture" part. Should our parents be largely blamed for our bad behavior? When we observe or read about a truly evil person, like a serial killer, one of our first responses is usually, "How was he/she *raised*?"[7] as if that person is obviously evil because they had terrible parents. There is no question that parental upbringing has both good and ill effects on children, however, there are too many bad people raised in good homes and too many good people raised in awful homes to allow us to make parents the primary explanation for evil. And yet if you talk to my son . . .

6. Although, truth be told, a lot of mischief originates from our jeans.

7. I should have just used the male pronoun because I've never met a female serial killer. Have you?

Lack of Conscience

I recommend a tantalizing little book titled, *The Sociopath Next Door*.[8] The author claims that fully four percent of the American public is sociopathic, which means they have no conscience. A sociopath, then, would never ask the question, "Why do we do what we don't want to do?" because a sociopath does not mind doing what other people do not want to do. In fact, they get off on it. And yet, while we might ascribe *some* of the evil activity in the world to sociopaths, psychopaths, sadists, folks with anti-social behavior, or Donald Trump, this does not account for why normal people do evil. Sociopaths may have a greater tendency to do evil things, yet we *all* do evil things.

Religion

Talk about a popular scapegoat for evil in the world! It is undeniable that religion can be a source of evil in the world. We see it every day on cable news. Terrorism of all varieties is often linked to a religious worldview—a warped religious worldview. This is nothing new. From the theologically inspired wars that overwhelmed Europe for centuries, to September 11, 2001, religion can spawn as much hatred and violence as any other potential culprit. At the same time, religion itself probably developed to *reduce* human evil, or, minimally, to create social order and the reduction of violence. While there are multiple scriptures from all religions that seem to condone evil, the overall message of the world's sacred scriptures is to condemn evil in all its many forms.[9]

Money and Power

There is the wide assumption out there that, as the Bible says, "The love of money is the root of all evil." There is certainly truth in that, although as an Uber driver once said to me, "The *lack* of money is the root of all evil," which might explain why he is moonlighting as an Uber driver. Lord Acton famously said, "Power corrupts, and absolute power corrupts absolutely," forever establishing the pursuit of power as a likely candidate for that which causes us to do bad things. The problem with this theory is

---

8. Stout, *The Sociopath Next Door*, Broadway Books, 2005.

9. Even as the producers of such scriptures did their share of naughty things.

that relatively few people in the world ever even get a chance to pursue a high level of power or a huge bank account, so it does not explain why the rest of us are no damn good. Also, some people seek money and power to do *good*. Those are the people who should be studied. Speaking of the pursuit of good . . .

The Pursuit of Good

Now here is a theory we almost never consider. Remember the old saying: "The road to hell is paved with good intentions"? Sometimes evil is caused by people who think they are doing good. While that is true, it is not true enough to discourage us from pursuing good.[10]

Evolution

As a modern person, I tend to explain evil scientifically rather than theologically.[11] If we evolved from a lower animal life form, then we have inherited our flawed morality from our pre-human ancestors. As I noted earlier, one of my religion professors asked his class, "When was the first sin committed?" and I blurted out the following answer: "The first time a caveman hit his cave-spouse on the head with a club and felt bad about it." In other words, the moment humanity developed a moral compass is the moment sin entered the world.[12] Therefore, my *best* answer to the question, "Why do we do what we don't want to do?" is that we are *animals* . . . but there is still one more point to make:

Evil is Non-existent

This is the craziest of all the theories out there (yet strangely reasonable): human evil does not actually exist. This is the notion that we humans have evolved in a way that arbitrarily separates good from evil. Not to sound too nihilistic, but since none of this (existence itself) has any inherent meaning, then our actions are meaningless as well, so no, evil does

10. Still, there's nothing worse than a self-righteous moralistic do-gooder who is doing more harm than good.

11. Confession: I am not a scientist, so ignore my bluster.

12. Notice how this sounds suspiciously like eating from the tree of knowledge of good and evil.

not actually exist. As far as theories go, this one has some philosophical merit, but it has little practical value. As Reinhold Niebuhr implied, we simply cannot go through life without distinguishing—arbitrarily or not—between good and evil. Unless we draw a line in the sand like Col. William Travis did at the Alamo, we cannot enjoy any semblance of civilization.[13]

So, there you are: Ten brief responses to the question, "Why do we do what we don't want to do?" As a pastor that struggles with issues of morality and ethics, I only have one relevant thing to say to my dear readers: Stop doing those things.

There are, of course, many more nuanced responses to the question, "Why are we no damn good?" including . . .

Because Doing Good is Difficult to Do

One of my inspirations for the study of ethics is the following words to the Thessalonians: "Brothers and sisters, do not be weary in doing what is *right*" (2nd Thessalonians 3:13). In the case of the writer of 2nd Thessalonians, he or she was addressing community concerns. Specifically, there were people in their community that were not "pulling their weight," so to speak. This was important because the early church was characterized by small communities that lived in what we might call "communes". Everyone shared everything with everyone else. The only way this can work, of course, is if everyone contributes according to their abilities. Apparently, the situation there was so severe that the writer felt compelled to say to them, "Anyone unwilling to work should not eat."[14]

Do you ever get weary in doing what is right? Do you tire from doing good? Maybe not. Most of us assume that doing the right thing comes naturally to us and we do not have to work very hard at it. However, my life's mission is to tell you that this is more difficult than we think it is.

13. The line drawn in the dirt at the Alamo, for the purpose of recruiting fighters, is morally questionable because the fight for Texas independence was largely a fight to maintain slavery and grab some land. Please don't tell my fellow Texans.

14. By the way, regardless of the passion of the extremist anti-welfare uncle spewing his nonsense all over the turkey at Thanksgiving, this should not be interpreted as a sweeping indictment of our modern welfare system, although it is a reminder that one of our ethical responsibilities is to not be an unnecessary burden to others (if we can help it).

Let us begin with the "small stuff." We do not sweat said small stuff too much, so even if we fudge a little on what is right or wrong in insignificant situations, we do not worry much about it. Even those folks who believe that doing right can tip the scales of heaven in their favor do not usually sweat the small stuff. For instance, deciding whether to tell someone a piece of green spinach is stuck in their teeth, or whether to grab a parking spot close to the store when you could park further away and allow someone else the closer spot, or whether to pay for the person's order behind you in the Starbucks drive-through after the person in front of you paid for yours. Small ethical decisions are not things we lose sleep about, nor do we grow weary of making them.

But then there are the "big things." These are the ethical decisions that could keep us awake at night. These are the things that can make us grow weary in doing what is right. Here are some examples: Deciding when it is time to move a loved one out of the home they love because it is not safe anymore for them to live alone. Deciding whether to "pull the plug" on a loved one. Deciding whether to adopt or give up a child for adoption, not to mention the option of abortion. Deciding whether to inform one's employer about shady or dishonest activities of a fellow employee. These are decisions that will make us tired. We should therefore be easy on ourselves. Ethical decision making can be very difficult, especially in terms of the "big things," and when we get weary or tired, we are prone to make mistakes.

Because There is Stiff Competition Between Ethical Decisions

The reason why it is so easy to grow wearing in doing what is right, especially in terms of important things, is because there is stiff *competition* out there. Let us imagine that "Doing What is Right" is the name of a team in a league called "Ethics." The main opponents in this league include teams with the following names: "Not Knowing What is Right," "Doing What We Want to Do," "Doing What is Popular," "Doing What is Easy," and "Doing What Seems Necessary." These are five of the strongest competitors against the team "Doing What is Right" in the Ethics League. Let me say a few words about each one of them:

"Not Knowing What is Right" is probably the fiercest rival of "Doing What is Right" because, well, to *do* what is right we first need to *know* what is right. This extremely dangerous competitor was eloquently articulated by Ben Kingsley in the movie, *The Confession*, where Kingsley's character says, "It's not hard to do the right thing; in fact, it's easy. What is hard is *knowing* what the right thing to do is. Once you know that, and believe it, doing the right thing is easy." I do not agree that once we know what the right thing to do is, it becomes easy, but knowledge is a good start.[15]

Even when we know what the right thing is to do, we still need to go up against one of the strongest players in the league, who goes by the name: *Cognitive Dissonance*. This refers to those times when there is a gap between knowing what the right thing is and doing it. We should not let cognitive dissonance defeat our ethics team. Once we know what the right thing is, we need to do it, and send cognitive dissonance to the end of the bench whimpering to the coaches about playing time and bad calls from the referee.

Another fierce opponent is the team, "Doing What We *Want* to Do." When we were growing up, this was probably our biggest competitor. Sometimes it goes by the names "Doing What Comes Naturally to Us" or "Doing the Selfish Thing." Even when we know what we should do, such as eat right and exercise, be generous, and love our neighbors as ourselves (thanks Bible!), we often fall back to doing what we want to do, what feels more natural to us, such as eating poorly, sitting on a couch all day, hording our resources, and ignoring our neighbors. Doing what we want to do is a powerful opponent.

When we are young, another team that is fiercely competitive against us is the team "Doing What is Popular." This is a difficult ethical team to beat because, by definition, it has a wide fan base. They are difficult to play against because no one wants to be unpopular and stand out like a sore thumb, go against the grain, or be made fun of. As adults, defending ourselves from the forces of doing what is popular is much more subtle, but it is still there. If we find ourselves agreeing with everyone around us about everything, then we should ask ourselves whether we are doing the right thing or the popular thing. We might be playing for the wrong team.

And then there is the team named "Doing What is Easy." This is the opponent that will come from behind and beat us every time if we are not careful. It is easier to do the easy thing rather than the right thing, right? One of the key players on the Doing What is Right team when opposing the Doing What is Easy team is "tough love." Tough love is a good player

15. Or not, suggests the Garden of Eden story.

to have on your team. This is the player you go to when Doing What is Easy is about to score and you need to stop them. If you have ever had to practice tough love on a loved one, you know what I am talking about.

A final worthy opponent in the Ethics league is "Doing What Seems Necessary." This is the sneakiest team of all because it often wears the same uniform as the Doing What is Right team. The Doing What Seems Necessary team is the one that tells us such things as "the only way to defeat violence is with violence," and "the only way to fight crime is to incarcerate people." Fortunately, most of the time that which is necessary *is* what is right, but we need to be aware of the times when the two are not playing on the same team, even if they are wearing the same uniform.

Perhaps you can think of other "teams" for a fantasy Ethics League, but all of this suggests that ethics—doing the right thing—is difficult if not wearisome. Ethics is a tough league to play in because the opposition to our team "Doing What is Right" is numerous and fiercely competitive.

Stiff Competition Illustrated: Ethical Wrestling

One of my fondest memories is going to a few professional wrestling matches at the old Coliseum in San Angelo, Texas when I was a young lad. My dad and his brother had an ongoing argument about whether the matches were "fixed" or not. My dad thought they were fixed, but my uncle Wilburn was a true believer. (I am almost certain the truth was somewhere in between. The outcome might have been fixed, and some of the punches might have been fake, but they must have felt the body slams and collisions.) I was particularly interested in tag team wrestling matches. Each team was made up of two contestants. Only one wrestler at a time from each team could be in the ring. When a wrestler in the ring got tired or was tired of getting whipped, he would slap hands with his teammate and leave the ring as his teammate entered the ring.

The tag team wrestling match is a good analogy for the "main event" in the world in recent years: the pandemic COVID 19 crisis. We are certainly in the "fight" of our lifetimes. I realize there are many skeptics out there, but there are always skeptics, Doubting Thomas's—or worse, deniers—about everything. My advice is to pay them no mind. My analogy might be a little confusing, so I suggest you grab a pen and paper and draw a picture showing COVID 19 and Mother Earth (or the environment) in the red corner and Homo Sapiens and the Global Economy in the blue corner. This is how I see our worldwide tag team wrestling match playing out:

COVID 19 is the youngest and, for now, the toughest, of all four wrestlers. It has a stranglehold on the wrestler it is currently fighting in the ring: Homo Sapiens. Homo Sapiens is taking a beating, but there are signs that it will eventually win. This is the pairing that has everyone's attention. Before this colossal match between COVID 19 and Homo Sapiens, Mother Earth and the Global Economy had been going head-to-head for decades. The Global Economy was winning that matchup. Mother Earth, in fact, was getting overheated from the Global Economy's relentless moves, including brain busters, piledrivers, backbreakers, and my favorite, the leapfrog body guillotine. (Don't ask.) Although Mother Earth was not very happy about having to join forces with the new villainous wrestler known as COVID 19, she was happy to get a break. In fact, while resting outside the ring her skies cleared, her cities grew quieter, and her wildlife had not been this cheery in a long time.

Meanwhile, over in the blue corner, while Homo Sapiens is taking a beating, the Global Economy is itching to get back into the ring. It is impatiently counting the days until Homo Sapiens can pin down COVID 19 so that it can get back into the ring against Mother Earth. Now, Mother Earth is not opposed to the Global Economy. She has tried to be partners with the Global Economy for several decades, but with little success. She just wishes the Global Economy would play nice and fair in the future. We know Mother Earth does not want to harm anyone, although she occasionally shows her own rather violent wrestling moves that go by names such as hurricanes, tornadoes, floods, droughts, wildfires, and earthquakes. Sometimes when Homo Sapiens and the Global Economy gang up against her, she lets everyone know she's not happy and wins a round or two.

Secretly, Mother Earth would love to see her current partner, COVID 19 permanently defeated, even if it means she will have to go solo against Homo Sapiens and the Global Economy once again (and likely lose). But she's hoping that if/when COVID 19 is down on the mat for good, she can join forces with Homo Sapiens and the Global Economy and create a wrestling match where everyone wins. As Mother Earth likes to say in post-match press conferences, "This doesn't have to be a zero-sum game." We can all be winners—there is no reason to fight. But first things first: COVID 19 needs to be thrown out of the ring . . . for good. So, get the damn shot.

Because We Are Doing the Best We Can . . . and It Ain't Great

I have a friend who is a Marriage and Family Therapist. He focuses on family systems theory. One day he summarized his approach to therapy and human nature by saying to me, "Generally speaking, people do the best they can with the tools they have."[16] Everyone, from the addict to the inmate, from the sarcastic to the sincere, is doing the best they can with the tools they have. Now, granted, we might not have the most qualitative tools in the human toolbox, yet we all work with what we have. No one wants to be a failure. No one wants to be a loser. If given the opportunity, we will succeed in the best way we know how. Even if we are no damn good, we will try to "be best."

This suggests that much of the time we are no damn good out of a sense of desperation. Speaking of that, a desperado was "a bold, reckless criminal or outlaw, especially in the early days of the American West." There is an obvious connection between the two words, "desperado" and "desperation," which implies that desperados were people who did something illegal out of a sense of desperation. Sometimes people seem to be no damn good because they feel they have no good choices to make. All of us, regardless of how "good" we might be, act out of a sense of desperation on occasion.

For instance, even today, Spanish speaking people attempt to come to America legally or illegally, often out of a sense of desperation. There are few other reasons to leave one's extended family behind and uproot their immediate family to travel with them through dangerous terrain to arrive at an unwelcome border. This has been happening for a very long time, although the news reports in recent years about children being separated from their parents and placed in various facilities has made us all more aware of the desperation of people who live in Mexico and Central America. Because of our government's interpretation and exercise of existing immigration laws, their desperation turned many of them into desperados.

A sense of desperation is everywhere. We see it on all sides of the cultural divide. For example, there is a large group of folks out there—mainly white men—who do not just own guns—they are passionate about owning guns. I believe this reflects a large degree of desperation. The statistics are startling. According to a 2018 *Washington Post* article,

16. Generals were not the only subjects of his research, just so you know.

there are more guns than people in the United States. While Americans make up just four percent of the world's population, we own forty-six percent of the world's firearms. Only forty-two percent of American families own guns. The average gun-owning household owns nearly eight guns. Furthermore, only three percent of American adults account for half of the nation's firearms.[17] All of this suggests that a very small percentage of people—mostly white men—are stockpiling weapons.[18] What is going on here?

One answer—although not the only answer—is a quiet sense of desperation. Studies indicate that in the gun culture there are very real fears about the white male ability to protect their families and maintain their place in the job market. Some of the fear is racially driven when they feel like they are competing with minority groups for jobs, including undocumented immigrants who work hard and who often work for less pay than their white counterparts. There is an old saying: "Desperate times call for desperate measures." Much of the gun violence in our country is almost certainly due to a sense of desperation and hopelessness on the part of the shooter, whether clinically diagnosed mental illness is a factor or not.

My rationale for using two widely divergent examples of desperation—immigration and gun ownership—is to show that hopelessness is not the exclusive domain of any one group of people. There is enough to go around for everyone. Take the recent uptick of suicide rates as another example.[19] People do not take their lives unless there is a profound sense of hopelessness and desperation. Mental illness is often a factor, although not always. Here are some statistics to ponder, and you will see a connection with the white male gun issue. In America:

- The annual suicide rate is 13.42 per 100,000 individuals.
- Men die by suicide 3.53x more often than women.
- On average, there are 123 suicides per day.
- White males accounted for 7 of 10 suicides in 2016.

17. *Washington Post* article written by Christopher Ingraham, June 19, 2018.

18. One of my favorite memes on social media asks the question "Who do most people assume is guilty for a mass shooting in America?" and the answer is a picture of Betty White. Say her name out loud.

19. When I first wrote about this topic, Kate Spade and Anthony Bourdain had just died by suicide.

- Firearms accounted for 51% of all suicides in 2016.

- The rate of suicide is highest in middle age — especially among white men.[20]

Most people who experience a sense of hopelessness and desperation do not uproot their families and try to enter illegally into another country, stockpile weapons and go on shooting rampages, or die by suicide. Most people do not allow their desperation to turn them into a desperado, but the desperation is there—and for many, many reasons.

The problem with laws—religious or secular—is that they do not always allow room for the truly desperate. When we say, "Laws are made to be broken," we mean that we *should* break them when we have no other way to show compassion for the hopeless and desperate. Maybe this is where we find God, hanging out among the hopeless, the dying, grieving parents of dying children, people with physical or mental chronic illnesses, undocumented immigrants in refugee camps, the suicidal, and yes, white men with guns, because God, as the writer Annie Lamott says, "is the gift of desperation."

By now I am sure some of you are humming in your minds the old song by The Eagles, called "Desperado." The song ends with the perfect message for the desperate and desperados among us:

Desperado, Why don't you come to your senses?
Come down from your fences, open the gate
It may be rainin', but there's a rainbow above you
You better let somebody love you . . .
You better let somebody love you
Before it's too late.

So . . .

So, why are we no damn good? I have no idea, or rather, I have no absolute answer. Maybe . . . some of us are bad due to some crazy theological twist of fate called "original sin." Maybe . . . we are bad due to some corrupt genes handed down to us through the process of evolution that led to an underdeveloped conscience. Maybe . . . there are outside forces that compel, persuade, or otherwise teach us to be no damn good, such as the devil, bad religion (not the band, necessarily), money and power, bad

---

20. *National Center for Health Statistics (CDC)*, Jun 2018.

parenting, or bad peers. Maybe . . . we are bad because it's just too darn difficult to be good, there is too much competition with the non-good, we are doing the best we can (so, what's the point?), or ethics is just a made-up category for people who want to think they are more precious than the rest of the animal kingdom. Maybe . . . we are bad because we often feel as if we have no other option.

Or maybe . . . we are bad because we are mad and sad that bad things happen to us . . .

3

God Has a Lot of God-splaining to Do

B ROADLY speaking there are two opposing positions to my ingenious thesis that people are no damn good. First, there is the theory that evil does not actually exist (or good for that matter), that any code of ethics we humans might create is simply a way to ease the stress of a chaotic world that seems to delight in arbitrary pain and suffering. This is a nihilistic view of the world. The other perspective is a little more on the sunny side of life, that we are, in fact, *good*. Rather than "bad to the bone" or "malignant to the marrow," we are, oh, I don't know, "kind to the kidneys," "holy to the heart," or "ethical to the endocrine system." According to this perspective, badness is like a rare disease. When it happens, it is newsworthy because it is not the norm. The ubiquitous "News" gives us the impression that planet Earth is a bad place to live. Of course, what other residential options do we have?

Stuff Happens

Let us assume, for one precious moment, the opposite of this book's claim, that we are indeed good to the glands rather than bad to the bone. If so, why do bad things happen to us? That is a question people ask me with regular frequency. That is a question that has been asked for as long as people have been stumping their toes or losing their kites in a strong wind.[1] I have no idea why bad things happen to, ahem, good people.

---

1. For people who wonder how God fits into the picture, there is the "theodicy" question, which asks how a good and providential deity could allow evil and suffering.

My cleaned up secular answer is "stuff happens." Rabbi Harold Kushner famously explored this question in his widely read 1983 book, *When Bad Things Happen to Good People*. He basically said, "I have no idea, either, but God cares."

Before Rabbi Kushner asked the question, the mythical character named Job, who has a book in the Hebrew Bible named after him, asked the same question (in so many words).[2] God (or rather the writer of the book of Job) gives an answer, which to me is sort of unsatisfactory, yet maybe is about as good an answer as one can give. Basically, God says to Job, "Who are you, and what gives you the right to be asking me such a deep and profound question?" Literally, God asks, "Where were you, Job, when I laid the foundation of the earth?" Where were you when I created stars, lightning, clouds, dust, animals, and human intelligence? God's answer to Job is sort of a "shut up and take it like a man" answer, which probably did not help someone who just lost all his children, servants, and livestock, and is suffering physical pain from head to toe. It is not the most satisfying response in the history of faith and philosophy. Then again, kudos to the writer of Job for not trying to B.S. us.

Although our pain and suffering rarely if ever reaches the level of Job's, we still want to know why bad things happen to good people. By the way, notice that this question assumes we are *good people*, an assumption I probably poo-poo with too much glee throughout this book. Nevertheless, here are my top ten answers to one of the most asked questions in the history of sentient beings:

1. God blesses the good and curses the bad, so if bad things happen to someone, they must be bad.

    This was a common view in the ancient world. In the Bible it is called "Deuteronomist Theology" because it is the theological premise of the book of Deuteronomy. It is still popular in some circles today, especially those who think hurricanes, pandemics and such occur only in places where sinners abound.[3] Fortunately, Jesus debunked this viewpoint. He said the rain falls on the just and

---

If you have the answer to that question, please give me a call.

2. Two things about Job. First, his name is pronounced "Job" rather than "Job" (I know, not much difference, right?) and as far as I can tell he didn't have a 9–5 job, but he had a lot of stuff that he hated losing. Job was a hoarder.

3. The interesting thing about a pandemic is that it picks *everyone* as a potential victim because, after all, we are *all* sinners, right?

the unjust alike, meaning that God's blessings and curses—if they exist—are *neutral*.

2. Human free will causes bad things to happen to good people.

This might explain why some bad people might do bad things to good people, but it does not explain why *nature* does bad things to good people. It also does not explain why we often use our free will (if that exists) to do evil. This theory, then, can sometimes be true, but it cannot explain every instance of evil against good people.

3. God is in control, so there must be a reason why bad things happen to good people.

This is the old "throw up the hands in the air and give up" answer. And it just does not fly. Try telling the parents of a child who has died that since God is in control there must be a good reason why their child died. If God *is* in control of everything, then logic suggests that God is responsible for all the bad stuff that happens. That is an uncomfortable viewpoint to say the least.

4. Even without God, everything happens for a reason, including bad things that happen to good people.

In a sense this is true. Because of the law of cause and effect, everything that happens *does* happen for a reason. However, not everything happens for a *purpose*. Natural disasters, for example, happen for a variety of reasons that can be explained by scientists, yet that does not mean they have an ultimate purpose. To have a purpose there must be a thought behind the action. Unless you believe that God is personally directing natural disasters, then there is no purpose to a natural disaster—other than to cause a disaster.

5. Because of the fall of humanity in the Garden of Eden, bad things happen to good people because we are bad people.

This answer suggests "we are all sinners" and therefore we all deserve bad things to happen to us because our ancestors did something really bad a long, long time ago. Eating from the forbidden fruit of the tree of knowledge was the "original sin." After that, as the story goes, everything—and everyone—went to hell in a handbasket. Now we are vulnerable to death, disease, and every other type of misfortune. As far as theories about why bad things happen to good people goes, this is a very creative story, but I am not sure that twenty-first century people can blame every instance of evil and suffering on the notion that our mythological ancestors ate a piece of mythological fruit.

6. The bad god or gods are responsible for why bad things happen to good people.

     In most religious traditions, including our own, we find a story that depicts a cosmological conflict between good and evil represented by divine or supernatural beings. In our religion Satan is the main culprit, although he seems to have an endless army of demons at his beck and call. Like the Adam and Eve "fall" story, this is also very creative, yet is it not also sort of a cop-out? There is a reason why Flip Wilson used to make fun of this by saying, "The devil made me do it." Again, in the twenty-first century, it is not very practical to blame everything bad on a red-toned man with horns and a tail.[4]

7. Murphy's Law—that's why bad things happen to good (and bad) people.

     Murphy's Law states that if a thing can go wrong, it will. Philosophers refer to this as a "logical fallacy" because it has no basis in fact whatsoever. Still, it is a fun way to explain why you tripped over your own shoelaces and fell and broke your hip.

8. Bad luck—that's why bad things happen to good (and bad) people.

     If Job had lived in our era, he might have told his friends that he had had a run of bad luck. Unfortunately, "luck" is not a real thing—it is only something we perceive or interpret. Luck is closely aligned with superstition, which is a way to explain things without having to resort to logic, reason, or even reality. But if you feel like you need to wear a lucky charm around your neck, feel free to do so. It will only hurt if it gets caught in a car door while you are standing outside as the car takes off for its next destination.

9. Bad things happen to good people who are accident prone.

     Some people truly believe they are prone to having more accidents than other people. This is true for some folks who are not very steady on their feet or are just naturally clumsy. Yet bad people can be accident prone as much as good people, and a lot of bad things that happen to good people are not the result of an accident.

4. Perhaps if he had made a better fashion statement . . .

10. No matter how much bad things happen to good people, this is as good as it gets.

This is a theory proposed by a philosopher named Leibniz. He said that among all possible worlds God could have created, this is the best one. Despite the existence of evil and suffering, this is the best of all possible worlds. He said that all other possible worlds could have had even greater amounts of evil and suffering. Of course, there is no possible way to prove or disprove this theory. I am sure someone out there is arguing that we exist in the *worst* of all possible worlds. If that is true, the Creator has a lot of mansplaining to do.[5]

They Are Trying to Kill Us

Those are my top ten explanations for why bad things happen to good people. In my mind, none of them are totally satisfactory, therefore, we are left with just one possible explanation, which is where I started: Bad things happen to good people because "stuff happens." Here is what I mean by that: Because *things* happen, the odds that something bad will happen to us—good and bad folks alike—at some point in our lives is, let's say, *100%*. Each one of us has a perfect 100% chance of experiencing some degree of evil and suffering in our lives. Does my math ring true?

To help answer the question about why bad things happen to good people, we can turn to the theory of evolution. According to the evolutionist, Richard Dawkins, every living creature has enemies that are working hard for its downfall. This includes me and you. At this moment, there are forces—human and natural forces—trying to kill or hurt us in some way. Here are some examples:

- There are people and nations out there plotting to wage war or terrorist attacks against us at this very moment.
- We participate in a win-lose economic system where people are competing with one another for jobs or money.
- The opposing team wants to beat our team.
- If we encounter a hungry bear, it will want to eat us.

5. If God is male, which might explain why bad things happen to good people.

- Parasites would love to get their hands on us, too. Tapeworms, bacteria, viruses, and cancer cells all want to feed off our bodies.

- As soon as we are born the aging (i.e., dying) process begins.

- Natural disasters are not out to get us per se, but if we happen to get in the way . . .

The odds are 100% that something bad or evil will happen to all of us at one time or another. Bad things happen to good people (and bad people) because stuff happens. We can choose to stay in our house all day to avoid bad stuff, but then our physical health will deteriorate from lack of exercise or sunshine and our mental health will likely suffer as well, and then . . . bad things *will* happen. We will never fully know why bad things happen to good people, but the question we should be asking is, "How do we continue to be, ahem, good people when bad things occur?"

Why Is God So Angry?

Another way to answer the question, "Why do bad things happen to good people?" is to argue that God is angry (i.e., "pissed off"). Do you think God ever gets angry? After all, anger is a *human* emotion. I would have to be convinced that the creator of the universe ever really gets angry. But maybe I am wrong. Obviously, the Bible suggests God is, on occasion, an angry God. But could it be that the biblical writers are merely describing God the only way they know how: in human terms? This is called anthropomorphism: attributing human characteristics or behavior to a god, animal, or object. The biblical writers have certainly attributed human characteristics to God, including anger, and most of us do the same.

Once we do that, then we are prone to do what the psychologists call "transference." Transference is the act of redirecting and applying to another person *our* feelings, desires, and expectations. A similar phenomenon is called "projecting." When we are self-absorbed, we tend to project onto another person what we are feeling rather than trying to understand what the other person might be feeling. In other words, because God is like me, and because I am angry, then God must be angry as well.

By the way, I am *not* saying that God *isn't* like us in some ways. I am reminded of the 1995 pop song by Joan Osborne, titled "What if God Was One of Us?" It is a thought-provoking song, but some people, me included, are thrown by the second line that claims God is "just a slob like one of us." I can bend theologically further than a lot of people (I am like a yoga master of theologians); yet suggesting that God is as slobby as I am, is taking anthropomorphism a little too far in my opinion.

For the sake of argument, let us allow that God does get angry on occasion. If this is the case, what does God get angry about? Well, in scripture God gets very angry about sin (i.e., people being no damn good). Just ask Adam and Eve and Noah's drowned neighbors. God's anger is directed at individuals, such as kings, and at the nation of Israel and other nations. How angry does the biblical God get, you ask? Hear the prophet Isaiah's description of God's anger in 30:27–28:

> See, the name of the Lord comes from far away, burning with his anger, and in thick rising smoke; his lips are full of indigna- tion, and his tongue is like a devouring fire; his breath is like an overflowing stream that reaches up to the neck—to sift the nations with the sieve of destruction, and to place on the jaws of the peoples a bridle that leads them astray.

Now, that is an angry God, especially if you read that with God's deep, menacing Old Testament voice. The writer of Psalm 80 was also convinced God gets angry. In verses 4–6, the psalmist writes,

> O Lord God of hosts, how long will you be *angry* with your people's prayers? You have fed them with the bread of tears, and given them tears to drink in full measure. You make us the scorn of our neighbors; our enemies laugh among themselves.

Then the psalmist attempts to calm down the divine anger by imploring, "Restore us, O God of hosts; let your face shine, that we may be saved." God's "shiny face" might be interpreted in contrast to God's red-faced anger.

So, yea, we get it. The biblical writers are mad and angry because life in the ancient world sucks, and they are very adept at transferring or projecting their own anger and emotions onto God.

I have already quoted from one 1995 pop song, so let me do another. In her biggest hit single, the Canadian pop artist Alanis Morissette asks, "Isn't it ironic?" That is an appropriate question for this moment. Isn't it ironic that a God the biblical writers (and we) have morphed into human form with human thoughts, actions, and emotions, *became* human through the birth of a child? We call this the "incarnation," which means "in the flesh." Did the incarnation happen because God was angry? Did God come to us in the flesh because God was getting weary trying to get through to us using more conventional methods such as the use of spoken words through prophets and written words through scripture?

Think of a CEO of a major company trying to get her employees to be more productive. She has tried sending word down the chain through her middle managers. She has tried writing memos and letters on company letterhead. Yet none of it is effective. So, what does the CEO do? She comes to them in person, and all hell breaks loose. Was God so frustrated, perhaps even angry, with us that God needed to come to us *in person?* If so, why would God be so angry?

From a first century Jewish perspective, God has every right to be angry. The oppressive Romans have occupied the land and there is no descendent of David on the throne in Jerusalem. There is a sense of desperation, so, to use a football analogy, God needs to throw a "Hail Mary" pass. Which is ironic, because, well, God *passes* through Mary's womb, so to speak.

We know the rest of the story: A divine-human child is born. Matthew's Gospel, utilizing Isaiah's words from long ago, calls this child "Emmanuel," meaning "God is with us" (if not actually *like* us). Mary's husband, Joseph, names the boy, "Jesus," the Greek form of the Hebrew name for "Joshua," which means "the Lord saves." Isn't it ironic that a God to whom we have attributed human characteristics, and to whom we have transferred and projected our own emotions, chose to be with us in human flesh? Is it because we are no damn good? I would say "you be the judge," but I don't want to make God angry.

There is a myriad of reasons for evil and suffering in the world, some of which I have briefly touched on in this chapter. Obviously, this is a topic beyond the scope of this book, and yet Rabbi Kushner's question, "Why do bad things happen to good people?" is, and always will be, a relevant question. We can sidestep the question by claiming such things as existence is meaningless or the question is meaningless because we are no damn good. But maybe we should consider one more alternative, which is that we are neither good nor bad; we are *morally ambiguous.*

4

Nailing Jell-O to a Wall

A FEW years ago, after yet another mass shooting in America, I was at a huge protest rally in downtown St. Louis. My wife kindly made a sign for me to hold so that I could feel like I was really contributing to the gun debate. A gentleman named Jerry Bruder liked my sign enough to approach me and hand me a flyer about an ethics seminar he was leading at a local high school. When I told him with as much humility as I could possibly muster that I have a PhD in ethics, he got excited and gave me his contact information. A week or so later, we corresponded through email, and he told me he was doing the same ethics seminar for a Senior Citizen's group in Ferguson later that month and asked if I would attend. I accepted his invitation, helped him with his PowerPoint presentation, and we became fast friends.[1]

The biggest theme I remember about Jerry's presentation is that ethics and morality are not cut and dry. There is much ambiguity in the human exploration and practice of ethics and morality. His presentation was titled, "Ethical Issues in a Changing World," which obviously underscores the biggest reason for ambiguous, gray-area, noncut-and-dry ethics: change. In his presentation, Jerry illustrates how difficult it is to name moral absolutes, as he challenges his audiences to continue to explore the depths of their personal convictions when faced with situations that test one's beliefs, principles, and values.

---

1. Jerry has been a world-class motivational speaker for over fifty years. He is also a fantastic pool player and one of those people who has never met a stranger. Ever.

After our first meeting he sent a letter to me, encouraging me to "think about the power of ethical behavior, the difficulty in deciding what *is* ethical, and the need for all of us to continually work together to examine the concept." He notes that defining ethics "often seems like trying to nail Jell-O to a wall." For Jerry, if "Ethical Decisions" had a middle name, it would be "Nuanced."

Captain Obvious is Not a Real Captain

There is very little I dislike more than a non-nuanced understanding of ethics and morality. To put it simply, I do not believe in a black and white binary ethical universe. I do not believe there are very many *obvious* answers to the great ethical dilemmas of this world. Ironically (thanks, Alanis), this is the reason Captain Obvious (along with Jerry Bruder) is my favorite superhero.

In the summer of 2019, I preached a series of sermons about "superpowers" based on the wonderful book, *Hope and Other Superpowers*, by John Pavlovitz.[2] Several years earlier, during my first "children's moment" at Immanuel United Church of Christ in Ferguson, Missouri, I erroneously claimed in a Michael Keatonesque manner that "I am Batman." Perhaps because I grew up as a skinny kid who would have had sand kicked in my face had I lived near a beach, I have allowed a slight, non-geeky fascination with comic book superheroes to fester in my soul.

Although Batman and Superman garnered most of my youthful attention, philosophically my favorite superhero is Captain Obvious.[3] I know, I know. Captain Obvious is not a real superhero, which is obvious because, as you know, there is no such thing as a superhero. "Captain Obvious" is a name invoked in conversation to draw attention to a self-evident fact. Someone might say, "It sure is hot today." Someone else might respond by saying, "Thank you, Captain Obvious!"[4]

Although Captain Obvious is obviously not a superhero, he has been spotted on television. Hotels.com had a character in its television commercials called "Captain Obvious" who said clearly obvious

2. Pavlovitz, *Hope and other Superpowers: A Life-Affirming, Love-Defending, Butt-Kicking, World-Saving Manifesto*, New York: Simon & Schuster, 2018.

3. Recently, I discovered that his brother is Captain Oblivious, and his main rival is Professor Subtle. Go figure.

4. For most of my personal history, I have said the same thing with the words, "No shit, Sherlock!" I'm sure you can guess why. #DrWatson

things such as "Saving money on a hotel is the same as saving money on anything that costs money." Not only is Captain Obvious obviously not a superhero, neither is he obviously a Captain. As one person wrote, "He does not hold the rank of Captain in the Army, Navy, Air Force, Coast Guard, Marines, the National Oceanic and Atmospheric Administration Commissioned Corps, the United States Public Health Service Commissioned Corps, the Salvation Army or any Police or Fire Department. Nor is he licensed to fly commercial or cargo aircraft or pilot fishing boats or cargo vessels, meaning that in a situation where he would have to pilot one of these vehicles and is asked by a duly authorized official to prove that he had the legal right to do so, he would not be able to."[5]

Obviously, Captain Obvious is not a Captain. Nor has he been very successful maintaining an important place in our culture. For instance, he has had a difficult time landing a role in a television series or in the movies, even movies about superheroes. An entire thirty minutes were cut from the first X-Men film to eliminate his role, due to the sheer predictability of his character. He tried his hand at comic books, too, but after three issues sales plummeted due to what critics called "predictable writing." He once appeared on The O'Reilly Factor for only about ten seconds because after he was introduced, he blurted out, "Wait a minute—this show isn't fair and balanced at all!"[6] Captain Obvious wrote, "I think my constant exclusion may have something to do with how I always say the obvious."

Wasteland of the Free

The Apostle Paul of first century biblical fame and Captain Obvious could have been good friends. In Galatians 5:19–21, Paul tells the ethically challenged Galatians: "Now the works of the flesh are *obvious*: fornication, impurity, licentiousness, idolatry, sorcery, enmities, strife, jealousy, anger, quarrels, dissensions, factions, envy, drunkenness, carousing, and things like these."[7] Paul may have been drinking from the Captain Obvious Kool-Aid when he wrote this, but his larger point is very important . . . and not so obvious.

---

5. https://uncyclopedia.ca/wiki/Captain_Obvious.

6. No shit, Sherlock.

7. That pretty much sums up a typical night out on the town.

At first glance it seems like Paul is trying to curtail human freedom by telling his readers what they should not do. He reminds me of a stern parent, pointing a finger at a child, telling them to behave. Ironically, Paul offers this list of things we should avoid doing in the context of "Christian freedom." He begins chapter five by saying, "For freedom Christ has set us free. Stand firm, therefore, and do not submit again to a yoke of slavery." He then talks about being slaves to the "Law". He is not suggesting we all turn into a bunch of anarchists, people who do not believe in any type of system of laws whatsoever. He is talking about freedom from two specific things: freedom from oppressive requirements of the Law of Moses (such as circumcision), and freedom from the power that the desires of the flesh have over us. He believed these are the things that were robbing the Galatians of their freedom in Christ. They were slaves to both the Law and works of the flesh.

Concerning the latter, anyone who has ever had an addiction of some sort—alcohol, drugs, food, sex, anger, etc.—knows exactly what Paul is talking about. Through Christ, however, Paul suggests we can free ourselves of the things that enslave and control us. That is a big claim and perhaps a little esoteric for most of us, but Paul had not been introduced to 12-step programs. Jesus was the only step he needed.

Our natural inclination is to seek freedom, and yet Paul warns us not to abuse our freedom. "For you were called to freedom," wrote Paul, "only do not use your freedom as an opportunity for self-indulgence" (Galatians 5:13). Instead, he says, use your freedom to love one another. This is a truth that I wish more of us understood, especially in a culture like ours that is rightly supportive of such things as freedom, individual rights, liberty, and independence. Yes, we live in one of the freest societies in history, and yet, because we are no damn good, we often waste our freedom on self-indulgences.

This reminds me of a great song from the country artist, Iris Dement, a timeless song about American culture titled, "Wasteland of the Free." Just as youth is sometimes wasted on the young, freedom is sometimes wasted on the free. And because we are no damn good, or, at the very least, morally ambiguous, we tend to use our freedom on self-indulgent things rather than for things that contribute to the well-being of society.

The Juice of the Spirit

The most obvious reason even the best of our species tends to be morally ambiguous is that we are naturally self-indulgent. This is the root of what we call "sin." Reinhold Niebuhr famously said, "The doctrine of sin is the only empirically verifiable doctrine of the Christian faith." The fact that we are not perfect is painfully obvious to most of us. Although the word "sin" seems rather archaic in more progressive circles today, it still resonates with many people in the fly-over states. We could find other words to replace it, yet the meaning is always the same: We are no damn good.

So, what is the alternative to self-indulgent "works of the flesh"? Again, Paul must have been hanging out with Captain Obvious when he wrote, "By contrast, the fruit of the Spirit (as opposed to works of the flesh) is love, joy, peace, patience, kindness, generosity, faithfulness, gentleness, and self-control." My response to this list is also "Duh".

But what about those things that are not so obvious, things that are more ambiguous? Paul was a genius at telling us what is obviously bad and good, but life doesn't always present us with such clear-cut choices, does it?[8] And yet, Paul was a "dualist." He tirelessly pits the spiritual world against the material world ("the flesh"). For Paul, reality is an either/or proposition. Either you are on the side of the spirit, or you are on the side of flesh. Either you wear a white hat or a black hat. Dualism has had the unfortunate result of giving us an unhealthy attitude about bodily issues, including sexuality. The flesh is bad while the spirit is good. And yet, again, reality does not always operate on such an obvious level. Life would be boring if it did. I believe it was Chuck Klosterman who said, "The juice of life is derived from arguments that don't seem obvious."[9]

It is not lost on me that juice is fruit in liquid form. Paul gave us an obvious list of the "fruit of the spirit," however, I'm just as interested in the "juice of the spirit," that is, the Spirit guiding us through things in life that are not so obvious or clear-cut, that are grounded in moral ambiguity (if that's even possible). As a pastor and a human being, the longer my existence continues to stretch toward the horizon, the more ambiguous,

---

8. For me, a clear-cut choice is defined as a chicken fried steak over tofu. I understand that, ethically speaking, tofu should be the proper choice for health, environmental, and animal rights reasons, so this is the most obvious evidence that I am no damn good.

9. Kosterman, *But What If We're Wrong: Thinking about the Present as If it Were the Past*, Simon & Schuster, 92.

disputable, doubtful, fuzzy, indefinite, muddy, obscure, uncertain, unclear, unpredictable, unsure, and vague life becomes. Freedom is cool, whether it comes from the U.S. Constitution or the Bible, and yet I am not always certain what to do with my freedom. Because I am inherently no damn good, sometimes I rope the wrong goat.

Whatever

Because we are morally ambiguous, if not no damn good, we often have a difficult time discerning between what is important and what is not important. For instance, when I get online, I like to see what's trending. Because I do not often recognize any of the names or words that are trending, I have decided that this is merely an exercise to keep me humble, to help me realize just how out of touch I am with what is going on in the world. After this brief self-deprecating moment, however, I realize that one reason I seem so out of step with reality is that I am not as prone to exaggerate the importance of certain people or events as many of my fellow human primates are. That is, I am not as likely to make a mountain out of a molehill.

I have what scholars, experts, and other know-it-alls refer to as a "whatever attitude." My wife will tell you this is my default setting. On occasion I try to steer away from it because I realize it gives others the impression that I do not care about anything, that I do not see any "mountains" out there at all, that all I see are "molehills." This is simply not true. I see plenty of mountains to overcome in our world: war, climate change, sexual harassment, racial injustice, Covid-19, and bad salsa, just to name a few. I have no trouble grabbing a bullhorn and telling the world that it needs to shape up or ship out, and yet, at the same time, I have no trouble looking at what is trending on the world wide web and saying, "Whatever. That is a molehill, not a mountain. Grow up."

"Making a mountain of a molehill" is an idiom that refers to making too much of a minor issue. When I was in grad school one of my professors used to call this phenomenon "majoring in minors," which is very confusing when one is studying the Old Testament or Hebrew prophets.[10] Also, one should not use the phrase "majoring in minors" while discussing

---

10. For those of you who studied more practical disciplines like Amazon finger painting or Literature of 16th century Scandinavian woodcutters, the Hebrew prophets are divided into "major" and "minor" prophets.

the complexities of baseball with a 33-year-old double A has-been ball-player either.

Why do some folks tend to major in minors, i.e., to make mountains out of molehills? Conversely, why do some folks often make the opposite mistake of making molehills out of mountains? In my humble opinion, the main culprit is *time*. There are two kinds of people in the world. First, there are those who have a *short view of time*, folks who live in the present. For short timers, everything that is happening *now* is of the utmost importance. These are the people who tend to make mountains out of molehills. Second, there are those who have a *long view of time*. These so-called long timers are less likely to ascribe exaggerated significance to something that is occurring in the present. The downside of the long timer, however, is that he or she tends to overlook the significance of something happening today that truly has consequences for the long term. These are the folks who tend to make molehills out of mountains.

Perhaps what we need is more balance in our understanding of time, the ability to know a mountain or a molehill when we see one and are not likely to confuse the two, the ability to observe what is "trending" on the internet and understand that things that are trendy, by definition, will be forgotten after the proverbial fifteen minutes of fame. In the mean*time*, if I see someone getting all worked up about something that has everyone's attention, do not be surprised when I look at them with a lazy frown and say, "Whatever."

We All Have a Little Weed in Us

Jesus had less of a "whatever" attitude than I do, yet I suspect that he understood moral ambiguity like a pro. He understood how difficult it is to discern between good and bad folks and even between mountains and molehills. To drive home his point, he tells a wonderful parable about wheat and weeds:

> He put before them another parable: "The kingdom of heaven may be compared to someone who sowed good seed in his field; but while everybody was asleep, an enemy came and sowed weeds among the wheat, and then went away. So when the plants came up and bore grain, then the weeds appeared as well. And the slaves of the householder came and said to him, 'Master, did you not sow good seed in your field? Where, then, did these weeds come from?' He answered, 'An enemy has done

this.' The slaves said to him, 'Then do you want us to go and gather them?' But he replied, 'No; for in gathering the weeds you would uproot the wheat along with them. Let both of them grow together until the harvest; and at harvest time I will tell the reapers, Collect the weeds first and bind them in bundles to be burned, but gather the wheat into my barn.'" (Matthew 13:24–30)

In this parable, a farmer is sowing good wheat seeds in a field, but at night someone comes along and plants weeds. The wheat and the weeds grow up together.[11] What does a farmer do with the weeds? The farmer's workers want to uproot the weeds before the harvest so that the harvest will only contain wheat, but the farmer says, "No, if you get rid of the weeds you will uproot the wheat as well. Just leave them alone and let the harvest sort them out."

Weeds are generally recognized as a problem. What should we do about them? We can pull them out individually, which is doable only in a small private garden. We can take a hoe and chop down the weeds, but if we do that, we will likely accidentally chop down some of the good plants as well, as Jesus warned. We could use some weed killer, but the biggest problem with weed killer is that it does not know a tumble weed from a tomato plant. I am not a farmer or a gardener, so I am not an expert on this, but I assume eradicating weeds is still a big problem.

Nevertheless, in this parable Jesus is comparing the kingdom of God to a garden that is infested with weeds. He is probably saying that there may be people in the kingdom of God that do not really belong. Although we say everyone is welcome in our congregations and everyone belongs, let us admit that some people can cause problems in the church just as weeds can cause problems in a garden.[12] Sometimes these people get so out of control that they are directly asked to leave a church, or they are indirectly run off from the church.[13]

I am not a big fan of eradicating the weeds from a congregation, but I have done it. I once sat down with a retired pastor on two separate occasions and asked her to leave my congregation. She refused to do so.

11. As the oldest and best child among three siblings, I understand the dynamic of wheat and weeds in the same household.

12. The "kingdom of God" and congregations are not necessarily one and the same.

13. For your entertainment, read Rediger, *Clergy Killers: Guidance for Pastors and Congregations Under Attack*, and Shelley, *Well-Intentioned Dragons: Ministering to Problem People in the Church*.

That weed is still growing in that congregation. I, on the other hand, was uprooted. Jesus' parable is telling us we need to be very careful about trying to uproot people from the church. In fact, Jesus suggests that if we do try to yank out such congregational weeds, we could do more harm than good.

As I indicated earlier, once upon a time *I was the weed* in a congregation, at least from the perspective of many of the parishioners. They wanted me gone. What those self-appointed weed killers discovered, however, is that by uprooting one weed—namely, me—they lost a big part of their wheat field. Many people left the church in protest of my departure. So, before you go grabbing your spiritual hoe or weed killer, remember this parable. After all, just who are the weeds and the wheat? On occasion we can perceive some obvious congregational weeds. Sometimes they stick out like a sore thumb. Other times, however, they are unidentifiable. There is usually no way to separate people into wheat and weeds—good and bad. Realistically, we are all hybrids. We all have a little wheat in us and a little weed in us.[14] We are all morally ambiguous.

Jesus Was No Captain Obvious

One of the best sermons ever preached on the above parable was delivered by Reinhold Niebuhr called, "The Wheat and the Tares." A "tare" is a biblical word for a weed that resembles wheat when it is young. That is the unspoken problem Jesus is trying to communicate in this parable. If tares resemble wheat, then how can we know what to uproot before the harvest? Niebuhr admits we need to make distinctions between good and evil. We cannot have a civilization unless we can draw the line somewhere between good and evil. And yet within our responsibility to distinguish between good and evil comes this parable of the wheat and tares, a parable where Jesus asks us not to uproot the tares or weeds. "Let both of them grow together until the harvest," says Jesus.

This is the great tension in which we are called to live. While we do have to make judgments to have a modicum of decency in this world, we need to admit that we are not the final decision-maker on who qualifies as wheat and who qualifies as weeds.[15] We do not always know who *obviously* qualifies as wheat or who qualifies as weeds.

14. Pot smokers are not excluded from this assessment.

15. That would be my mom.

Such is the ambiguous moral life of a follower of the one who told the parable of the wheat and weeds. Jesus was no Captain Obvious, as much as fundamentalists might hope for. Sometimes we cannot see the distinctions between good and evil in people or institutions until the final harvest. Furthermore, to make matters even more confusing, good often lies in the heart of an evil person or self-serving business, and evil often lies at the core of a benevolent person or institution. Just ask Tony Soprano, Walter White, Saul Goodman, and countless other cinematic or television characters about their own moral ambiguity.[16] At the end of the day, and against our moral instincts, sometimes we need to "let both of them grow until the harvest." This is not an excuse for moral laziness. It is, however, a reminder that we ain't God, and moral ambiguity is always part of the equation.

16. Concerning Saul Goodman from both the *Breaking Bad* and *Better Call Saul* television series, I have a theory about his name. "Saul" is the name of the Apostle Paul before he converted (and the name of the first king of Israel who had both positive and negative qualities). Paired with his surname, "Goodman," i.e., "good man," we get a sense of the moral ambiguity that Jimmy "Slippin" McGill's character was trying to portray.

5

Searching through the Moral Kiosk

A ND now, a musical interlude from my favorite band, R.E.M., a song to put us in a morally ambiguous mood, called *Moral Kiosk*, from the 1983 *Murmur* album:

> Scratch the scandals in the twilight
> Trying to shock but instead
> Idle hands all orient to her
> Pass a magic pillow under head
> It's so much more attractive inside the moral kiosk
> Inside, cold, dark, fire, twilight
> Inside, cold, dark, fire, twilight
> They scratch the scandals in the twilight
> She was laughing like a Horae
> Put that knee in dour landslide
> Take this step to dash a roving eye
> It's so much more attractive inside the moral kiosk
> Inside, cold, dark, fire, twilight
> Inside, cold, dark, fire, twilight

Yep, you're right. The lyrics make no sense whatsoever, which is R.E.M. and specifically Michael Stipe at their finest, although most of the responses I read pointed to a subtle critique of hypocrisy. Maybe. But we all know what a kiosk is—"a small structure in a public area used for providing information." In this chapter I invite you to pick up a few pamphlets, sort through them to find something that piques your interest and try to stop being no damn good.

Historically, there are a multitude of attempts to explain the human ethical enterprise, both descriptively and prescriptively. I thought it would be helpful to offer a sample from my own moral kiosk, a.k.a. file cabinet, full of notes from lectures I used to offer in my Introduction to Ethics courses at the community college and local prisons. I will begin with the Godfather of Western Ethics, Mr. Socrates himself.[1]

Socrates (470–399 BCE)

The ancient Greek philosophers thought we as a species have potential. We do not need to be no damn good. To paraphrase an old Army commercial, we can be, with careful logic and reasoning, all we can be. The Greeks believed we are a reasonable species, and if we are reasonable, then we can be good.

Socrates is the first reasonable philosopher to pop up on our on radar screen. Even if the use of reason leads to unpopular and dangerous results, we should allow our convictions and conscience a fair hearing. He taught us how to follow the popular method of reasoning that is named after him: The Socratic Method.[2] If anything, Socrates was a sneaky man. He would engage someone in dialogue who believed they thought they were correct in their assertions. He did this knowing that the other person was, to be blunt, full of crap.[3] After he set up the other person by coaxing them to state their wayward and faulty opinion, Socrates would begin a series of probing questions, going deeper than a colonoscopy as he responded to each answer, always requiring the other person to give precise definitions of his or her key terms. According to the mythological greatness of Socrates, his line of questioning would invariably reveal logical inconsistencies on the part of his opponent. At the end of the debate, Socrates would offer his own opinion with laser beam logic. As someone once said to another person sitting in a bar, "Here comes Socrates. Don't argue with him. You can't win."

Of course, this did not win him enough friends to keep him out of trouble. In 399 BCE, the Athenians voted to condemn the

---

1. Not to be confused with the "Western Ethics" of Wild Bill Hickok and Wyatt Earp.

2. Not to be confused with the Kominsky Method.

3. This is historical fiction at its finest. I have no idea whether Socrates ever spoke the words "full of crap" about another human being (in the Greek language of course), but he sure must have thought something very similar.

seventy-seven-year-old Socrates to death, basically for being able to win every argument against every opponent, even when the opponent was correct.[4] He believed in the democratic system so much that he accepted his death sentence, calmly drank some hemlock, and then, while his own personal Titanic was sinking, engaged his friends in philosophical conversation. Socrates was probably better than no damn good, which is why we killed him.

Plato (428ish–348ish BCE)

Now let us turn our attention to the guy that reminds us of that malleable gooey multi-colored stuff we played with when we were small children. Even after twenty-five centuries, Plato's name is more recognizable today than even John Doe. We consider him the benchmark for Western philosophy. Like Socrates, he was great at knowing the right questions to ask and the wrong answers to avoid. Like a kid with Play-Doh, he was very creative in possible answers for life's difficult questions. He understood that knowledge did not necessarily consist of what people had already said or done. For Plato, reflectiveness trumped tradition.

In an opinion that should give all of us pause, Plato did not think very highly of the Greek form of democracy because he saw what happened to Socrates when the majority rules. He was not a "might makes right" kind of guy. He preferred, instead, a governmental system ruled by a "philosopher-king."[5] Only a philosopher, he suggested, is well-trained and able to grasp objective truth enough to know what is genuinely good for all people.

Perhaps because there were not endless ways of being entertained in the ancient world, the Greeks key ethical question concerned the *eudaimonia*—the "good life." For Plato and Socrates, the good life consists of an abundance of wisdom and its companion, knowledge. To be a good person requires one to have knowledge that leads to virtue. Virtue was understood as "excellence in function." A virtuous teacher, for instance, is a knowledgeable teacher because teaching knowledge is their key function. Plato surmised that when people are ignorant, they cannot control their desires and passions, so I assume Plato would agree that ignorant people are no damn good.

4. Socrates was the Tom Brady of philosophy.
5. Not to be confused with a Tiger King.

The Greeks loved virtues such as wisdom, temperance (or modera-tion), justice, courage, and piety, all of which led to *eudaimonia*. Notice that the word "pleasure" is absent from that list. Plato's philosophy was in direct contradiction to the ethics of the Sophists, who believed that the good life is a hedonistic life filled with pleasure. Plato argued that plea-sure could not be the standard of morality.[6] Furthermore, committing an injustice (robbing people of the good life) damages one's character and soul. To bring this back full circle, Plato suggested that we commit acts of evil and injustice due to ignorance. Thus, when I say, "People are no damn good," the elitist Plato inside me adds, "*Ignorant* people are no damn good." But at least they are blissful.

Aristotle (384–322 BCE)

If anyone should know whether people are good or evil, it is the person who served as a personal tutor to Alexander the Freaking Great. The latter had a penchant for conquering the known world. Aristotle was certainly qualified to be Alex's personal tutor because he learned his craft from Plato at the latter's Academy. Aristotle was not a typical butt-kissing student because it is known that he would challenge the elder Plato when he found flaws in his reasoning.[7] His position as Alexander the Great's tutor came about because of family ties to the throne of Greece.[8]

Aristotle was a first-rate ethicist. In his book, *Nicomachean Ethics* (obviously a nod to his daddy), Aristotle wrote the first genuinely system-atic analysis of ethical questions in Western philosophy. Like all good Greek philosophers, he wanted to know what we need to do to have a "good life." Rather than ask what rules to follow, however, he wanted to know what sort of person we should be, thus introducing us to the concept of *virtue* or *character* ethics.

He began his search for the good life by asking what ultimate end or goal people desire. He concludes, like Plato, that it must be *eudai-monia* (well-being or happiness). Applying his well-honed Greek skill of reasoning, he concludes that happiness is the goal because 1) happiness

6. Even today we tend to separate the desire for pleasure from an ethical life. We have Plato to thank for making us so dull at parties.

7. This may be why he did not have a career teaching in Plato's Academy.

8. Aristotle's father, Nichomachus, was the personal physician for the King of Macedonia, whose son would become known as Philip the Great, who, in turn, was the father of Alexander the Great.

is intrinsically desirable; 2) it is not a means to attain anything else; 3) by itself it satisfies human beings; and 4) wise people are able to attain it.

Then he digs deeper: "What is the nature of happiness?" he asks. He argues that *human* happiness must be explained in terms of that unique function or activity which distinguishes human beings from other animals.[9] Aristotle concludes that the ability to *reason* is at the top of the list. Interestingly, this means that such things as physical pleasure does not bring as much *eudaimonia* as the ability to reason because even animals derive pleasure from physical activities (we assume). Like Plato and Socrates before him, Aristotle seems to be saying, "Smart people are ethically superior and happier than not-so-smart people."

Virtue and reason are key ethical concepts for Aristotle. A virtue is related to the function of something, so if a person or thing performs its main function properly then it is said to have virtue. Virtues stem from tendencies, dispositions, or habits, therefore for a human being to be virtuous he or she must have a disposition or habit to live according to reason. This equates to intellectual virtue, which is distinguished from moral virtue. Morality does not require reasoning; it consists of dispositions or habits to act in a right manner. For Aristotle, practice makes perfect, so a virtuous disposition is formed in a person that practices right actions.

Aristotle is also the world's greatest moderate. He suggests that virtues are found at the mid- point between excess and deficiency. This is called the "golden mean," the optimal point between "too much" and "not enough." "Moderation in everything" is therefore an Aristotelian concept stolen by Oscar Wilde. This does not mean, by the way, that moderates are ethically superior to folks on the left or the right, but it does mean they are much less likely to get plastered at a Greek party.

Epicurus (341–270 BCE)

Another dead Greek philosopher that does not get quite the airtime as Socrates, Plato, and Aristotle, is their archnemesis, Epicurus, although

---

9. I have spent most of my career trying to understand the intrinsic differences between humans and other animals, and I have narrowed it down to three things: 1) humans like to play baseball—animals like to play with the ball; 2) humans like to drive cars—animals like to chase cars; and 3) humans like to eat their food from on top of the table—animals like to eat food that falls from the table. Note: my analysis is limited to the dog that lives with me.

the latter was more a lover than a fighter. Epicurus founded an institution of higher education called "The Garden of Epicurus," which competed with the Academy of Plato and Aristotle's Lyceum.[10] Unlike the other two, the Garden of Epicurus admitted men and women, free persons and slaves, and landowners and those who owned no property. I hope he gave a tuition discount for the women, slaves, and renters.

The curriculum must have been intellectually accessible because Epicurus emphasized a life of quiet seclusion. He and his followers lived simple lives, consisting of a bread and water diet, and an occasional glass of wine for special occasions. His philosophical-ethical system can be reduced to a few fundamental insights: cultivate lasting friendships, live simply, do nothing to excess, seek to maximize peaceful and harmonious pleasures, and use critical thinking to minimize superstitious fear and pain. He also—and this is what his students were graded on—focused on the study of philosophy and nature.

Epicurus is rightly labeled a "hedonist," but not because he ate at Chinese buffets and hosted nightly orgies at his condo. He stressed instead seeking the pleasures to be found in abstract thought, not sensual pleasures, such as food, sleep, and sex. He gives straightforward advice: Adopt a simple life where our wants are few and long-term pleasures of the mind are preferable to short-term pleasures of the flesh. To live this way, he says we need to cultivate the virtue of prudence rather than overindulgence. The "good life" is a life of peace of mind or serenity. Furthermore, we cannot avoid pain and suffering altogether, but we can avoid the sorts of pains that arise because we have foolish, superstitious, or mistaken beliefs. Scientologists do not fare well at an Epicurean weekend retreat.

Immanuel Kant (1724–1804)

Let us fast forward through the biblical era and the Dark Ages to find some more interesting Western thinkers. Obviously, the focus of the moral and ethical life has changed from happiness to . . . something else. If there was ever a guy who was not all that concerned about happiness, it was Immanuel Kant. Kant was a moralist in the sense that he was certain

10. Wouldn't it be great to focus on intellectual and philosophical competition between schools today rather than what occurs on football fields and basketball courts, although I must admit that I would love to see the Dallas Cowboys hire "cerebral" philosophers for their coaching staff rather than guys with damaged brains.

we could determine what was right and wrong. Furthermore, he was certain we could apply our conclusions to every person in every time and place. There wasn't much wiggle room in Kant's ethical universe. We label Kant a "deontologist," which comes from the word *deon* or duty. He was a do-your-duty-dude, no matter the consequences. Hence, we also refer to him and his fellow deontologists as "non-consequentialists."

For Kant, the end (result, consequences) never justifies the means because rightness or wrongness is based on the act itself. Thus, one can do the "right" thing and have a bad result, or one can do the "wrong" thing and have a good result. Like the Greeks, Kant believed in the power of reason, which he believed we can use to work out an absolute consistent set of moral principles, applicable to everyone—from caveman to CEO.[11] There are no exceptions to the rules, even if following the rules might cause harm to someone. Kant therefore refers to the standardized rules as "imperatives" or "commands."

His absolutist views led him to propose a couple of gnarly imperatives called, creatively, the "Categorical Imperative" and his "Second Formulation of the Categorical Imperative."[12] The first formulation of his Categorical Imperative is this: "Act only on that maxim whereby you can at the same time will that it would become a universal law." Translation: A rule is good for you if it is good for everyone. His second formulation seems to be his most important Categorical Imperative: "So act as to treat humanity, whether in your own person or in that of any other, in every case as an end and never as merely a means only." He could have just said, "Don't use people," but then the length of his books would have suffered.

I love Kant. I really do. I think he would have made a great neighbor so long as you stayed off his lawn. Yes, his Categorical Imperatives might lead to the occasional absurd consequence, but he did not care about consequences anyway.[13] He just wanted to make sure we have a way to determine when someone is being good and when someone is being no damn good. Fair enough.

---

11. I do not mean to demean our hairy cave-dwelling ancestors by suggesting they ever stooped to the same moral standards as today's CEO's. I apologize, although the pictures on the walls of the caves suggest that cavemen and women did not have good posture.

12. Kant was never asked to name babies, pets, or even hurricanes.

13. He is the guy who coined the phrase, "To hell with consequences!" No, he's not.

John Stuart Mill (1806–1873)

One cannot mention Mill without giving a nod to his predecessor and mentor, Jeremy Bentham (1748–1832). For lack of a better phrase, Bentham was the first of the great "bleeding heart liberals." He was concerned about what was good *for everyone*, not just the whitest and wealthiest. Like the Greeks before him, Bentham (and then Mill) used "happiness" as a goal or consequence worth pursuing.[14] With that in mind, they set out to reform such things as parliament, prison reform, women's suffrage, and democracy itself.[15]

Mill's father raised him to defend the political theories of Bentham. Together, their stress on social utility has been described as the purest form of a genuine teleological system because it focuses on results or consequences. Hence the name "consequentialism" is also applied to their ethical system. It is the consequences of our actions that determine whether they are right or wrong—ethical or unethical. The preferred consequence, of course, is the "greatest happiness for the greatest number." In fact, the cornerstone of Mill's teaching is called "the Doctrine of Utility" or "the Greatest Happiness Principle."[16]

For Mills, happiness is equated most closely with pleasure, which has been termed "the hedonistic calculus." Math nerds should love Mill. A choice is calculated to be ethical by adding up the positive pleasures and subtracting the pains and going with the choice that has the greatest balance of pleasures over pain. One can see here influences from both Aristotle and Epicurus. Mills combines the former's claim that the good life is happiness with the latter's claim that pleasure is intrinsically valuable.

Humorously or derogatorily, Mill's critics accused him of a "pig philosophy," suggesting that pigs in the mud are the most ethical creatures on the planet because they are, well, as happy as pigs in the mud. Mill counters this critique, however, by pointing out that human pleasures are higher than that of animals. "Higher pleasures" include such things as

14. Have you ever noticed that the U.S. Constitution guarantees the right to a "pursuit of happiness"? The founding daddies knew, as the Netflix series, *Happyish*, suggests, that happiness is stupid slippery. We can engage in the chase but not the catch.

15. Some say he invented rock and roll, which is not possible. However, this is an understandable fabrication, given the fact that rock and roll is responsible for the most amount of happiness for the most people.

16. When Major League Baseball awards a "utility player" with the MVP someday, then we can claim that MLB has happily become a Millsian game.

intellectual pursuits, poetry, art, literature, music, dance, creativity, imagination, spirituality, objects of nature, architecture, composing, history, and NASCAR.[17] One of the most-utilized quotes in Mill's writings is this: "It is better to be a human being dissatisfied than a pig satisfied; better to be Socrates dissatisfied than a fool satisfied." I am sure bacon connoisseurs agree.

Aristotle Revisited: Virtue or Character Ethics

In contrast to consequentialist and non-consequentialist ethics is a focus on virtue or character. Virtue ethicists argue that a person's character traits, habits, and virtues determine the proper standard of conduct whenever there is a need to make a moral decision. Any moral action taken by an individual who has the proper moral virtues and character traits will be a good action. In 1958, the British philosopher, G.E.M. Anscombe published an article called "Modern Moral Philosophy," in which she argued that we should stop thinking about obligation, duty, and rightness, and return to Aristotle's approach.[18]

A partial list of virtues includes: benevolence, civility, compassion, conscientiousness, cooperativeness, courage, courteousness, dependability, fairness, friendliness, generosity, honesty, industriousness, justice, loyalty, moderation, reasonableness, self-confidence, self-control, self-discipline, self-reliance, tactfulness, thoughtfulness, and tolerance . . . pretty much everything Donald Trump is not.[19] As implied above while discussing Aristotle, the virtues are means poised between the two extremes of excess and deficiency. Let us take "courage" as an example. Courage is a mean between the extremes of cowardice and foolhardiness.[20]

I appreciate virtue or character ethics, and yet for me the basic problem with this theory is that it does not work all that well for people

---

17. I added "NASCAR" because now that they have eradicated the confederate flag and racism from their race events, they will almost certainly begin to attract philosophers, artists, and poets to their deafening contests.

18. Anscombe was a real gem!

19. I seriously cannot think of one Trumpian virtue. If you can, please write to me at sherlockspal@yahoo.com.

20. An alternative perspective on courage comes from the pen of Jeremy Goldberg: "Courage is knowing it might hurt and doing it anyway... Stupidity is the same. And that's why life is so hard."

who are genuinely no damn good. The racist redneck in the woods is not going to change his or her character by merely acting according to their character. For that person, a list of rules or laws (deontology) and/or an awareness of the consequences of their actions (teleology) might be in order before we hope that the redneck in the woods does not attempt to resurrect the South or invade the U.S. Capital (again).

Ayn Rand (1905–1982)

If there was ever an approach to ethics that proves beyond a shadow of a doubt that people are no damn good, it is a category known as *ethical egoism*. The heroine of this approach is Ayn Rand, who seems to take the ancient Greeks' emphasis on happiness to an extreme, if not logical, conclusion. Ethical egoism is defined as the notion that each person *ought* to pursue his or her own self-interest exclusively. This is a prescriptive view of morality rather than a descriptive view.

In contrast, *psychological egoism* is the notion that we are always motivated to do what we perceive is in our own self-interest—a descriptive theory of humanity. The ethical egoists, in other words, are saying that even if we do not normally act out of our own self-interest, we *should*. Thomas Hobbes (1588–1679) suggested that egoism is the proper foundation for the moral and political life, which means he would have made a great American politician. Because we are naturally self-interested creatures, it makes no sense to ask anyone to be altruistic. If anyone acts altruistically, they are doing it out of self-interest.

This "morality of self-exaltation," as ethical egoism is often called, is a consequentialist ethical theory because it seeks consequences that are good for us, even at the expense of others. One can see why this ethical theory is a favorite among self-described capitalists. Adam Smith (1723–1790) and his followers argue that "enlightened" self-interest leads, as though by an invisible hand, to competition in the marketplace, which causes us to make better products, which is good for everyone.[21] We call this "a rising tide lifts all boats" perspective.

Rand and her followers often take this a step further by arguing that everyone ought always to serve *my* self-interest, a theory known as

---

21. "Enlightened" self-interest sounds suspiciously egoistic, which I guess is the point. It is also like saying, "I know I'm a sociopath and yet I'm using it for the good of all." Uh huh. Right.

"individual ethical egoism."[22] Selfishness is a virtue, while altruism is a vice, although wouldn't the egoist want others to be altruistic so that they can benefit from the goodness of others? At the end of the day, even if we are self-interested creatures (i.e., no damn good), we should at least strive to do better, to minimally give an impression to the world that we are better than that, so that our odds of being shot in the face while the shooter says, "You're an asshole," is less likely to occur. Now, *that* is in our self-interest.[23]

Feminist Ethics

If there is an approach to ethics that is in direct contrast to ethical egoism, I nominate Feminist Ethics for the prize. Although a woman, Ayn Rand does not represent the kind of ethics that is typically associated with a feminine touch. I should offer a word of warning before I continue with this: As a man writing about feminist ethics, I might come across as sexist without even realizing it. There may be "microaggressions" leaking out of my misogynistically-formed brain. If I were completely "self-aware" as a male, I would raise the bar for men so unusually high that there would be no choice but to build a monument in my honor.[24]

Feminist ethics is associated with women, such as Mary Wollstone-craft, Olive Schreiner, Carol Gilligan, Nel Noddings, the suffrage movement, the feminist movement of the 1970s, and even male ethicists such as David Suzuki and Peter Singer. Collectively, they propose an "ethic of care" that is often ignored in institutions such as politics and religion, where male influence has enjoyed much power and privilege. Feminists rightly assert that women have a distinctive perspective in many arenas, such as ethics, politics, and religion, and therefore we should hear their voices more often and more loudly.

In a nutshell (which is an ironic term to use in this context), an ethic of care argues that we should treat everyone as we would treat our loved

22. I would agree with this approach if only I could make it work in my own home. I cannot. I am way down the line in terms of having the power to do things out of self-interest. My dog is even ahead of me in the pecking . . . I mean barking order. Therefore, I reject it as a viable theory.

23. By the way, if you are wondering whether Rand Paul, the Libertarian Senator from Kentucky, is named after Ayn Rand, you get a gold star for the day. If he is not, he ought to be.

24. Which is a typical masculine thing to do.

ones. It therefore focuses on small-scale, personal relationships, although not to the exclusion of the greater society. Interestingly, an ethic of care applies to more than just people; it applies to our care of creation and creatures, which is why feminist ethicists are often involved in the environmentalist and animal rights movements.

The Rider and the Elephant

As we continue to search through the moral kiosk looking for an acceptable pamphlet—although we can't go wrong with an ethics of care—we might pause and ask about the psychology behind ethical decision-making. What is going on in our minds?

Like most people I assume that my political, social, religious, and ethical views are totally unbiased, informed, and rational. I assume that my views are therefore correct. If I assumed otherwise, wouldn't I change them? Of course, you know what happens when we assume too much. I do not need to sound it out for you. However, my political, social, religious, and ethical views are *not* totally unbiased, informed, and rational. My views are just how I have come to perceive things. As I have heard many times in my life, "My perception is my reality."[25] To be consistent, even that comment is just a perception. But I digress.

Not long ago I read *The Righteous Mind: Why Good People are Divided by Politics and Religion* by Jonathan Haidt.[26] Before I dove into this book I assumed (there is that word again) that I knew why people are divided by politics and religion. I assumed (ahem) people are divided by politics and religion because some people are unbiased, informed, and rational while others are, well, ignorant stupid morons.[27]

Haidt taught me that in truth *none of us* are completely unbiased, informed, and rational. And even if we have mastered a high degree of these characteristics, it would not matter. We do not use our big rational brains to make moral decisions anyway. According to Haidt our First Responder (a.k.a. our mental police officer, firefighter, and EMT) is not the illusive facts that we can pluck from the intellectual atmosphere like picking a cherry from a low-hanging branch or selecting a brochure from

25. Always from people who think I'm out to lunch (in a non-eating way).

26. Haidt, *The Righteous Mind*, Vintage, 2012.

27. Please note that some of my best friends are morons. There is nothing like a moronic BFF for kicks and giggles. And some of my best friends say the same thing.

a kiosk in the mall. Our First Responder is our intuition that is rooted and formed within our social environment.

Haidt uses the analogy of "the rider and the elephant" to explain what he means. The rider is a controlled process that consists primarily of our reasoning abilities. The elephant is our automatic processes, including emotion and intuition. He says we come to moral (including political and religious) conclusions first through our intuition, our elephant. The rider, our rational mind, is just trying not to get thrown off.[28] This suggests that we cannot change people's minds by strongly refuting their arguments. If we want to change someone's mind about a moral or political issue, we need to appeal to their intuition, i.e., elephant, first. Find out what makes a person tick. What is their moral foundation? At the end of the day, we are not trying to win arguments; instead, we are trying to win friends and influence people. (Thanks, Dale Carnegie.) The next step, I assume, is world peace. But I digress.

Moral Foundations

Haidt and others refer to an approach called *Moral Foundation Theory* (MFT). If you take seriously what you are about to read, then you will never ever debate ethical theory, moral decision-making, or political partisanship again for as long as you live on this planet or the next. Or, if you are like me, you will read this and then conveniently forget about it so you can argue freely with that favorite conspiratorial uncle at holiday meals, you know, the one who thinks FOX News is too liberal.

MFT basically says that we are who we are because there is something built into our DNA either through nature or nurture or a combination of the two in the form of . . . you guessed it . . . *moral foundations*. At minimum, there are six foundations, listed below. These innate foundations help determine what we feel, think, believe, and how we behave or act. It helps us understand why there are differences in morality, yet similarities as well—differences and similarities that are cross-cultural. According to MFT, ethics are intuitively based on these foundations. Our virtues, narratives, and institutions are all built on top of these foundations. Here are the six foundations, listed with their opposites:

28. The analogy of "the rider and the elephant" is very appropriate for Republicans; therefore, I suggest that any Democratic readers should change their image to that of "the rider and the *donkey*." Libertarians, obviously, can use any animal they darn well please because this is their right, so long as it is not a porcupine or a skunk.

1. Care (harm) – This foundation builds kindness, gentleness, and nurturance.

2. Fairness (cheating) – This foundation builds justice, rights, and autonomy.

3. Loyalty (betrayal) – This foundation builds patriotism and self-sacrifice for the group.

4. Authority (subversion) – This foundation builds leadership and followership, deference to legitimate authority and respect for tradition.

5. Sanctity (degradation) – This foundation builds religious notions of striving to live in a moral, i.e., less carnal, way.

6. Liberty (oppression) – This foundation builds feelings of resentment toward those who dominate and restrict liberties and feelings of solidarity with those who oppose oppression.

Much of the MFT research involves applying the theory to political ideologies that lean left or right. They argue that the American culture war is explained by the fact that liberals try to create morality relying primarily on the Care foundation, with additional support from the Fairness and Liberty foundations. Conservatives tend to use all six foundations to one degree or another. To test this 6-point theory, think about how they connect with social issues such as abortion, LGBTQ+ issues, racial issues, gun control, and taxes.[29]

There is much wisdom to this approach to morality and ethics. If we buy into the notion that every moral perspective is based on a foundation of virtues that are inherent in humanity either through nature or nurture, we could certainly minimize the number of heated arguments that currently tend to dominate our (un)civil discourse. My primary criticism of MFT is that it does not encourage us to judge which foundations are preferable to others. I need this. I need to be able to say to my opponent that I am right and "you, my friend, are no damn good." So,

29. Just for fun, we should develop a game called "MFT" with six Foundation cards and dozens of cards defining moral and ethical issues, both personal and social. A player has one minute to make an argument about an issue and the other players need to guess which foundation or foundations the player is utilizing to make their argument. Okay, maybe this game would not be "just for fun," but it would help us all see that every argument is based on virtues that derive from moral foundations . . . even if the foundations should be broken up by a jackhammer.

please, MF'ers, build on your wonderful theory and help us find a way to be morally superior.

Ethical Relativism

I shall give another nod to Captain Obvious here and suggest that my claim that "people are no damn good" is a generalized and thus largely meaningless statement. Of course, people do not always measure up to the highest ideals of ethics and morality, and yet we must consider the fact that we will not always agree on what are the highest ideals in the first place. Ethical or moral relativism is the theory that there are no universally valid moral principles. Moral principles are only valid *relative* to cultures or even individual perspectives. Ironically, moral relativism might be an absolute truth.[30]

Many people deny moral relativism even as they subconsciously build up an ethical system in their minds that relates most acutely to their own culture or individual preferences. Perhaps the height of self-awareness is to be convinced that one is morally operating within a system that he or she is only minimally aware and in control. We might be uncomfortable with moral ambiguity, and yet it is this awareness that offers us the best chance we need to be more ethically evolved. After all, change does not start with the end-product; it begins with an awareness of the need to change, although, if relativism is true, then one can never be certain one has "arrived."

There is, of course, multiple downsides to moral relativism—if taken to an extreme. First, we can no longer say with absolute certainty that the customs of other societies or subcultures within our own society are morally inferior to our own, even if these folks seem to break every decent moral principle we support. Second, moral relativists almost always judge the standards of other societies by consulting their own, which can be self-serving. Third, reformers could be considered as wrong because they are operating against the established moral principles of their own culture. Fourth, if moral relativism is taken to an extreme, any hint of moral progress is called into question. Finally, if moral relativism is the only guide in our ethical arsenal, then our laws are without a firm foundation.[31]

30. Wrap that around your head like a tight bandana for a couple days.
31. Weaponized law enforcement officers have the luxury of not worrying about

Despite the weaknesses of extreme relativism, the strengths are, first, not assuming that our moral standards are always absolute and beyond reproach, and second, teaching us that we need to be open-minded about the standards of other societies. As an attempt to add some balance to ethical relativism, I shall turn briefly to W.D. Ross's *prima facie* principles or "near absolutes." His list suggests strongly that although there might be some moral wiggle room in the world, there are some principles that are generally agreed upon. These are:

1. Do not kill innocent people

2. Do not cause unnecessary pain or suffering

3. Do not cheat or steal

4. Keep your promises and contracts

5. Do not deprive another person of his or her freedom

6. Do justice, treating equals equally and un-equals unequally

7. Tell the truth

8. Help other people, at least when the cost to oneself is minimal

9. Show gratitude for services rendered; that is, reciprocate

10. Obey just laws

If we adhere to these Ten Near Absolutes, then we might qualify as people who are "near damn good."[32] In the meantime, feel free to sort through the moral kiosk the next time you visit the mall.

---

the moral superiority of the laws they are hired to uphold. Bullets are very firm foundations.

32. Do I think this is a better list than the Bible's Ten Commandments? You betcha.

6

It's Time to Put the 10 Commandments in the Garage

A FTER I made it through my very rewarding university career learning about Christian ethics, I became more familiar with philosophical or secular ethics as I prepared to teach Intro to Ethics at Howard College and the local prisons in Big Springs, Texas. It was there that I was introduced to many of the topics discussed in chapter five, from Socrates to Moral Relativism. However, to be clear, I do not concern myself with the strict categorization of ethics that separates the discipline from "sacred" to "secular." As a pastor to people who operate in both worlds, I feel that every aspect of the ethical enterprise is open to me for study and utilization. If Jesus said something, that's great, but I'm not limited to just what Jesus said . . . or did.[1] Nevertheless, this chapter is devoted to a few things I have learned about the Judeo-Christian ethic, i.e., biblical ethic, in my long journey as a non-Bible thumping Christian pastor.

Ten Anachronistic Commandments

First, let's get something out of the way . . .

I believe in the rule of law, so long as they are good laws. There can be no civilization without laws, rules, regulations, or standards. I am not

---

1. "What would Jesus do?" is a great and relevant (if not unanswerable) question to ask, yet it has been usurped by too many Christians who have an extremely underdeveloped understanding of the Jesus ethic. But at least they get to wear those cute little bracelets.

an anarchist by any means.[2] In fact, I tend to think we need *more* laws, or at least better enforcement of laws that are already on the books. For example, I strongly believe that due to recent chaotic changes in weather patterns, including hurricanes and floods, heatwaves, droughts, and wild-fires, there should be tougher environmental laws. I also strongly believe that in response to the absurd level of gun violence in this country, there should be tougher gun control laws. As a citizen I want our country to be more pragmatic and practice a "better safe than sorry" approach to laws and regulations, without, of course, taking away our basic freedoms. By the way, I do not believe destroying the environment for economic gain is a basic freedom, nor do I believe owning weapons that can mow down dozens of people in a crowd is a basic freedom. But that's just me.[3] That's who I am as a citizen of these United States of America.

In terms of my religious life, however, specifically as a Protestant Christian, I am less enamored with laws, rules, regulations, command-ments, etc. I am more of an anarchist in terms of my religious orientation. My faith is less about laws and more about God's grace.[4]

In 2017 we celebrated, or observed, the five hundredth anniversary of the Protestant Reformation. One of the great insights of the Refor-mation is that religion should not be based on laws or commandments. Instead, it should be rooted or grounded in a relationship with God through Jesus Christ. Our emphasis should be on our relationship with the love giver rather than the law giver.

Unfortunately, many Christians, even Protestants, have a difficult time weaning themselves from a law-based religion, one that is too often illustrated by our love affair with the Ten Commandments. Interestingly, the Ten Commandments are from the Old Testament, or Hebrew Bible, not the New Testament or Christian scriptures, and Jesus himself did not seem to think the Big Ten were "all that and a bag of chips." Just read his Sermon on the Mount.

Why do Christians, especially Protestant evangelicals, then, like to have signs in their yards or monuments in their courthouses depicting the Ten Commandments, and yet not the Beatitudes or some other list

2. I would only be an anarchist if I were the only anarchist in the world and every-one else had to follow the rules.

3. No, it's most of us. I woke up one day in my adulthood and realized that I am now "mainstream" in my political and social views. Weird. It's like I'm old now.

4. You know, the "amazing" kind, not the conditional kind we find in congrega-tions that would burn a witch if you let them.

from the New Testament? I suggest it is because we are addicted to the rule of law, even in terms of our faith. But that's not Protestant. After five hundred years, you think we would finally get it right. But sadly, no. Therefore, I will offer a brief response to our love affair with the Ten Commandments.

Although hundreds of laws or commandments are found in the Torah, the first five books of the Bible, the Ten Commandments became the symbol of ancient Israel's laws and ethics. Many Christians assume the Ten Commandments are the foundation of Christian morality, and even the basis for our legal system, but they really are not. In fact, the first four commandments are *theological* commandments, which have nothing to do with morality or our legal system. Let us take a gander at each one briefly:

1. You shall have no other gods before me.

    This commandment comes from a polytheistic culture, one that believed in the existence of many gods, or else why would it mention "other gods." This commandment is of little value to us today because we no longer believe in the existence of multiple gods. We are about as monotheistic as one can be.[5]

2. You shall not make for yourself an idol.

    This commandment also applies to people who believe in the existence of many gods. If you believe in the existence of only one God, you do not need to create idols. Only if you need a way to distinguish the various gods from one another do you need to make little idols or figurines that reveal what that specific god looks like. Do we need this commandment today? No, and in fact if we did not have this commandment hanging over our heads our arts and crafts assignments in Sunday school would be much more interesting.

3. You shall not make wrongful use of the name of the Lord your God.

    The old King James Version says, "Thou shalt not take the name of the Lord thy God in vain." Almost all of us have been led to believe, erroneously, that this is referring to the utterance of a particular curse word we use when we hit our thumb with a hammer. It is not. The original intent of this commandment was more complex. Possible intentions include: 1) attempting to cast a spell using God's

---

5. Although Christians are often accused of being "Tri-theistic" (Father, Son, Spirit)—a well-deserved criticism if you ask me.

name; 2) giving false testimony in God's name; and 3) doing bad deeds in God's name. So, if you go to war in God's name, invoke God's name at a KKK rally, or pray for victory at a football game, you are probably transgressing the third commandment. But again, I do not think we need any laws about this, do you? Public shaming works wonders.

4. Remember the Sabbath day and keep it holy.

Orthodox Jews, who practice a law-based religion, take this seriously, but we do not. If we did, we would have to lay aside all our chores from Friday at sunset through Saturday at sunset, which we will not do.[6] We used to have "blue laws" that tried to regulate a Sabbath for us, but we did not even get the day right. Obviously, resting for an entire day once a week is a great idea, but most of us oppose legislating a religiously sponsored day of rest. That would violate the First Amendment's establishment clause. Besides, we like our restaurants to be open on Sunday. Especially, Mexican restaurants.

These are some of the problems associated with the first four commandments. But what about the last six? Here we go. Put on your seatbelt. If you are riding a motorcycle, put on your helmet.

5. Honor your father and your mother.

This is the commandment every parent loves. It was even more important in ancient Israel, a semi-nomadic tribal culture in which elderly folks were often more of a burden than a blessing. This commandment protected them from being abandoned once they were no longer productive members of the tribe. Today, this commandment is a nice sentiment to express, although the honor needs to go both ways. In a world in which parental abuse of children abounds, perhaps a more practical commandment would be "Honor your children."[7]

6. You shall not murder.

This is almost hypocritical coming from a people that carried out the death penalty for even minor offenses and practiced genocide on occasion, although they may have been more evolved

---

6. Well, lazy people will. For lazy people, every day is a Sabbath day. Lazy people are thus holier than thou.

7. i.e., spare the rod. Children *should* be spoiled.

than some of their even more violent neighbors. Originally, this commandment meant, "You shall not murder one of our own unless they do something wrong." By the way, every legal system on this planet has laws against murder. So, meh.

7. You shall not commit adultery.

No one would argue that adultery is a good thing; however, do we really want people to be arrested for it? Ancient Israel was a polygamous society, so this commandment was primarily directed at women. And it carried the death penalty. I think we can safely say that this commandment is a good one to teach in principle, but not to legislate. And for goodness' sake, do not even think about being the first one to cast a stone.

8. You shall not steal.

Once again, doesn't every legal system in the world have laws against stealing? If they do not, then they must have super sturdy padlocks.

9. You shall not bear false witness against your neighbor.

For the third time, doesn't every legal system in the world have laws against lying in court? A better commandment would be, "You shall not allow the wealthy to get off scot-free."

10. You shall not covet your neighbor's (stuff).

The problem with this commandment is obvious. Our entire economic system depends on coveting our neighbor's stuff.[8] Of course, if you literally take your neighbor's stuff, that would be stealing, and stealing is already covered in the Ten Commandments.

So, why does it feel like I just dissed the Ten Commandments? I did not. Okay, I did. However, I am trying to say two things: First, the Ten Commandments are a far cry from being the bedrock of our morality and legal system in America; and second, in terms of the Christian faith, we are not a law-based religion. We are a relationship-based religion. As the Apostle Paul writes in his letter to the Philippians, noting that he was once part of a law-based religion: "As to the law (I am) a Pharisee; as to zeal, a persecutor of the church; as to righteousness *under the law* (which included the Ten Commandments), blameless." And then he goes on to

---

8. Especially the Jones's stuff.

say that he regards all of that as "loss because of the surpassing value of *knowing* Christ Jesus my Lord" (Philippians 3:8).

Our religion is based on a relationship, not a list of rules. At one point, Paul even calls the law "rubbish." I would never be so insensitive to tell folks that the Ten Commandments sign in their yard is rubbish, but it might be a good way to start a bonfire. By the way, do not get the idea that the Old Testament or Hebrew Scriptures are just one rule or law after another (although there is a good amount of "dos and don'ts" in the elder scriptures.) There are good reasons why the followers of Jesus continued to study and utilize what came to be known as the Old Testament, especially those who play baseball . . .

Hitting a Triple

Professional baseball is a lot like the Old Testament. In the Old Testament there are major league prophets and minor league prophets. The difference is that the minor prophets' books are not as lengthy as the major prophets' books, but they are just as important. A good example is the "minor" prophet known as Micah. Micah was an eighth century BCE prophet who wrote around the time of the Assyrian conquest of Israel. His book might be short and sweet compared to Isaiah or Jeremiah, yet it contains one of the best lines in the entire Bible.

Micah 6:8 is one of the greatest hits of the Bible: "He has told you, O mortal, what is good; and what does the Lord require of you but to do *justice*, and to love *kindness*, and to walk *humbly* with your God?"[9] Frankly, we could build an entire religion on that one sentence. In recent history Micah 6:8 has been one of the most celebrated verses within all of Scripture. Like anything else that becomes popular, however, the danger is that it becomes too familiar. When Bible verses or anything else become too familiar we sometimes hear them with mental detachment. We hear the words, but we are not really listening.

According to everything I have read about it, the popularity of Micah 6:8 is a recent fad. It does not seem to have been that popular in the Early Church. There are very few references to Micah 6:8 in letters, sermons, and other works in antiquity.[10] It seems to have become more popular in conjunction with our modern emphasis on social justice.

9. I'm pretty sure this is a rhetorical question.

10. I would offer some references, but I can't, which is the point.

Like many passages of scripture that are worth their salt, Micah 6:8 is a counterargument or critique of what was happening at the time it was written. In this case, Micah had noticed that the religion of his people had become little more than a religion of rituals. It was a religion of burnt offerings—crops and animals—and such things as anointing with oil. It remembered a not-too-distant past when first born children were sacrificed to the gods. Micah asks, "Shall I give my firstborn for my transgression, the fruit of my body for the sin of my soul? (Micah 6:7)"[11]

The trouble with religion that is based on the ritual of sacrifice is that it is a religion with no real substance and no life-changing power. Ritualistic religion often has little to do with the human heart. Possible parallels with our religion today are our practice of the sacraments of communion and baptism, reciting the Lord's Prayer and the creeds, and singing the Doxology and the Gloria Patri. If or when these kinds of repeated things in our worship become so routine that they lose all meaning, then we might be subject to the same type of criticism Micah leveled against his people.

Recently I heard someone talk about two opposing things that are threatening the long-term viability of religion in the world today: Extremism and Routine-ism. Extremism produces such things as cults and terrorism. Routine-ism does not produce anything but complacency and dying congregations. Extremism and routine-ism are both examples of bad religion. Micah 6:8, on the other hand, tells us what is *good*. It offers a very simple and straightforward list of requirements for "good religion."

Not everyone agreed, of course. People were convinced that sacrifices were absolutely required. Later, as the Jewish faith developed, hundreds of laws became requirements. The early Christians, all of whom were Jewish, at first struggled with whether they should continue to obey certain laws, such as circumcision and food laws. Human nature often seems to require a list of, well, requirements. As Christianity developed, however, it soon cast aside hard and fast laws for other, softer, requirements, such as "You shall love the Lord your God with all your heart, and with all your soul, and with all your strength, and with all your mind; and your neighbor as yourself."[12]

---

11. Can you imagine growing up as a first-born child (as I am) in that context? I would have been on the first bus out of town.

12. You know, "snowflake" stuff.

Another one of these soft laws was the Golden Rule, which is incorporated into almost all the major religions in the world today: "Do unto others as you would have them do unto you." The need to simplify religion is illustrated very clearly when a heathen approached the famed Jewish rabbi, Hillel, and asked him to summarize the entire Law while standing on one foot. Hillel answered, "What is hateful to you, do not do unto others."

Religion is at its best when it can be narrowed down to a brief teaching or statement, which is why church growth experts today tell us that our Mission Statements should be so short and memorable that our children should be able to tell us what it is. Perhaps we should just borrow Micah's Mission Statement: "And what does the Lord require of you but to do justice, and to love kindness, and to walk humbly with your God." To use a baseball analogy, doesn't this cover all the bases? Well, technically baseball uses four bases, but I am sure you get my drift. Even though Micah only covers three bases in his Mission Statement, in my opinion he hit a homerun.[13]

Micah 6:8 is based on three important Hebrew terms. The first, *mishpat*, which means "justice," is the basic word used by Israel's prophets to describe the fairness and equality they believed should govern all social relationships. Even today, thousands of years later, that sounds like a great idea. And yet we still have a long way to go before we can claim that our world is rooted in justice. If Micah were alive today, he would have the same criticism of us that he had of his people.

Perhaps the reason animal and crop sacrifices were so popular was because they were so easy. To make everything right with God all you had to do was bring in the first fruits of your crops or a spotless animal for sacrifice. Even today we prefer a religion that is focused on sacraments and rituals and beliefs because that is much easier than changing the world. We convince ourselves that what God really requires is getting baptized, taking communion, singing hymns, saying prayers, and being generous. In other words, Sunday morning worship. But God does not require those things. God requires *mishpat*, justice.

The second word in Micah's list of requirements is *hesed,* which is usually translated as kindness or mercy. When Micah says we are to "love kindness," he means that we should be passionate about our kindness.

---

13. Perhaps I should have used a basketball analogy so I could say, "Micah is the Michael Jordan of Old Testament prophets," although I do not want to upset LeBron James's fans.

There are two types of kindness. There is perfunctory kindness, which is being kind in a way that requires very little effort. For example, back in Kentucky people like to say, "Well, bless your heart," which sounds like a kind statement, but it is not. The second type of kindness is what Micah is talking about: heartfelt kindness. If kindness is heartfelt, then we will go out of our way to do kind things.

The third word or phrase in Micah's list of requirements, *hatsnea' lekhet*, means to walk humbly. By the way, nowhere does it say, "walk humbly and carry a big stick."[14] It does say, however, "Walk humbly *with your God*," which could be interpreted as a big stick . . . As important as seeking justice and loving kindness is, walking humbly might just be the most important part of Micah 6:8 because humility colors everything else we do. Humility is the one ingredient that holds the recipe of requirements together. After all, a person who seeks justice or loves kindness *without humility* is never going to be respected for their justice seeking or kindness. Humility tells others that this person is willing and able to put the interests of others before themselves. It makes their acts of justice and kindness more authentic.

So, here is my bottom line: It is good to simplify religion and morality in the sense of making it easy to articulate; it is not good to simplify religion and morality in the sense of making it easy to *practice*. Doing justice, loving kindness, and walking humbly with God is a good and simple Mission Statement, and yet it is much more difficult to do than routine rituals on Sunday morning. But it is not as hard to do as baseball. Baseball is hard. Even with a big stick.

The Ethics of Jesus

I would be remiss not to include Jesus' understanding of ethics in a book written by a Christian pastor. Admittedly, this is presumptuous if not pretentious on my part. I am not claiming, however, that I can fully get inside the mind of Jesus. His ethical worldview is surprisingly sophisticated and complex. Entire books have been written about it, so here I will offer a summary of my understanding of the Jesus ethic.

The first thing to note about Jesus is that he was a teacher that employed something akin to the Socratic Method on many occasions to engage others in dialogue. He makes heavy use of literary devices such

14. That would be "*speak* softly and carry a big stick" #TheodoreRoosevelt

as parables, proverbs, and aphorisms. He was keen on using hyperbole to draw attention to what he was saying. His primary objective seems to have been to stimulate his listeners to think for themselves and to act accordingly. Metaphorically, he was a shepherd, but we are not supposed to be mindless sheep.

Perhaps the primary reason Jesus has "aged well" and remains relevant is the fact that he preferred principles over laws and legalism. Much of the conflict he endured (if not sought) in his brief ministry is due to his elevation of ethical principles over the Mosaic Laws, many of which had become oppressive to many people. Jesus was a forerunner of what we now call "situation ethics," which, again, is why scholars and Sunday school teachers alike continue propagating his words in our context. Of course, many of his moral ideas can be found in the treasure trove of his tradition. He was, after all, Jewish to the core.[15] And yet Jesus seems to have taken these treasures and added a few jewels to make them more valuable for his generation.

The most important characteristic of Jesus' ethical framework is that it is radically theocentric. With Jesus, the buck stops on God's desk. He never loses sight of the Jewish notion that God is the measure of all morality. God's righteousness is the norm rather than the customs and mores of his community. Jesus' "kingdom of God"—as John Dominic Crossan famously characterizes it: "the way God would rule the world if he were the king"—is the goal of his ethical worldview. With that as his foundation, Jesus' ethical "theory" can be summarized in the following manner:

1. He stressed the importance of the inwardness of morality and human motives rather than just the outward act.

   In his "Sermon on the Mount" in Matthew 5, Jesus offers some illustrations of this principle, including his view that to be angry at someone is to be guilty of murder, and to look lustfully upon someone is to commit adultery in the heart. What we "do" is important but not as important as our motives. We might do the wrong thing for the right reasons, and we might do the right thing for the wrong reasons. The former is more ethical than the latter.

2. He stressed the value of every individual.

15. "The core" is not meant to be a euphemism for circumcision.

The identity politics we see playing out in our era owes much to the Jesus ethic. Although he did so not without a few old prejudices rising to the surface, for the most part Jesus was comfortable interacting with children, the physically and mentally challenged or disturbed, heretics and schismatics, the politically incorrect, rejects, and immoral sinners. If Jesus was ever critical of anyone, it seems to have been the "good" people rather than the no damn good people (the former not understanding that they are the latter).

3. He stressed positive rather than negative morality.

Judeo-Christian ethics is traditionally articulated negatively in terms of "do nots." In contemporary evangelical-fundamentalist culture, for example, ethics and morality tend to focus on what they believe we should not do *with our bodies*, such as have sex outside of marriage, have an abortion, or engage in same-sex relationships. There seems to be a fair amount of projecting going on in these Christian circles.[16] Instead of focusing on what we shouldn't be doing, Jesus focuses on what we *should* be doing, which is perfectly articulated in his rendition of the Golden Rule: "In everything do to others as you would have them do to you; for this is the law and the prophets" (Matthew 7:12).

4. He stressed love above everything else.

I see a progression in Jesus' love ethic from love of God to love of self to love of neighbor to love of enemy. His love ethic might be the most inclusive ever proposed on this planet. His love ethic is the most epic mic drop in the history of moral thought.

5. He stressed service.

In one of his many upside-down principles, Jesus said, "Whoever wants to be first must be last of all and servant of all" (Mark 9:35). This might be the clearest indictment of our culture, one that stresses power, hierarchy, and value based on wealth, education, and other ways to measure one's social standing.

I said earlier that Jesus has "aged well." The most important reason he remains relevant is that we are like a dog chasing the car—the Jesus

---

16. In the last episode of *Shameless*, season 10, Frank Gallagher's youngest son, Liam, asks Frank if all homophobes are gay. Frank answers in the affirmative. Not all gays are homophobic, just to be clear.

ethic—and we rarely catch the car, but it is in our nature to keep trying. If we do catch it the world tries to run us over. Just ask the martyrs.

Hitting the Trifecta

Other than the Jesus ethic, the New Testament is full of ethical insights, still relevant today. One of my favorites is from the book of *James*. Here we find another triple of sorts—a trifecta.

I am not a frequent gambler at the horse track; however, I do know what a trifecta is. A trifecta occurs when someone selects the first three finishers of a race in the correct order. I have never won a trifecta, but I know it is a good payout. I would like to apply the trifecta to a great little passage from *James*. In his letter, James writes in the vein of Character or Virtue ethics. As we learned earlier, according to Virtue ethics, a person's character shapes their behavior and decision-making process. A person with good character traits will make good ethical decisions and engage in good behavior. Everything stems from our character, so we should work on developing good character traits.

Before I studied ethics in school, I came face to face with my own character issues and went through a mini moral crisis. One day my new brother-in-law and I drove to the nearest golf course to play a round of golf. I was teaching him how to play. (Today he beats me regularly, but that is beside the point and shall not be discussed any further.) This course was a small operation. Nobody was in the clubhouse, but there was a slot in the door in which players were asked to deposit their green fee. Unfortunately, we did not have the correct change or a checkbook with us, so we decided to start playing and then try to catch someone in the clubhouse after the first nine holes.

When we made the turn after the front nine, there was still no one there, so we proceeded to play the back nine. Again, when we returned to the clubhouse no one was there, so we looked at one another and said, "Well, it looks like we just played a free round of golf." Afterwards, I went to a friend's house and told him how "lucky" I was that I did not have to pay my green fee that morning. His wife heard me and said, "Jimmy, you lack character." That comment stung. Ever since then I have tried to understand and practice what it means to have good character.

What does good character look like? I will ask it this way: What is the *trifecta* of good character? If we were to list the top three traits of good character in order of their importance, what would they be? Obviously, there is no wrong list or order. We could all come up with our top three good character traits. So, I decided to examine what the letter of James might say about this. James is full of good, sound ethical advice, still applicable today among shifty golfers. Here are James' top three traits of good character: *openness, integrity,* and *compassion.*

James 1:19 says, "Let everyone be quick to listen, slow to speak, slow to anger." This is a description of *openness,* and it might just be the foundation, the starting point, of good moral character. We need to be open to other people, other perspectives, new experiences, etc., because if we are not open, we cannot grow as a human being. But how can we be open?

First, as James says, we need to "be quick to listen." Listening is the primary way to be open to other people. We need to hear what others have to say. To quote the late Aretha Franklin, we need to show some R-E-S-P-E-C-T, and the best way to do that is with a posture of listening. If we are "quick to listen" we will be "slow to speak," that is, slow to respond if we hear something we do not like or agree with. Listening helps us put the brakes on our emotions because if we are slow to speak or respond, then we will also be "slow to anger." Listening is like the "governors" we use on automobiles to keep them from going too fast. Is this the foundation of a good moral character, the first of the trifecta: to be quick to listen, slow to speak, and slow to anger"? I think James is right on here. In the horse race of good character traits, openness needs to cross the finish line first.

The second-place character trait for James is *integrity.* He says in verse 22: "Be doers of the word, and not merely hearers." Listening to others is the first step. The second step is to act on what we have learned; to do and not just hear. This is integrity. We heard the word "integrity" quite a bit after the passing of Senator John McCain. McCain was one of those politicians that had the ability to make just about everybody mad at one time or another, but at the end of the day you knew that he was operating from a place of integrity. And when he failed to do so, he would usually come back later and say how wrong he was. He was a rare politician indeed.[17]

Integrity is the opposite of hypocrisy, which occurs when we do *not* act according to what we have heard and learned. When I heard that young lady all those years ago tell me that I lacked character for not paying for my round of golf, she was saying to me that I had no integrity.

17. Although . . . Sarah Palin.

At that point she became my moral instructor. I was obviously *open* to what she had to say because it affected me so strongly. The question is: did I learn to practice what she taught me? Did I just *hear* what she had to say, or did I become a "doer of the word?" Is integrity the natural follow-up to openness? Is it the second-place finisher in our trifecta of good moral character? I think so.

The third character trait in James' moral trifecta is *compassion*. James illustrates compassion in a very specific way by saying, "Religion that is pure and undefiled before God . . . is this: to care for orphans and widows in their distress." Obviously, James is referring to the most vulnerable people of his day. In response to that, allow me to make a bold statement: I do not believe anyone can claim to have good moral character unless they have compassion for the needy. Abigail Van Buren once said, "The best index to a person's character is how he treats people who can't do him any good, and he treats people who can't fight back."[18] Compassion completes the trifecta. Without it, our race is incomplete. Too often people think that integrity is all that is needed to have good character. "I am a person of my word," they might say, without ever moving to the next level of character, which is compassion for the most vulnerable among us. Compassion might be the third horse that crosses the finish line, but it is the one that works the hardest. It is the proof that we are open and that we have integrity.

The Ethics of Augustine (354–430 CE)

As I noted earlier, the New Testament is full of moral and ethical insights and advice, perspectives that we continue to chew on and wrestle with even today. However, ethical insights and advice from a Christian perspective did not end with the last book of the Bible. Folks who came from that tradition continued and continue to bring new parcels of ethical food to the table. We will never go hungry. Some of those folks even went on to become "saints."

Augustine of Hippo would one day become both a saint and the inspiration for a thick carpetlike grass. He is generally recognized as the greatest theologian of the first millennium of the Christian era. Harkening back to the Greek philosophers, however, Augustine argued that

18. Although her language is not inclusive of women, I'm almost certain Abigail thought women could have good character.

happiness is the goal of all human beings. How one attains happiness, of course, is the big question, and the answer to that question is how one arrives at a worldview or ethic.

For Augustine, happiness is not found in physical pleasures, therefore perfect happiness will never be found in this physical world. God reveals the secret of happiness to us, and thus God alone can satisfy the desires of the soul for eternal and perfect happiness. Augustine's ethical worldview may be more theocentric than Jesus's. Certainly, it is more Christocentric.[19] He believed any morality not rooted in the Christian religion is essentially immoral. He could be judgmental that way.

While Augustine firmly believed that God is omnipotent, omniscient, omnibenevolent, and the sole creator of everything that exists, evil *does* exist. That is, as one of his spiritual descendants would one day proclaim, people (and all of creation) are no damn good. The Christian, then, is tasked with finding solutions to the problem of evil. Augustine explains the existence of evil in a way that has reverberated down through the history of the church. You may recognize your pious aunt Molly's words in his explanation:

1. The apparent unfairness and injustices we find in this world (evil) are fair and just, and human beings deserve them.

2. Evil is a consequence of the Fall of Humanity due to original sin.

3. Evil is a deficiency, the absence of good.

4. Since God is perfectly good, and since God created everything, therefore it is good that evil exists.

5. Evil is due to human free will.[20]

His list leaves a lot to be desired, and yet it gave Christianity the building blocks for developing a moral and ethical worldview. His basic solution is to choose to do good rather than evil. The former lands one in the City of God and the latter lands a person in the City of Man.[21] Our ethics begin with our relationship with God rather than such things as success, knowledge, or power. Again, in contrast to the Greek

19. If you believe Jesus' ethic is "Christocentric," you need to start over in your theology.

20. Which does not explain natural evil, such as hurricanes, wildfires, and alien invasions, but, oh well.

21. I would need to wait and see which City of Man he is referring to before I judge too harshly. Also, does this include the suburbs?

philosophers, happiness is the goal, yet it cannot be found in this world, even if we focus on such things as prudence, justice, courage, and wisdom, because these all belong to the City of Man.[22] All I can say in response to Augustine is, "good luck." I hope you made it to heaven.

The Ethics of Aquinas (1225–1274 CE)

For Thomas Aquinas, the Father of modern Catholicism, the existence of God is the only clear basis for morality, so he set about to prove God exists. I imagine him sitting around a campfire one night, looking up at the stars, when he formulates the "cosmological argument" for the existence of God. Aquinas surmised that something or someone had to start all this and put it all in motion, so he theorized that God is the Uncaused Cause of everything that exists and the Unmoved Mover of everything that moves. This is the groundwork for his ethical theory. The Uncaused Cause and Unmoved Mover is responsible for the creation of everything, including the laws of nature and the laws of morality. Humanity's ethical task is to follow these laws to the best of our ability.

These laws are part of God's "eternal law," which no one can know except through the use of reason to understand patterns and laws of nature, known as "natural law." Confusing? Perhaps, but what makes this joyride through life even more interesting is that we can choose to follow God's laws or not, because we have free will. If we choose not to follow God's laws, well, there might be hell to pay.[23] The conclusion of Aquinas' ethical system is that through natural inclination and reason—not scripture, revelation, or God—we can find moral reasons for all the things we should and should not do. To a degree, I agree with Aquinas that human

---

22. This explains why theologically educated conservative Christians, who are very Augustinian, are critical of social justice and progressive politics. And no, "theologically educated conservative Christians" is not (always) an oxymoron.

23. If you have ever wondered why the Catholic Church is so fiercely against homosexual behavior, look no further. The church claims that it is against "natural law" because gays and lesbians, etc., cannot reproduce if they engage only in homosexual activity. Other than the fact that many non-human animal species engage in same gender dilly-dallying, and most sexual activity among heterosexuals does not lead to reproduction (by choice or not), the Catholic church and many of her Protestant siblings are forgetting one very important fact: homosexuality is "natural" for those who are indeed homosexual. Also, many of the unmarried priests in Catholicism are gay. So, there's that.

beings can "figure things out" on our own, but we should not use the natural law argument to justify our "isms" and "phobias."

The Ethics of Kierkegaard (1813–1855 CE)

The nineteenth century Danish theologian, Soren Kierkegaard, included ethics in his list of "the three stages on life's way." The first stage is the aesthetic, wherein one lives for enjoyment. The second stage is the ethical, in which one lives in such a manner as to promote the good of the community. The third stage is the religious, which is rarely achieved. Only the best of us, those of us who are "damn good," can claim to have reached the third stage.

It is in the third stage that one may commit an act that is, at first glance, *unethical* because God has instructed us to do so. Such an act is "teleological" (i.e., goal-oriented) in that it serves the goal of obedience to God. Ethics, as commonly understood, is suspended for the moment. Kierkegaard famously gave the example of Abraham's near sacrifice of Isaac. From an ethical perspective, child sacrifice is wrong, and yet sometimes God's wisdom and will can transcend our concept of right and wrong. Whereas the choice to live an ethical life binds us to a strict moral code, the religious life allows one to go beyond the normal rules that apply to everyone else. There are occasions, in other words, when God calls us to do something that the world views as unethical. Kierkegaardian scholars refer to this as "the teleological suspension of the ethical," which is a smart way of saying "the end justifies the means." Obviously, in the wrong hands (i.e., people who are no damn good), Soren's system needs to be suspended.

While you might be spending a great deal of your spare time surveying the field of Judeo-Christian ethics, I recommend that one always ask not, "What is the *Christian* thing to do?" but rather what is the *right* thing to do. The two do not always play for the same team.

7

Like Porn, We Know It When We See It

I F this book reveals anything at all, if it uncovers any not-so-hidden truth about humanity, it is that goodness is not as easily defined as one would think, and yet I am convinced *we will know it when we see it.* Ironically, this suggests that goodness is much like obscenity, at least in terms of how we answer the questions, "What does goodness look like?" and "What does obscenity look like?" The latter was famously answered in a 1964 U.S. Supreme Court case in which Justice Potter Stewart argued that the material in front of him was not obscene. He wrote,

> I shall not today attempt further to define the kinds of material understood to be embraced within that shorthand description ("hard-core pornography"), and perhaps could never succeed in intelligibly doing so. But *I know it when I see it*, and the motion picture involved in this case is not that.[1]

Goodness looks different than obscenity or hard-core pornography (I assume), and yet describing goodness requires looking at it from different angles, much like porn is best observed from multiple angles, or so I've heard. The following essays are a collection of the ways I have concluded goodness looks like, although I have never seen the dusty, hidden-in-the-closet VHS videos per se. Let us begin with the most basic level of human (and animal) thought and activity: instincts.

---

1. The motion picture in question was Louis Malle's, *The Lovers* (1959).

Goodness Looks Like Evolved Humanity

We typically think of non-human animals when we think of instincts. We think about a spider spinning a web, a bear hibernating for the winter, a bird building a nest, and yes, a skunk protecting itself by spraying an awful perfume in the direction of a potential enemy. Instinctive behavior is unlearned natural behavior. Because we are also animals, human beings have instincts as well. An obvious example is the suckling of a newborn baby. Like other animals, most of our instincts are related to survival: fright, fight, or flight, and the instincts to eat, drink, and procreate. Minimally, the goal of living is to live. It is all about survival of the species.[2]

Of course, life for us people-animals is not only about survival. We have a higher calling or purpose in life. Even as we keep an eye on our survival, sometimes our instincts need to be ignored or overcome so that we can be good people. Sometimes we just need to be a little bigger than our instincts. We need to be *distinct from instinct* because sometimes our instincts *stink*.[3] There are instincts that have helped humanity survive for a very long time, and yet, from a faith perspective, they occasionally need to be ignored or overcome. Sometimes we need to evolve beyond our evolutionary status. In no certain order or logistical scheme, some of our more stinking instincts include:

Revenge

Throughout history there have been times when people may not have survived if they had not acted out in a revenge mode against people who had wronged them. Admittedly, we cannot always let people get away with doing wrong, and yet the story of Joseph in Genesis 45 teaches us that we can rise above the need for revenge.

As a young man, Joseph's brothers sell him into slavery, and he ends up in an Egyptian prison cell. Through good fortune and God's help, and his own instinct to survive, he becomes Pharaoh's right-hand man and helps to prepare Egypt for a famine. The famine reaches Palestine where Joseph's family still resides. They come to Egypt for help and unknowingly need to deal with their long-lost brother, Joseph. They do not know it is

2. I almost wrote "survival of the fittest," but then I looked at myself in a mirror . . .

3. There is a skunk connection in there somewhere.

him. He could have been vengeful and had them killed or put in prison. Instead, he overcomes his instinct for revenge and helps his family. He tells his brothers, "God sent me before you to preserve for you a remnant on earth, and to keep alive for you many survivors. So, it was not you who sent me here, but God" (Genesis 45:8).

Jesus likewise grapples with the revenge instinct in his sermon from Luke 6. He says, "If anyone strikes you on the cheek, offer the other also." In other words, rather than get into an eye for an eye vicious cycle of violence, it is often better to be the first to say "enough, I will not strike back." Furthermore, Jesus says, "Forgive, and you will be forgiven." Again, someone needs to be the first to offer forgiveness rather than continue with a potentially endless cycle of revenge. Joseph and Jesus both understood that forgiveness is distinct from instinct. They were damn good people.

Hatred

Hatred is a natural thing. It is human instinct to dislike if not hate people who are different from us. In the ancient world, to defend your village from outsiders and invaders, you needed to have a strong dislike for them. You needed to dehumanize them so that it was easier to kill them if necessary. We have seen this same instinct play out in every war we have ever fought, where we come up with dehumanizing names for our enemies.[4] It is easier to kill a hated enemy than a mere acquaintance. The same kind of hatred—although less intense—applies on our athletic fields, courts, and rinks. The hate instinct makes it easier for us to cheer for our team and against the other team.

At its worst, hatred leads to violence and "hate crimes." Some people do harm to other people simply because they hate them. No other reason is necessary. Hate is instinctual, but to be distinct from instinct we need to eradicate the need to hate "the other." Jesus said, "Love your enemies, do good to those who hate you, bless those who curse you, pray for those who abuse you" (Luke 6:27–28). Again, Jesus was a damn good person, but we knew that already.

---

4. The same phenomenon occurs on every playground in the world. Creating dehumanizing names for our merry-go-round nemesis just seems like a good way to impress other third graders.

Greed

One can easily understand how this has also helped us survive as a species. After all, if we give away everything we have, we will have nothing. We need to be careful, if not stingy.[5] One of my parishioners once gave away most of her furniture to a family who had lost everything in a house fire. This person acted in a way that is distinct from instinct. In various passages from Luke 6, Jesus is recorded as saying, if anyone "takes away your coat do not withhold even your shirt," and "Give to everyone who begs from you; and if anyone takes away your goods, do not ask for them again." If that was not clear enough, he then doubles down on his anti-greed tirade and says, "Give, and it will be given to you. A good measure, pressed down, shaken together, running over, will be put into your lap; for the measure you give will be the measure you get back." Whether that literally happens or not, to be generous is to be distinct from instinct. My parishioner is a damn good person.

Judgmental

Obviously, we should practice good judgment. The human species will not survive if it never judges between good and evil. After the mass shooting in a Baptist church in Sutherland Springs, Texas, my congregation held a Church Safety Seminar, taught by a former FBI agent. Rightly so, he said we need to be on the lookout for folks who come here and look a little suspicious. We need to follow our *instincts* about people, he said. But again, at some point our actions need to be distinct from instinct. Jesus is clear about this: "Do not judge, and you will not be judged; do not condemn, and you will not be condemned" (Luke 6:37). Here is the hard and tricky part: We should strike a balance between being instinctively judgmental and being nonjudgmental and indiscriminate. At the end of the day, we should seek a higher purpose. We can all be damn good if we just let go of the merry-go-round of judgmentalism (that goes round and round), which goes against every instinct in our bodies.

To be distinct from instinct means, among other things, to forgive rather than practice revenge, to love rather than hate, to be generous rather than stingy, and to be non-judgmental rather than judgmental.

---

5. We need to "bee stingy." (Yep, I made that up.)

None of this is easy, normal, or natural, especially in terms of how we have evolved. But we are not animals.[6]

Goodness looks like Hospitality

I have lived my entire life on the edge of the American South, but not really in it. Most of my years in Texas were spent on the west side of I-35, which is the unofficial border between the South and the West.[7] I have lived in Indiana, which is a northern state that often behaves like a southern state.[8] I lived for a while in Louisville, Kentucky, which is known as a city that teeters on the edge of the South and the Midwest. And now I am in St. Louis, the "Gateway to the West," with its complicated cultural history and diversity, some of which includes a Southern flair, including a truckload of racism and racial disparities.

While I have never been a Southerner per se, and I do not drink sweet tea, I do have some affinity for Southern culture. One of the primary characteristics of the South is their knack for *hospitality*. They are also known for their etiquette and politeness. You will hear a steady stream of "yes ma'am," "no sir," "please," "thank you," and "you're welcome" in the South. And do not forget "bless your heart," which sometimes means something entirely different altogether.[9]

My denomination, the United Church of Christ, has done its best to try and cultivate a culture of hospitality. We often use the phrases "extravagant hospitality" or "extravagant welcome." Many UCC congregations use the slogan, "No matter who you are or where you are on life's journey, you are welcome here." Why the emphasis on hospitality and welcoming? Obviously, we want new members, and we rightly believe that a focus on hospitality is a good first step—although I would argue that it is not enough. If we do not have something authentic to offer people after they walk through our church doors, then all the hospitality and extravagant welcoming in the world will not be enough.

Hospitality is at the center of the Christian witness. It is a spiritual discipline. It has roots in the ancient Middle East, from the place our

---

6. Okay, we are animals, but we cook our food.

7. I learned that while residing in Waco, Texas, which is physically on I-35.

8. Indiana's posture and position in American culture and geographical location looks like it is giving the North the middle finger, metaphorically speaking.

9. Especially if you add "little" into the phrase.

religion was born, and our holy scriptures were written. It is a discipline practiced by Jews, Christians, and Muslims alike.[10] Christians, for instance, are called to welcome the stranger in their midst as they believe they have been welcomed into God's realm through the love of Jesus Christ. When we practice extravagant welcome, we believe we are imitating God's extravagant welcome.

The following passage from Matthew 10:40–42 is an insight into the ancient Middle Eastern practice of hospitality. As you read this, try to imagine hearing these words as if you live in an extremely hospitable culture:

> Jesus said to his disciples, "Whoever welcomes you welcomes me, and whoever welcomes me welcomes the one who sent me. Whoever welcomes a prophet in the name of a prophet will receive a prophet's reward; and whoever welcomes a righteous person in the name of a righteous person will receive the reward of the righteous; and whoever gives even a cup of cold water to one of these little ones in the name of a disciple—truly I tell you, none of these will lose their reward."

There is plenty to unpack there, yet I prefer to focus on the practical side of these words, which is: "Whoever gives even a cup of cold water" will be rewarded. In case we are wondering what hospitality or extravagant welcoming looks like, this is a good place to begin: giving water to the thirsty. This is where hospitality *begins*, but this is not where hospitality *ends*. That is an important distinction. I do not think for one minute that Jesus believes hospitality begins and ends with a cup of cold water. If someone just needs a cup of cold water, fine, but if the needs are much greater than a cup of water then we should expand our application of the principle of hospitality to a point where the word "extravagant" comes into play.

If hospitality begins with a cup of cold water for a thirsty individual, what does hospitality look like for hundreds or thousands of people who have even greater needs? Immigration is a hospitality issue that is at the heart of the social and political disagreements in many countries around the world, including our own. From a Judeo-Christian perspective, immigration is a serious test of our hospitality. Before, during, and after

10. I love to tell the story about a Palestinian shop owner in East Jerusalem that I visited in the summer of 1988. He sold religious paraphernalia from all three monotheistic faiths, so I asked him what his own faith perspective is. In a thick accent, he answered, "I am a Muslim, a Christian, and a Jew." Obviously, he had a lot of stuff to sell.

the Trump era, the immigration issue was, and still is, front and center around the world. We have seen the issue play out in Western Europe in a very serious manner as well. Brexit was, at heart, an anti-immigration vote and we are seeing heightened immigration concerns in other countries such as France and Germany.

For Americans, the issue is even more personal. More so than any other nation on earth we are a nation of immigrants. Most Americans can trace their lineage back to a time when someone crossed a dangerous ocean (voluntarily or involuntarily in the case of African slaves) or walked across a border in the desert heat. By the way, concerning those who come here by crossing our hot and dry southwestern border (legally or not), doesn't Jesus' admonition to give people a cup of cold water hit a little too close to home? The death count related to illegal immigration and thirst along the southern border is astronomical.

The ancient stories and teachings of our Bible sometimes serve to prick our consciences in very uncomfortable ways. The stories about people who migrate from one place to another, stories about former slaves who spend a long time in the wilderness before they cross a border to their new homeland, and stories about people in exile who find their way home and discover an inhospitable place, speak to us directly in a world grappling with the same issues and concerns.

Hospitality and extravagant welcome, is, admittedly risky and sometimes dangerous. It is not always a tame practice, such as an opportunity to shake a stranger's hand or offer a cup of cold water. Sometimes it is downright scary. Years ago, I was driving down a rural highway in Missouri. Rain was coming down in sheets. I saw a young man walking alongside the road, holding a pile of books. He was drenched. I pulled up beside him and yelled at him to get in my car. It was one of those moments when the opportunity to show hospitality seemed like a no-brainer. *I need to do this.* It would be inhumane not to. Unfortunately, this soon became a dangerous moment for me. After a couple of minutes, the young man asked me, "Would you be willing to die for me?" This freaked me out because I did not know why he asked that question, so I hem-hawed around for a while as he kept talking about people dying for others. I then calmly drove to the nearest town, found a crowded parking lot, put the car in park, took my keys and quickly jumped out of the car. I told him to get out. My hospitality had run its course.

Extravagant hospitality is not easy. If it is so difficult on a personal level, how much more difficult is it on a national or international level?

Despite our views about such things as immigration in this era of "terrorism," isn't it true, however, that you and I are called to be extravagantly hospitable? We should have compassion for those in power who need to make such tough decisions. We should also have compassion for ourselves as we seek to balance our desire for safety and security with the spiritual discipline of hospitality and welcome. We can start by reminding ourselves that our mantra should be, "No matter who you are or where you are on life's journey, you are welcome here."[11]

Goodness Looks Like Humility

Every Palm Sunday a young donkey or colt plays a very significant role in the story. Other than Jesus, this young donkey plays the most significant role in the story because of what it symbolizes: humility. I therefore created a new phrase for humility: "Borrowing the burro." That has a nice ring to it, does it not?[12]

People often wonder what the difference is between a donkey (or burro), a mule, an ass, and a horse. Because of the World Wide Web, I think I can answer that question. Horses and donkeys are members of the same genus, biologically speaking, and yet they are regarded as being completely different species. The scientific genus name for the horse is *Equus Caballus*. You may notice the connection with the word "equine," which we use to refer to horses. You may also notice the connection with the Spanish word for a horseman, a *caballero*.

On the other hand, the scientific genus name for the donkey is *Equus Asinus*. Now you know why donkeys are often referred to as "asses." They are not called "asses" because someone decided to use a bad word for the donkey, although I guess we could say that its name hints at a deeper truth because donkeys do exhibit a large degree of stubbornness. A "jack" is a male donkey, which is where the word "jackass" comes from. A male donkey, a jack, is crossed with a female horse to produce a mule. A male horse can be crossed with a female donkey (called a "jenny") to produce a hinny. (Clear as mud, right?) Because of the differences in chromosomes between the donkey and the horse, nearly all mules are sterile. I do not

11. Unless you are in my car, sopping wet, asking me if I am ready to die. Then, no, get out.

12. "Burro," of course, is the Spanish word for "donkey." No, a burrito is not made from donkey meat. At least, I don't think it is.

know if this information makes the Palm Sunday story more interesting . . . but Jesus borrowed a burro. This was a gesture of humility that
should not be overlooked.

Let me share some thoughts I have about humility. First, in my
exceedingly humble opinion, when a person thinks they are humble they
probably are not. A lot of folks tend to go out of their way to prove their
humility. Ironically, some of us even tend to be proud of our humility.
What this means is that we can act in humility, and yet we might not
actually be a humble person, that is, we might not have a *condition of
humility*. I suspect that a person is either born with a condition of humility or is not. Our condition of humility is not a choice. It is part of who
we are. That is, some people are naturally humble, and others need to
make a conscious choice to act in humility. When we say, therefore, that
someone is humble, we can mean that the person is naturally humble, or
we can mean that the person is trying to act in humility.

My second point is that humility is most clearly observed in people
who have every reason *not* to be humble. Most of us—just average
people—can get through life without worrying too much about whether
we are humble or not. We might be average people *because* we are naturally humble people. We are not out there stepping on people to get
ahead. We are not out there showing off because, quite frankly, we do
not have that much to show off. I do not mean that in a disparaging way.
I just mean that when we do achieve something important or momen-
tous, we probably *should* show off and let everyone know what we have
accomplished. Why hide our light under a bushel if we do not have many
opportunities to shine our light in the first place? A part-time bragger
is probably a humble person who just needs a little pat on the back now
and again.

I will give a personal example here. Although I enjoy the office of a
pastor, an office that used to be held in high esteem, no one is throwing
any parades for me or my colleagues these days. My previous books are
not on the *New York Times* best seller list either. I am not on the list of
America's most popular preachers. After I die, I will probably be forgotten in about three generations, just like everyone else. Therefore, when I
retire, I will not need to borrow and ride a burro into the sanctuary in
an act of humility like Jesus did. In fact, I might even take a moment or
two to pat myself on the back and say, "Thirty-five years as a pastor? No
one saw that coming!" Yes, I can be a little self-deprecating, which is just
a form of false humility.

Jesus was one of those rarefied souls who, if he had lived today in our world of social media and twenty-four-news coverage, would have been more famous than Donald Trump, LeBron James, and the Pope combined. Even without the aid of Facebook and Twitter, CNN and FOX News, Jesus had become so popular in his day that when they had an opportunity to throw a parade for him, they did. Jesus knew that would happen, so he does what every authentically humble person does when the spotlight is about to shine brightly upon them: He borrows a burro.

Bible readers like to suggest that borrowing this burro was an "act" of humility. I do not think that is the best way to state it. I like to think that Jesus borrowed the burro because he was naturally a humble person, and he was about to be treated in a way that threatened his natural humility. If he had not been naturally humble, he would have ridden through the gates of Jerusalem on the back of a more majestic animal, such as a white stallion. He would have sought a war hero's welcome. He would have driven the Jaguar rather than the Pinto. He certainly would have demanded better optics or visual effects than poor people's cloaks and leafy branches spread on the road. Clearly, he welcomed the people's attention *for their sake*. He wanted them to have their moment of joy and hope. And yet, because his natural human condition consisted of humility, he was content to ride into Jerusalem on the back of a young burro.

Humility is a big theme in our faith tradition. It is considered one of the most important virtues of followers of Christ. Unfortunately, some of us have it and some of us do not. For those of us who do not have it, we need to borrow the burro. We need to hop on Jesus' humility as best we can, as often as we can, and as authentically as we can because people are watching. They have lined the streets watching our parade through the march of history. And they want—and need—something to celebrate. We just need to make sure we do not make an ass of ourselves.

Goodness Looks Like Compassion (Part 1)

Wouldn't you like to know if your religion is the right one? One of the reasons people belong to a religion is because they believe it is more correct or truthful than other religions. The main reason we belong to a particular religion is because we were raised in that religion, or we belong to the dominant religion in our culture. Regardless of how we got here, we would not stay here if we thought we were in the wrong pasture.

To use the imagery Jesus uses in Matthew 25:31–46, we believe we are the "sheep" and not the "goats." This imagery is near and dear to my heart. I grew up in sheep country. In fact, the place of my berth, San Angelo, Texas, has been called "the Wool Capital of the World." The mascot for the local university, Angelo State, is the Ram, and at last count there are forty-eight fiberglass sheep statues around the city of both the ewe and ram variety.

Sheep are held in high esteem where I live. Goats . . . not so much. In fact, one of the most derogatory things to call someone where I was raised is the aforementioned "goat roper." As I described at the beginning of this book, a goat roper is a wannabe cowboy. They drive pickups and wear cowboy hats and boots, but they have no cattle, horses, or land. They are also the ones who tuck their pants into their boots to show off their boots, thus showing their ignorance about the purpose of boots. Every true cowboy knows that you need to wear your pants over your boots so that snow, mud, and manure do not get into your boots.

Apparently, Jesus was like a shepherd with West Texas sensitivities because he tells us that someday he will "separate people one from another as a shepherd separates the sheep from the goats, and he will put the sheep at his right hand and the goats at his left." It turns out well for the sheep, but not the goats.

This is one of those places in the New Testament that refer to what we call "the Second Coming of Christ." Is this a real thing? I will inform, you decide. Perhaps these references to a Second Coming were written because the early Christians were still mourning the death of Jesus and they needed a Messiah who would come and shake things up. As a people who were oppressed at the hands of the Roman Empire, they yearned for a new king, a Jewish king: "When the Son of Man comes in his glory, and all the angels with him, then he will sit on the *throne* of his glory." Clearly this reflects the notion that early Christianity understood Jesus as a king figure.

The "angels" seem to be his army. They will help him occupy a throne—a coup? Opposing Jesus, of course, is the devil and *his* angels. The entire scenario is set up as a cosmic showdown between the forces of good and evil, Jesus and the devil, and angels and demons. Obviously, Jesus will win and then the sorting between the sheep and the goats begins.[13] This is a great image, although perhaps a little too simplistic.

---

13. This reminds me of the "scripted" outcomes in pro wrestling.

We should not take it literally. Can you imagine just the people who are alive on earth today, about eight billion, lining up to receive either their sheep promotion or their goat demotion?

This passage, if taken literally, ruffles my feathers, or better yet, my wool, in other ways as well. First, the "kingdom" Jesus establishes here sounds like a meritocracy, that is, people are judged based on their merits. I, on the other hand, have been conditioned to read the Gospels through the lens of grace. Grace does not judge people based on merits, so is this an anti-grace passage?

Second, I need to admit that, as someone who has been referred to as a goat roper on occasion, I do not really appreciate how harsh it is against goats. Why are sheep better than goats? Goats seem a lot more independent to me. But they are also a little meaner than sheep. They are b . . . a . . . a . . . a . . . d.

The third thing that ruffles my wool about this story is how it pits the right hand against the left hand. Doesn't this reveal a bias against left-handed people? Doesn't Jesus know that since Gerald Ford, most of our presidents have been left-handed? Doesn't he know that there is some evidence to suggest that left-handed people have better cognitive skills than righties, although teachers used to suppress left-handedness because they thought these students were disabled? Doesn't Jesus know that southpaws are invaluable for a pitching rotation or bullpen?

Nothing ruffles my wool, however, as much as the seemingly un-Jesus-like practice of separating people. Didn't Jesus believe in God's unconditional love and mercy? I realize it is very easy to label some people, like Charles Manson or Adolph Hitler or people who drive Hummers, as goats, and yet we are not the ones doing the labeling. Jesus and/or God get that job (presumably) and I want the divine to show much more grace than we do.

Furthermore, this passage compels me to ask *myself* whether I am a sheep or a goat. The criterion Jesus uses to distinguish between the two groups is troubling to me because I do not think I measure up very well. Imagine spending what seems like eternity waiting in line to be judged only to discover that the criterion is exactly what I do not want it to be. Jesus will judge us based upon whether we fed him when he was hungry, gave him water when he was thirsty, welcomed him as a stranger, clothed him when he was naked, and visited him while he was in prison. My response will be the same as some rather unassuming, unpretentious, humble folks in the story who say to Jesus, "Lord, when did we see you hungry, thirsty, a stranger, naked, or in prison?" And he will tell me, and you, that if we did these things for the least of them, the truly needy, then effectively we have done these things for Jesus, and therefore we get to spend eternity with the sheep shearers rather than the goat ropers.

So, which is it? Are we to be counted among the sheep or the goats? This is troubling to me. If we take this literally then unless we spend our entire lives working in homeless shelters or refugee camps or holding AIDS babies, we might as well call ourselves Billy Goats and start head-butting our neighbors. We can do that and drive ourselves crazy with guilt or we can focus on what the passage is really saying to us. Once we cut through the literalness and the exaggeration, the underlying message of this story is that Jesus puts a high premium on compassion. That's it in a nutshell. Jesus is simply trying to tell us that there is nothing more important in this life than helping those who are truly in need.

We also need to acknowledge that we live in a different time and place, and so the needs are often different, although not *that* different. We have a greater social safety net than existed in Jesus' day, yet there are still people in our midst who are hungry and thirsty and in need of clothing. Because we are an immigration nation, there is no shortage of strangers among us. And because we have the highest incarceration rate in the Western world, there is no shortage of prisoners to visit.

Compassion can show itself in many other ways as well. It might be sitting with the dying or the bereaved. It might be caring for animals. It might be helping to stop bullying or teaching ballet to a child from a disadvantaged home. It might be in the form of Habitat for Humanity or the Heifer Project. No matter who we are or what we do, compassion *is* humanity's finest virtue. As Albert Schweitzer said, "The purpose of human life is to serve, and to show compassion and the will to help others."

If Jesus could literally sit on a universal throne his priority would be to encourage and enable his subjects to be compassionate toward those who are less fortunate. If we are compassionate, then yes, we do belong to the right religion, no matter what we call ourselves. If we are compassionate, then yes, we can say we are the sheep and not the goats, and by that, I mean no disrespect to goats.

Goodness Looks Like Compassion (Part 2)

One day I took the liberty of goofing off for a few hours. While driving in my pickup I heard a variation on the "Why did the chicken cross the road?" joke on the radio and decided, you know what, I can do better than that. So, I set about the task of coming up with new comedy material, inventing several new variations on the popular joke. Much to the chagrin of my Facebook audience, I shared all of them on social media. The first one that popped into my head was:

Why did the playground equipment salesperson cross the road? To get to the other *slide*.

I followed up with:

- Why did the duck cross the road? Because she wasn't *chicken*.

- Why did the Protestant cross the road? Because he didn't know how to cross *himself*.

- Why did Donald Trump cross the road? To comb his hair on the *other side*.

- Trying to be fair, I could not come up with a Hillary joke, although I have one now: Why did Hillary cross the road? She didn't. She used *email*.

- After that I got a little too big for my britches and came up with one that few people "got":

Why did the chicken cross the road? Because she had yet to be introduced to *the poetry of Robert Frost*.

I do not mean to be condescending, but I am referring to Frost's poem, "The Road Not Taken."

That same evening, I was sitting in my screened in back porch as I read the Parable of the Good Samaritan (Luke 10:25–37). This parable is about someone who is willing to *cross the road* to care for someone who had been robbed and beaten half to death. It did not take two seconds for me to realize that my sermon title that Sunday would be, "Why did the *Samaritan* cross the road?"

Jesus never calls him the "Good" Samaritan. He did not need to. The Samaritan's goodness is implied in the story. Another reason Jesus does not call him the Good Samaritan is because this would have been an oxymoron, a contradiction in terms. No Samaritans were good from the perspective of Jesus' listeners. To refer to the Samaritan as good would have created a reaction at best of rolled eyes and a dismissive smile and at worst the lawyer would have spat on the ground, cursed, and walked away. A good storyteller, as Jesus was, would not want to sabotage his story by turning off the listener at such a critical point in the story.[14]

According to first century standards, Samaritans were ethnically and religiously below par.[15] They had Jewish ancestry yet may have comingled with some gentiles during the time of the Babylonian exile over five hundred years earlier, when the "best and brightest" Jews were forced into exile. The irony is that the word "Samaritan" means "Guardian of the Law" (or Torah). The Samaritans saw themselves as religious purists who believed they kept the original version of Judaism intact. But to their neighbors to the north in Galilee and to the south in Judea, the Samaritans were ethnically and religiously impure and therefore looked at with contempt.

Because of that, their morality was suspect as well. Some folks might compare them to a specific ethnic and cultural group today called the Romani. They are pejoratively called "Gypsies," which has a connotation of being illegal and irregular. In fact, the label "Gypsy" is where we get our word "gyp," which means to cheat or swindle. We have all heard the stories.[16] I suspect that Jesus is telling the lawyer a story about a Samaritan who is willing to cross the road to help a man that not even a priest or a Levite is willing to help. It would have sounded to him much like it would sound to us if someone told a story about a Gypsy crossing a dangerous road to *help* someone rather than *rob* someone who is lying there half dead. Listeners today might roll their eyes as well.

In some ways, the Samaritan is symbolic of the "other" in our midst, and the "other" is defined by who *we* are. If we are white, the other is a person of color. If we are straight, the other is gay. If we are Christian, the other might be a Muslim. If we were Jewish in the first century, the other was a Samaritan. The parable of the Good Samaritan is just as relevant today as it was then because the other does not seem to want to go away.

14. A third reason not to refer to the Samaritan as "good" is, as I've been suggesting, people are no damn good. All people, including Samaritans.

15. In this case, "below par" is bad, whereas in golf "below par" is good, although I would not know that through personal experience unless we are talking about Putt-Putt.

16. There is probably an element of truth to the Romani stereotype, yet we should be careful not to paint them with a broad brush and acknowledge that much of the less than desirable characteristics attached to this stereotype is due to the economic hardships of a (sometimes forced) nomadic lifestyle.

And the one thing that can rock anyone's world is the notion that the other can be morally superior to *us*, no matter who "us" is. Crossing the road, therefore, is a metaphor for engaging the other when the others are bleeding to death, both literally and metaphorically. Crossing the road is also a metaphor for recognizing the good in the other.

We are called to cross the road, no matter how dangerous we might think it is.[17] So why is the road dangerous? The parable mentions the road from Jerusalem to Jericho. This road follows a "wadi," specifically the Wadi Qelt, which is a deep ravine. Crossing a wadi to get to the other side of the road is dangerous because either wild animals or bandits could have attacked them as well, which is one reason the priest and the Levite in the parable are afraid to cross the road. It was not like crossing a path or a modern paved street. It really was not like jaywalking at all. It was climbing down into a ravine and climbing up the other side. Anything could happen. Yet, the Samaritan does so, courageously, and does four things: He stops the man's bleeding, takes him to a safe place, spends the night with him, and then leaves money for his care. This is the reason there are hospitals and many other charitable organizations around the world that have utilized the name "Good Samaritan" in their official titles.

So, why did the Samaritan cross the road? My first thought was, "To avoid the priest and the Levite." But this is really a question about what motivates us as human beings. The Samaritan was motivated by compassion. The priest and the Levite were motivated by self-preservation. They understandably did not want to risk getting robbed and beaten themselves. Also, according to their laws they were not even allowed to touch a corpse or blood, both of which would make them ritually unclean. The last thing a priest or Levite wants to do is become ritually unclean because they would have to miss work for a few days. A Levite, by the way, was a priest that worked primarily in the Temple in Jerusalem.

At first glance, one might think the Samaritan did not need to worry about either one of those problems—getting robbed or becoming ritually unclean. To the contrary, a Samaritan outside of his region would be in even *more* danger of physical harm. To be brutally honest, here are a couple of modern parallel examples: a white person who is afraid to drive through a predominantly African American neighborhood, and a black person who sees the lights of a police car in their rearview window. That

---

17. I came up with a new phrase to use for our "calling" to cross the road: "Jaywalking for Jesus."

is what it was like for a Samaritan to be traveling between Jerusalem and Jericho.

Also, remember that the Samaritans saw themselves as religious purists—they are the Guardians of the Law. So, they would be even more concerned about touching blood or dead bodies. And yet, according to this oxymoronic story, the Samaritan, with so much at stake, is the one who crosses the road or ravine to get to the half dead man. The question is, then, why would such a purist of the law be the one that sidesteps the law to practice compassion? Perhaps *because* he was a purist, he knew the *essence* of the Law better than the priest or the Levite. Perhaps he knew that obeying the Law should never get in the way of showing compassion.

So, why did the Samaritan cross the road? Because someone needed him.

Goodness Looks Like Mercy

Now, let us apply that story to a contemporary problem, which is, "Should we offer treatment for Covid-19 to those who refuse to get vaccinated?" To heal, or not to heal, that is the question. Believe it or not, this is an ethical question that people have been grappling with since vaccines for Covid-19 have become available. From hospitals and public health institutions considering medical rationing or triage, to a doctor in South Miami who will not allow unvaccinated individuals to come to her office, to a doctor in Alabama who decided to no longer treat unvaccinated persons, to a Colorado-based health system that denies organ transplants to the unvaccinated, to insurance companies who want to charge higher premiums for the unvaccinated, to the Australian government which will not provide welfare benefits to parents who do not vaccinate their children, the issue of providing health care for the unvaccinated is fiercely debated.

The reason this is even an issue is because our health care system has been overwhelmed—stretched to the limit. This has become a pandemic of the "unvaxxed." Vaccinated people cannot help but be frustrated and even angry at those who refuse to do their part to put an end to this pandemic. So, what do we do about this? I believe the Parable of the Good Samaritan offers some guidance on this.

Not long ago, I began to think about the healing stories in scripture, which are many. Most of them, of course, are stories about Jesus or the

Apostles performing *miraculous* healings. Stories where the lame walk, the blind see, the deaf hear, and the lepers are cleansed. These are fantastic and inspirational stories. But I don't believe we relate to them very well. I don't know about you, but my attempts at miracle healings have failed to land me a gig as a slick-haired televangelist. I simply do not have the "gift" to pray away the pain, to help others cast away their crutches, or to cancel out the cancer in someone else's body. I wish I could, but I can't.

I began to realize, however, that from a Christian perspective, healing is not about performing miracles. That's the route taken by con artists and charlatans. Instead, in the Christian tradition, healing is like the service provided by the unnamed character in Jesus' Parable of the Good Samaritan. Healing is more mundane than miraculous, more gory than glamorous, as it was for the Samaritan in this story.

I soon realized that this parable has something very specific to say to us about the question of caring for the unvaccinated amid a pandemic. To heal, or not to heal? I believe the answer is "heal," which means I had a change of heart, because, like many people, I was inclined to think that choices have consequences. I was leaning toward the old saying, "You've made your bed, now lie in it," which sadly often means a bed in ICU.

In the story, Jesus responds to a couple of questions from a lawyer, one of which is, "Who is my neighbor?" He answers that question in the conclusion to the Parable of the Good Samaritan: A neighbor is "the one who shows mercy," which is a much better answer than, "My neighbor is the person that lives next door to me." Mercy is defined as "compassion or forgiveness shown toward someone whom it is within one's power to punish or harm." This is interesting, because the parable does not give us any indication that the man who had been beaten and left for dead *deserved* to be punished or harmed. And yet, isn't that what the priest and the Levite do? By passing by on the other side of the road to avoid the half-dead man, they are essentially punishing him for being in the wrong place at the wrong time. They choose not to show mercy to this man.

The reasons why the priest and the Levite do not go out of their way to help this man are obvious. They are religious men who are trying their best to adhere to the Law of Moses, which states that touching blood or a corpse makes one religiously unclean. The priest and the Levite cannot go to work that day if they are unclean. If they touch this man, they will need to *quarantine* for a while. So, they decide to socially distance themselves from the man lying half-dead on the side of the road. The Samaritan, by contrast, did not worry about touching blood or a corpse and being declared unclean, although he knew what the consequences are for doing so. Like the priest and the Levite, I'm sure he would have loved to have kept his distance rather than offer a helping hand. Instead, he risks exposure, he risks his personal safety, knowing that the robbers who beat this man could still be as close by as a deadly virus.

As I reflected on the applicability of this story to our situation today, my mind almost exploded. This parable speaks to us today in a life-affirming way about how we should treat the unvaccinated—the "unclean"—among us. It teaches us that health care is sometimes a selfless act, requiring an act of courage. The practice of health care should have no borders or boundaries, as the organization "Doctors without Borders" reminds us. Certainly, there are political, philosophical, and physical lines drawn between the vaccinated and the unvaccinated, but the Parable of the Good Samaritan tells us that the only choice we have is to treat everyone for everything, even if we are angry and frustrated with them. Health care is a right, not a privilege for the well-behaved.[18]

Goodness Looks Like Non-Violence

The preaching business can be a frustrating enterprise. Sometimes it feels like the art of banging my head against a wall. We "sermonators" talk about how to change the world and make it better by using key biblical texts that seem to have been written to make us better people. But does the world ever get better? Do *we* ever get better (or damn good)? That is debatable. Part of the problem is the Bible itself. If we are honest in our assessment of the Bible, we will admit that it offers some mixed messages. I realize this is tricky terrain to traverse (say that five times fast), but I am going to try anyway.

Not long ago I read a book with the great title: *How to Read the Bible and Still be a Christian*, written by the renowned biblical scholar John Dominic Crossan. The premise of Crossan's book is that reading the Bible is like traveling on two Express Trains that are thundering along on twin and parallel rails. One of the trains is traveling on a rail of nonviolence or peace; the other train is traveling on a rail of violence. Crossan suggests the Bible presents two competing visions of God and God's kingdom. One is a vision of peace and the other is a vision of violence. He notes

18. Would we deny lung cancer treatment for a smoker? AIDS treatment for needle-using addicts or the sexually promiscuous?

that the Bible offers us a "bipolar God." Admittedly, that is probably an unfortunate and ill-advised label.

Perhaps we could say it this way: God is depicted as having a "split personality" in the Bible, a bit of a Jekyll and Hyde identity crisis. The same could be said about Jesus. There are also two similar visions of Jesus in the New Testament, according to Crossan. Most people rightly assume that the primary view of Jesus in the New Testament is that he proclaimed a nonviolent Kingdom of a nonviolent God. Jesus is the Prince of Peace. We find this view of Jesus most clearly in his Sermon on the Mount, where he talks about "loving enemies" (rather than destroying them). Jesus' God is one who "makes his sun rise on the evil and on the good, and sends rain on the righteous and on the unrighteous."

The assumption that Jesus is depicted in the New Testament as purely a man of peace has led some to make the odd claim that the God of the Old Testament is a violent-loving God of vengeance and punishment, while the God of the New Testament, as proclaimed through Jesus and his followers, is a peace-loving God of forgiveness and mercy. In fact, the second century heretic named Marcion believed that the wrathful Hebrew God of the Old Testament was a separate and lower entity than the all-forgiving God of the New Testament. It is possible that Marcion thought the God of the Old Testament was Satan himself.

These assessments are nothing more than anti-Semitic propaganda. After all, the New Testament, especially in the book of Revelation, portrays a God that engages in as much or more violence as anything the Old Testament God ever did. Jesus himself is also characterized as having a bit of a "mean streak." His primary persona might have been closer to the good guy, Dr. Jekyll, and yet Mr. Hyde pops out on occasion. Here is some evidence of that:

Jesus' first press agent, John the Baptist, was not exactly known as a flower smelling peacenik. He viciously calls the Pharisees and Sadducees a "brood of vipers," and talks about cutting down and throwing into the fire any tree that does not bear good fruit, which is a metaphor for people who are no damn good. John the Baptist certainly believed in divine violence. He says about Jesus: "His winnowing fork is in his hand, and he will clear his threshing floor and will gather his wheat into the granary; but the chaff he will burn with unquenchable fire" (Matthew 3:12). This is not the picture of a man who oozes peace and love. Jesus may have ridden the peace train for the most part, and yet the New Testament is not shy about putting him on that parallel track of violence either.

At the same time, although many people believe the God of the Old Testament is almost always riding the train of violence, the truth is that the Old Testament God is oftentimes poetically portrayed using some of the most majestic and peace-oozing words and phrases in all of Western literature: "The wolf shall live with the lamb, the leopard shall lie down with the kid, the calf and the lion and the fatling together, and a little child shall lead them" (Isaiah 11:6) . . . is just one example. The editor of the book of Isaiah felt so strongly about this future vision of world peace that he repeats it again in chapter 65. Of course, to be fair, immediately before Isaiah presents such a beautiful portrait of peace, he claims that God will "kill the wicked with the breath of his lips" (Isaiah 11:4).[19]

A violent and a nonviolent God are present in both the Old and New Testaments. In the New Testament Jesus is primarily nonviolent, and yet the Gospel writers do not mind adding a little violence to his resume. So, forget the bad cop/good cop stereotype of the Bible. If you believe that the God of the Old Testament is all about slapping down his opponents on a whim and the God (and Jesus) of the New Testament is all about loving enemies and turning the other cheek, you are guilty of selective reading.

What do we do with all this? Where do we go from here? If there are parallel tracks running throughout the Bible, which train should we ride? In other words, do we accept both trains—the train of violence and the train of peace—and ride whichever one seems best at the time? We might call that the pragmatic approach. Or do we choose to ride the Peace Train . . . all the way . . . wherever it takes us? Do we take an uncritical approach to the Bible and accept all of it as "true," even the parts that depict a God that is violent, murderous, and inflexible? Or do we take a more critical approach to the Bible, as John Dominic Crossan does in his book, and conclude that the violent images of God and Jesus in both Old and New Testaments reflect the human authors rather than the divine author.

Perhaps what we need are "Content Warning" stickers on our Bibles. You know what I mean. Have you ever finished watching a television program and at the end the following words pop up on the screen, "The views and opinions expressed in this program do not necessarily reflect those of this network"? This explains why reading the Bible is so difficult. In my humble opinion the views and opinions expressed in the Bible

19. Divine halitosis can be a deadly thing.

do not always reflect God's views and opinions. Not everyone will agree with me, of course, and that is okay. Some people are comfortable with a violent, vengeful, wrathful God and Jesus. I am not, primarily because our view of God influences how we treat one another. People who are no damn good tend to worship a no damn good god.

Goodness Looks Like Self-Denial

Peter's confession that Jesus is the Messiah is sometimes called the "Petrine Confession." This came after Jesus asked his disciples, "Who do people say that I am?" and the disciples gave a few answers such as John the Baptist, Elijah, or one of the prophets. Mark, Matthew, and Luke all give similar, yet slightly different accounts of this story.[20] After Peter gave his answer, Jesus "sternly ordered them not to tell anyone about him" (Mark 8:30). In Mark's Gospel this is called the "Messianic Secret."[21] For some reason, Jesus did not want his disciples going around the countryside blabbing to everyone that he was some sort of messianic figure. He knew this was a sure-fire way to get the unwanted attention of the paparazzi or worse, end up on a Roman cross.

Jesus may have known that his days were numbered. He tells his disciples that "the Son of Man must undergo great suffering and be rejected by the elders, the chief priests, and the scribes, and be killed, and after three days rise again" (Mark 8:31). This is called a "passion prediction," and is the first of three in the Gospel of Mark. All this death talk did not set well with Peter, the man who had just given the correct answer to the question of Jesus' identity. Messiahs are supposed to be victorious, especially in battle, and would never be defeated as Jesus' death talk implies. So, arrogantly, if not stupidly, he rebukes Jesus. At that moment, Jesus realizes that Peter has completely misunderstood the nature of messiahship. He has his mind set on "human things" rather than "divine things," which is a common human weakness.[22] He is not thinking about

20. However, it *really* happened this way: Jesus asked his disciples, "Who do folks say that I am?" His disciples answered him, saying, "Master, Thou art the supreme eschatological manifestation of omnipotent ecclesiastical authority, the absolute, divine, sacerdotal monarch." And Jesus said, "WTF?"

21. Attention was first drawn to this motif in 1901 by William Wrede in his book titled, you guessed it, *The Messianic Secret.*

22. "Human things" is a nice way of saying "no damn good things."

Jesus' ministry in terms of the Kingdom of God, but rather the Kingdom of Israel. He wants Jesus to be a military leader.

Imagine Peter's consternation when Jesus launches into a mini sermon that begins with these words: "If any want to become my followers (not soldiers), let them deny themselves and take up their cross (not swords) and follow me" (Mark 8:34). Hearing the word "cross" would have been enough to send shivers up and down their spines. To them, this meant literal death. Taking up one's cross did *not* mean (as it does for us) patiently bearing our burdens, as when we sometimes speak of "our cross to bear," such as a physical difficulty or a troublesome mother-in-law.[23]

Although the disciples may have heard no words other than "take up their cross," I tend to think the most provocative thing Jesus said to them was, "Let them deny themselves." Self-denial is at the heart of what it means to follow Jesus, and yet nothing is more unnatural to a human being than self-denial. Jesus is telling his disciples (and us) that to be a follower of Jesus means to deny one's self-interest. That seems rather harsh, does it not? We can deny just about anything else in life without batting an eye, but *self*-denial is another matter. We are not very good at that. The human animal is a self-interested animal precisely because we have a highly developed sense of *self*. We are more likely to deny things that do *not* serve our self-interest. For example, if we are involved in a minor fender bender—and we are technically at fault—we are likely to deny our guilt as much as we possibly can because denial serves our self-interest.

Sigmund Freud had an explanation for why we are prone to deny things, even minor, insignificant things. He famously argued that denial is a defense mechanism. This mechanism is triggered when a person becomes too uncomfortable with the overwhelming evidence of a truth or fact and becomes worried about the repercussions of that fact.

I hate to tattle-tell on my kids, but when they were growing up there were exactly three minor incidents where I asked them, "Who did this?" Even with the promise that the guilty party would not be in trouble they would not come clean. Here were the three incidents: First, someone turned down the thermostat. Second, someone took a bite out of a bagel and threw the rest of it away (they obviously did not like it). And third, we had a toilet that kept running if we did not jiggle the handle after flushing. I came home and the toilet was running. I asked who used the

23. If my mother-in-law is reading this, note that I am only generalizing.

toilet last and not one of my three precious offspring was willing to admit it, just like in previous weeks no one would admit to turning down the thermostat or throwing away the bagel. One might think that my kids were just terrified of the consequences of admitting their guilt. However, I was never a traditional disciplinarian. In all three cases I asked the question, "Who did this?" with only mild curiosity (at first). But I should confess that their denials *did* make me angry.

If people will deny such insignificant things, then it goes without saying that we will deny big, important things. For example, people addicted to substances such as alcohol or drugs often deny their addictions, and yet for recovery programs to be successful, the addict needs to abandon the denial. Back in the 1980s the phrase "in denial" was popularized primarily in relation to the sex abuse scandals that are still rocking the Catholic Church and other institutional expressions of Christianity. We learned that many adults remained "in denial" of the abuse they suffered as children. In that situation the denial swings both ways, of course. The church itself is in trouble for denying the abuse that has taken place in every diocese in the country (if not the world).

Elisabeth Kubler-Ross famously argued that denial is the first of five stages in the grief process of a dying patient or the death of a loved one. So, Freud was right. Denial can be a defense mechanism. We need to have some way to psychologically deal with uncomfortable information in the face of overwhelming evidence.[24]

Sometimes the act of denial can get rather humorous, as in the case of the Flat Earth Society, which denies that the earth is round. Did you know that there are members of the Flat Earth Society all *around* the world? There are also those who deny the moon landing. By the way, the Flat Earth Society began the rumor that the moon landing was a hoax. That makes sense. And don't forget the folks who are in denial about Elvis Presley's death.

Other groups of deniers are not so funny. I would include in this group Holocaust deniers, climate change deniers, and, more recently, COVID-19 pandemic deniers. Again, as Freud said, people will deny things that are uncomfortable to them despite overwhelming evidence to the contrary. On some level, the denial in question is due to self-interest. Jesus, however, steers us in another direction: "If any want to become my followers, let them *deny themselves* and take up their cross and follow

24. Such as, "The South lost" and, more recently, "Trump lost." If January 6, 2021, taught us anything, it is that denial on a social scale can be dangerous.

me." Is anyone capable of doing this? What is the use in trying to follow Jesus if we know we cannot do it?

There are people who disagree with Jesus on this point. As noted earlier, there are those who argue that people *always or often act* according to their own self-interest, that we are psychologically constructed to do so, called "egoism." And then there are the folks who say that we *should* always act according to our own self-interest, called "ethical egoism." Obviously, Jesus was not an ethical egoist. He taught the exact opposite, which is that we should *deny* our self-interests. But how does that work? How does that play out in real time? There is no way we can always, at every moment, deny our self-interest. All of us have been acting in our own self-interest as soon as we got up this morning.[25] We need some perspective on this, some nuance, to make this more doable.

To offer some perspective I turn to a contemporary Christian ethicist, J. Philip Wogaman. Wogaman argues that the problem is not acting out of self-interest. Instead, the problem is acting out of self-interest when it conflicts with the interests of others. Wogaman says that when our self-interest conflicts with the interests of others, our *presumption* should be for the interests of others. This, he claims, is what Jesus means when he says we should deny ourselves. We are not so much denying ourselves as we are *not denying the interests of others.* This is what it means to love our neighbors *as ourselves.* As best we are able, the interests of our neighbors should come before our own interests when there is a conflict between us.[26]

Our presumption should be for the interests of others. This principle can play out in all manner of ways in many circumstances. For starters, it means that if we are involved in a minor fender bender, we should do our best to make sure we are not unfairly putting all the blame on the other driver. So, the next time you rear-end the vehicle in front of you, you will have a good opportunity to see if you are no damn good or a decent human being. Choose wisely.

25. Hygiene and nourishment, as examples, are pursued for the sake of self-interest.

26. Wogaman practiced what he preached when he surrendered his ordination in the United Methodist Church in May 2017 to stand up for the full inclusion of the LGBTQ+ community in ministry.

Goodness Looks Like Self-Demotion
and Other-Promotion

I am constantly being told I need to do better at self-promotion. So, not long ago I decided to try my hand at it. I wrote a bio for my "author's page" on my book publisher's website after the publication of my second book, *An UnDevotional*. Here is what I wrote:

> Jimmy R. Watson writes books and columns that are insightful, personal, unconventional, accessible, and at times humorous. A native West Texan, Watson's writings are best read on the back porch with a favorite beverage in hand and the sprinkler running or on the tailgate of a pickup next to a creek and an un-baited fishing pole. His two works explore the intersection of the Jesus genre with whatever he is thinking about at that moment. Watson is the Senior Pastor at Immanuel United Church of Christ in Ferguson, Missouri. (Yes, *that* Ferguson.) In the last thirty years he has pastored congregations in Texas, Missouri, Indiana, and Kentucky. He does a mean (i.e., good) funeral sermon. In 1996 he somehow managed to procure a PhD in Theology and Ethics from Baylor University. He and his wife, Annie, a priest in the Roman Catholic Women's Priest movement, live in a gingerbread house in St. Louis. Their five children and five grandchildren are spread here and yonder with no discernible migration pattern.

Wouldn't you read a book that guy wrote? I admit that writing this playful bio made me feel a little narcissistic.[27] Like most people, I am a little too narcissistic for my own good, which is why we need Jesus to occasionally knock us down a notch or two—humiliate us—and put us in our place.

In the fourteenth chapter of Luke's gospel there is a story about a Pharisee inviting Jesus to his home to eat a meal on the Sabbath. While there, Jesus notices that people are narcissistically choosing the best seats, i.e., places of "honor." This either means they are jockeying for the head of the table (next to the host or food line), or for the most comfortable

---

27. Some folks saw a Facebook post after one of my trips to Texas in which I am standing in front of a full-length mirror photographing myself. An ironic sign above the mirror reads: "Only you can stop narcissism." I wrote, "I tried to stop it, but I just made things worse." What made that mirror I found in a used book and record store in Denton, Texas so appropriate is the fact that in Greek mythology, Narcissus, who was known for his beauty, fell in love with his own reflection in a pool of water.

pillow to sit on because in those days people often sat on the floor to dine. And yes, their pillows were flagrantly decorated with food stains.

Regardless, Jesus tells a parable about a comparable event, a wedding banquet. In Jesus' parables, the wedding banquet symbolizes the kingdom of God. Jesus loved to use this analogy for a couple of reasons. First, wedding banquets were the most festive of occasions, and second, coming into the kingdom of God is like making a marriage covenant. It is all about commitment and faithfulness. In this parable he warns against gobbling up the seats of honor at a wedding banquet "in case someone more distinguished than you" arrives, in which case the host may have to ask you to change seats, which would be embarrassing.

Can you imagine all eyes on you as the host tells you to take a lesser seat? Presumably, the next available seat will be the lowest seat at the banquet, whatever that means—probably stuck in a corner somewhere—which is where you will have to park yourself. This is like the opposite of a recent St. Louis Blues hockey season: Rather than go from worst to first, as the Blues did, a narcissistic, self-promoting person will have to go from first to worst. Jesus' advice is very simple, yet hard to swallow for all the self-promoters out there: When you go to a wedding banquet, choose the lowliest seat so that the host *might* tell you to find a better seat. He might not, but he might. In that scenario, there is no embarrassment, there is only honor.

If Jesus had stopped right there it would only be a parable about a narcissistic person who is trying to figure out a way to get a good seat at the banquet, that is, more *power*. Between the two choices of either starting at the top or starting at the bottom, Jesus' advice is to start at the bottom—an act of humility—that might possibly conclude in one's favor. In other words, start with self-demotion rather than self-promotion and see what happens. That is just good, practical advice, and we could imagine a variety of settings where we might apply Jesus' words. By the way, this shows that Jesus knew his scripture. Proverbs 25:6–7 says, "Do not put yourself forward in the king's presence or stand in the place of the great; for it is better to be told, 'Come up here,' than to be put lower in the presence of a noble."[28]

But that is not the end of Jesus' teaching moment. He then turns his attention to the host of the Sabbath dinner party and gives an even more important lesson. Here he is no longer telling a parable for the entire

---

28. Jesus was the Bible Trivia king in his Sunday school class.

room to hear. He is speaking directly to the host. He castigates the host for inviting to his dinner party only those people in his close circle: his friends, relatives, and (more importantly) his rich neighbors. If you do that, Jesus says, you will be repaid in kind, yet there is nothing morally noteworthy about doing something for someone to be rewarded for it. Then Jesus delivers the punchline: "But when you give a banquet, invite the poor, the crippled, the lame, and the blind. And you will be blessed, because they *cannot* repay you, for you will be repaid at the resurrection of the righteous" (Luke 14:14). I am certain that ruined the dinner party.

This little section in Luke's gospel contains two messages, one for those of us who have no power, and another for those of us who do have power. For those of us who have no power and are tempted to promote ourselves to gain power, Jesus tells us to practice self-demotion rather than self-promotion. Humility is the only path to authentic power and honor. Power that is not supported or propped up by humility can only be sustained through further acts of power, which often has disastrous consequences.

On the other hand, for those of us who already have power, like the host in this story, Jesus wants us to lift-up the powerless. For the powerful, the Christian faith is practiced not by self-promotion or even self-demotion; it is practiced by *other promotion*. For those of us with power, the Christian faith is all about giving our seats to those who do not already have a seat at the table. *Self-demote* if you are powerless so that any power you attain will be authentic; *other-promote* if you are already powerful so that you can lift-up the powerless in an authentic way. There is no room for self-promotion or narcissistic falling in love with one's reflection . . . unless you are writing a short bio.

Getting Ready for One's Funeral

As you may have noticed, in recent years I have been thinking about how we should live. I do not want to exaggerate and give the impression that I am so busy with esoteric thoughts that I do not have time for domestic chores. My wife ain't havin' none of that. It is not like I sacrifice my nightly couch-potato activities for the ultimate exercise in self-reflection either. Furthermore, I have sermons to write, so I do not want to waste too much of my aging and fading mental energies on philosophical flights of fancy.

Yes, some of my sermons address the question, "How should we live?" at least in indirect ways. In fact, I should probably do more of that. A gentleman walked by me after worship one Sunday morning and quietly exclaimed, "I heard what you said, but you never told us what to do about it." This reminds me of a parishioner years ago who walked out the door of the sanctuary muttering, "So what?" I think she was referring to my lame attempt at a sermon that day.

Preachers should not be the only folks who dabble with ultimate questions. All of us, from plumbers to preachers, philanthropists to philanderers, should be asking the question about how to live. We should all be heeding Socrates' proclamation: "The unexamined life is not worth living." My favorite secular ethicist, Peter Singer, published a book in 1993 with the title, *How Are We to Live?: Ethics in an Age of Self-Interest.*[29] Sounding very much un-Ayn Rand-like (or Rand Paul for that matter), Singer argues that doing the right thing involves putting others first. We must consider the sufferings and preferences of other beings, including sentient animals. In contrast to the popular view in our society that acting according to self-interest is good for us and for society, Singer suggests otherwise.

As I have argued with more nuance earlier in this chapter, I agree with Singer that we should look self-interest in the eye and tell it to take a hike, and yet I also understand that for most of us, most of the time, this is highly unrealistic. Most of us do have the altruistic ability to show compassion and empathy toward others, yet there is very little chance that our needs of self-interest will ever take a backseat to the interests of others, not without a lot of self-strongarming.

I am not a fan of bumper sticker life lessons unless they are pithy and prophetic enough to make a difference in people's lives. Two of my favorites include: "Be the person your dog thinks you are" and "Live your life so the Westboro Baptist Church will want to picket your funeral." These quotes remind me of the columnist David Brooks and his distinction between "resume virtues" and "eulogy virtues." The former includes the things one would put on a job application to impress a potential employer. The latter includes the good things people will (hopefully) say about you at your funeral.[30]

---

29. By the way, calling Peter Singer my "favorite" ethicist is much like calling Meryl Streep or Robert De Niro my favorite actors. It does not exactly separate me from the pack.

30. Brooks, "The Moral Bucket List," *The New York Times*, April 11, 2015.

Therefore, if your life reflects your dog's overly optimistic opinion of you, if the goofballs from Topeka, Kansas think you are worth the trouble of spewing hate speech, and if someone will be able to crank out a good eulogy for you when your busy life is hushed, then I can stop my arcane crusade to get people to straighten up their act. Now I can return to my chores.

Goodness Looks Like a Greater Sense of "We"

As we dabble with the question of right and wrong, here is a question worth asking: What is the purpose of the church? Obviously, there are many possible answers to that question. One of the best answers I can offer is this: The purpose of the church is to move us from a "me" to a "we" attitude. This means that the church is working against human nature, which is notoriously me-focused. But "me and we" is a very fluid notion. All of us fall somewhere on the scale between people who are totally me-focused and people who are totally we-focused (which is probably impossible).

Jonathan Sacks, the late chief rabbi of Great Britain, said the following as a criticism of BREXIT and what is happening here in the United States: "We've moved, in Britain and America, from being a 'We' society—'We're all in this together'—to an 'I' society: 'I'm free to be whatever I choose.' The bad news is that this leaves people vulnerable and alone. The good news is that we can turn it around and become a 'We' society again." I am not convinced his premise is correct, that we were ever a "We" society in the first place, yet I do appreciate his optimism that we can be more of a "We" society.

Let me share with you one reason I believe the purpose of the church is to move us from a "me" to a "we" attitude. This comes from my reading and understanding of Paul's first letter to the Corinthians. In chapter 8, Paul responds to something that has the potential of tearing apart the Christian church in Corinth. The specific issue is whether it is okay for Christians to eat food that has been offered to pagan idols. Corinth was a gentile city, and therefore pagan religious practices were common. The Christians were in the minority. Presumably, much of the food one could find in Corinth had been ritually sacrificed to pagan idols before the food went to market. I believe he is primarily talking about meat. So, if you are a Christian who does not believe in the pagan gods, are you allowed to eat this meat? Paul's characterization of this dispute is that the most recent converts to Christianity, i.e., those whose faith is still "weak," believe that it is unquestionably wrong to eat meat that has been offered to pagan idols, even if that means you and your children will experience food insecurity.

This level of fanaticism is common among new converts to religion. Let me offer a parallel example from my young adulthood. I converted to a charismatic form of Christianity when I was twenty-one years old. I was young and impressionable and had been told that rock music is "satanic." Therefore, I participated in an album burning ritual, something I came to regret as the years went by.[31] The point is, I was a "weak" Christian then. My conscience was easily "defiled," as Paul said. These days, when I get in my car, I am very likely to crank up the Led Zeppelin because I am no longer easily offended. My conscience is not defiled by something as silly as the song, "Stairway to Heaven." I no longer believe that one can hear the voice of Satan while spinning the song backwards, something we referred to as "backmasking." However, if I am with a new, i.e., "weak" Christian who is easily offended by such things as listening to secular music, then I will refrain from doing so in their presence. I will wait until they are out of my car before I crank up my Pandora radio again.

This is what Paul is talking about when he concludes, "Therefore, if food is a cause of their falling, I will never eat meat, so that I may not cause one of them to fall" (1 Corinthians 8:13). Sometimes we need to sacrifice the "I" or "me" for the "we." And to a large degree, this is the purpose of the church: To help us become more aware of the feelings of others, to help us become more empathetic and thus, sympathetic, to help us learn how to walk in another person's moccasins, to help us see humanity as a collective "we" as much or more than an individualistic "I" or "me."

This is not easy because, if you are like me, sometimes you just want to smack people on the head and say, "grow up" or "stop being so sensitive" or "just eat the food and turn on the Rolling Stones and get over yourself!" so that you can keep doing your thing without worrying about someone getting offended. However, as Americans, lovers of such things as freedom, independence, liberty, and individual rights, the church has put us in an awkward position. With its handy manual called the Bible, the church takes the rights afforded to us from the Constitution of the

31. Primarily because I spent a lot of money replacing those charred albums with CD's.

United States and tells us to make sure we interpret and practice our individual rights with the community in mind. None of us have perfected this selfless approach to individual rights and freedoms, so one important purpose of the church is to oversee and guide our journey toward perfection.

I discovered some literature on this issue. The first one is a book titled *Pendulum* by Roy Williams and Michael Drew.[32] They argue that societies swing back and forth like a pendulum between a "we" society" and a "me" society about every *forty years* (which is kind of "biblical," right?). They claim that 1963 was the pinnacle of a "we" focus and 2003 (40 years later) was the pinnacle of a "me" focus." If we do the math (and if they are correct), in 2023 we will be halfway through the pendulum from a "me" focus to a "we" focus. In other words, we are heading in the right direction. We can see this happening, can we not? From the "Me too" movement, which is, despite the word "Me" in its title, a movement about the collective feminine "we," to the "Black Lives Matter" movement, which is also about the wellbeing of a collective or community of people of color, to the pandemic, which has brought us all together in a powerful way. All these things—and more—are slowly shaking us out of our *me moments* to *we movements*. And the task of the church is to help us do our part to move this process along.

Another source I found is a book titled *The Upswing* by the great Harvard political scientist, Robert Putnam.[33] Putnam says that in the last century, from the "Gilded Age" of the 1920s to the 2020s, what he calls the "New Gilded Age," we have "swung" from an "I" to a "we" back to an "I" society. The trick now, he says, is to get us back to a "we" society, what he calls an "upswing." Putnam describes an "I" society as one that suffers from economic inequality, polarization, isolation, cultural individualism, narcissism, and self-centeredness. (Does any of that sound familiar?) As we move back toward a greater sense of "we," Putnam says, the key is to pay more attention to who counts as "we." Is it just white males, as it has been throughout most of our history, or can we now be more inclusive in our "we-ness"?

32. Williams and Drew, *Pendulum: How Past Generations Shape Our Present and Predict Our Future,* Vanguard Press, 2012.

33. Putnam, *The Upswing: How America Came Together a Century Ago and How We Can Do It Again,* Simon & Schuster, 2020.

Goodness Looks Like Creation Concern

I love a good bumper sticker. I had to laugh one day when I saw one that said, "Watch out for the idiot behind me." I was, of course, behind his vehicle. Sometimes bumper stickers make me shake my head. Another one I saw said, "Worship the Creator, not the Creation." This made me shake my head and scratch it at the same time. Personally, I have never met *anyone* who seriously worships Creation—and by "Creation" I assume they mean such things as mountains, rivers, vegetation, and animals.[34]

I know many people who are *concerned* about Creation, that is, the environment or nature. I have even met a few people who are self-described "tree-huggers," but I do not think any of them worship trees, nor are they particularly fond of bark scratches on their arms. They just think trees are important for the survival of life on this planet. I concur with that. And even if people *do* worship trees or nature, I do not think they are people we need to worry about. I am pretty sure nature lovers and environmentalists—even the more radical ones—are less likely to set off bombs in public places, crash airplanes into buildings, or go on shooting sprees in public schools. I do not perceive that there is a large group of people out there who worship the Creation rather than the Creator and who are therefore *creating* problems—pun intended. Yet, for some reason, people get all "bugged out" about environmentally conscious folks—pun intended again.

Years ago, when I first became a pastor, I read a fair number of books about "creation spirituality," primarily from the author, Matthew Fox. Creation spirituality understands the universe as a blessing from God and therefore we are called to take care of our little corner of the universe as best we are able. There is much more to it than that, of course, but I concluded that creation spirituality is not in conflict with traditional Christian theology in any way—it only enhances it by making us more aware of the beauty and value of what God has created around us. Nevertheless, I once wrote a newsletter article about creation spirituality for my congregation. One of my colleagues from a sister congregation read it and was "deeply disturbed." He thought I had turned into a worshiper of trees, frogs, and creeks. I told him he was an idiot and he needed to stop driving so close behind me.

34. And, of course, slimy worms.

That episode in my life inspired me to think more deeply about Creation and try to understand how we should relate to the Creation, that is, nature and/or the environment. I was also inspired to read what the biblical writers had to say about the Creation, and I learned that they have quite a bit to say. In the early days of the environmental movement, showing support for the environment was considered sort of a fringe thing to do—you either had to be a scientist or a hippie to be concerned about such things as pollution or the hole in the ozone layer. These days even the crustiest of souls recycle, pick up litter, and support alternative energy sources. Concern for the environment has become the norm. *Cleans streams have become mainstream.*[35]

We cannot talk about Creation without mentioning two controversial topics: evolution and climate change. On both topics, I am inclined to go with a cool little concept called *scientific consensus*. There is no need to belabor the point, but evolution is the dominant scientific theory of biological diversity, which is good enough for me. Likewise, most climate experts—97% to be exact—claim that human activity is creating devastating changes to the world's climate. Something is happening, and I choose not to put my head in the sand. I am a better-to-be-safe-than-sorry kind of guy.

Even if the scientific consensus about evolution and climate change proves to be incorrect someday, we still need to have a good "theology of creation." For Jews and Christians, it all starts with the Creation story in Genesis. Do you remember what the writer of Genesis claims was God's reaction at the end of each day of creation? "God saw that it was *good*." Hence, the first point we can make in a theology of creation is that creation is good. Or is it? In 1850, the poet, Alfred Lord Tennyson, famously wrote that nature is "red in tooth and claw," and he is certainly correct about that. Nature is bloody and dangerous in its finer details, and yet when we look at the big picture, we can conclude that it is *good*. Damn good. Existence is better than non-existence.

We could draw upon many other biblical texts to develop a theology of creation, beginning with Psalm 148. Outside of Genesis 1, Psalm 148 is the crown jewel of a biblical theology of creation. The message of this psalm is simple, yet powerful: Everything—every aspect of creation—compels us to praise the Creator God. Everything in the heavens, from the angels to the stars, compels us to praise the Creator. Everything on the

---

35. You're welcome.

earth compels us to praise the Creator, including the chaotic forces in the sea, powerful weather phenomena, majestic landscapes, the diversity of vegetation and animal life, civilized human beings, and yes, even uncivilized human beings.[36]

Psalm 148 implies that when we look at the Big Picture, when we observe nature in all its wonderful complexity and variety, our only appropriate response is to praise the Creator. I once heard Carl Sagan, the great cosmologist, answer Johnny Carson's question about whether science and religion are compatible by saying, "Science flatters God." I concur with that even as I paraphrase Sagan's words and say, "The Creation flatters the Creator." And of course, the more we can make a connection between the Creator and the Creation, the more we will be *concerned* about the Creation.

Acts 11:1–18 also contributes to a theology of creation. The Apostle Peter was, at first, a little resistant to take the message of the gospel to the gentiles. Peter had been raised to believe there are certain people in this world that are not clean enough for God, just as there are certain animals that are not clean enough to eat. Peter had been raised on "purity laws," which means not everything created is of equal worth and value—people included. His mind changed, however, when he had a vision of a "large sheet coming down from heaven," containing unclean animals—animals that Peter and his people were not supposed to eat. Peter hears a voice telling him several times that "What God has made clean, you must not call profane." He gets the message. The voice is not just talking about animals; it is referring to people as well, namely, the gentiles. Therefore, share the gospel with the gentiles. Don't be an idiot.

Acts 11 contributes to our theology of creation by telling us that every aspect of creation is "clean," in the sense of being a valuable part of God's sacred Creation. From muddy creeks to fresh spring water, it is all clean. From microbes to mountains, it is all clean. From Jews to gentiles, it is all clean. Like the writer of Genesis says, "It's all good." And it compels us to praise the Creator. Despite the inherent violence in nature, "red in tooth and claw," despite the chaos of weather phenomena, despite the decay and death of all living things, despite the scientific consensus of evolution and climate change, God's Creation is good and clean and compels us to praise the Creator.

36. i.e., no damn good people.

One of my favorite theologians is Sally McFague. She is noted for promoting the metaphor of "the world as God's body."[37] What would happen if we took that metaphor seriously? How would our care of Creation be better if we could make a more substantial connection between the Creation and its Creator—the world as God's body?[38] Despite what that bumper sticker claimed, no one ever said we need to worship Creation, but how can we earnestly worship the Creator if we do not value the Creator's Creation? This is only a conundrum for those who are afraid that showing any concern for the Creation is as idolatrous as melting down a ton of gold and fashioning it into a golden calf. That sort of thing really pisses off the Creator.

Goodness Looks Like Playing Safe Bets

One of my doppelgangers, Kenny Rogers, died in 2020. I am a fan of his song, "The Gambler," and those iconic lyrics, "You've got to know when to hold 'em, know when to fold 'em." I come from a poker-playing family, although, because I am a clergyperson, I did not exactly follow the family path. After Rogers died in 2020, I noted that with everyone wearing face-masks even in casinos, due to the pandemic, folks did not have to worry whether they have a good "poker face." The facemask puts everyone on a level playing field, or rather a level card table.

I am also a fan of another famous "gambler," although I do not think he played poker. Blaise Pascal was a seventeenth century French philosopher, mathematician, physicist, inventor, writer, and Catholic theologian.[39] I refer to him as a "gambler" because he came up with what we call "Pascal's Wager." This is a rather simplistic philosophical argument that claims we humans bet with our lives that God either exists or does not exist. His conclusion was that a rational person should live as though God exists and that we should seek to believe in God. If God does not actually exist, he claims, then people who have chosen to believe in God might lose only a few things, such as a few hedonistic pleasures or unnecessary luxuries. On the other hand, if God *does* exist, and we believe in God, then the "pot gets sweeter" (to use a poker term). If

37. McFague, *Models of God: Theology for an Ecological, Nuclear Age,* Philadelphia: Fortress Press, 1987.

38. Is this the divine version of a "dad bod"?

39. He was also very clever at padding his resume.

God exists and we believe in God, then, says Pascal, we will be infinitely rewarded (meaning heaven) and we will avoid infinite losses (meaning hell). In other words, it is better to be safe than sorry.

As a young man, still working for my parents in their little grocery store in West Texas, I had this conversation with my best friend at the time. I was a new convert to evangelical Christianity, and I was most definitely getting on my friend's nerves, constantly trying to get him to "see the light." Without knowing what I was doing, I used Pascal's argument on him. This was several years before I was introduced to Pascal's Wager, so I guess all seventeenth century minds think alike (because that is about how archaically sophisticated my thinking was at that time). By the way, my friend eventually moved to California and became an evangelical Christian, and I became a mainline Protestant ecumenically minded Christian, which is an odd turn of events or twist of fate if you ask me.

These days, I am not a big fan of applying Pascal's Wager to the question of God's existence because I think his theology is too simplistic. The notion that if people cannot make themselves believe in God, they will land in eternal punishment is not exactly an enlightened view of God, even if many Christians still believe that. I choose to believe that God is not quite so petty. Nevertheless, I do think Pascal's logic in his famous "Wager," which I simplistically call the "better to be safe than sorry" argument, *can* be applied to other things in our place and time. His wager is better suited for some of the major ethical dilemmas of our day.

Not long ago, for example, I used Pascal's Wager to suggest that we need to get behind the science of climate change. I am not the first to do so. Since at least 1992, scholars have applied Pascal's Wager to decisions about catastrophic climate change. Some would argue that his logic works even better for climate change because while there is *no* scientific evidence for the existence of God, there is *plenty* of evidence for the reality of climate change. And, as Warren Buffett once said, "If there is only a 1% chance the planet is heading toward a truly major disaster and delay means passing a point of no return, inaction now is foolhardy."[40] In terms of climate change, is it not better to err on the side of caution?

The same argument could be used in our debates with an interesting group of people known as "anti-vaxxers." Drawing on Pascal's Wager, rational people should take the advice of science and have their children vaccinated. There is little or no evidence that vaccinations are harmful,

40. Why Warren Buffett Doesn't Think Climate Change Is His Problem | AJOT. COM

but there is enormous evidence that vaccinations have saved millions of lives. We have everything to gain, and very little to lose.

COVID-19 brought us another health crisis, and once again there are people that were and are willing to wager that the pandemic does not really exist, or if it exists, it is not a big deal. To these people, I think Blaise Pascal would say, "You are making a terrible bet. Stay away from poker tables because you will get your clock cleaned." It is not a good bet to ignore what the scientists and epidemiologists are telling us because the potential upside of going back to business as usual does not outweigh the potential downside of a long-lasting pandemic. Therefore, get your "Fauci ouchie."

By the way, the word "pandemic" ought to be a clue to those who do not think this is a big deal. The Latin word "pan" means "all" and the word "demos" means "people," so "pan-demic" literally means "all people." There is no excuse for folks out there making bad wagers on the health and wellbeing of themselves and others by not wearing masks, practicing social distancing, or getting inoculated. So, my friends, let us combine our inner seventeenth century philosopher, mathematician, physicist, inventor, writer, and theologian with what our twenty-first century scientists are telling us and get the damn shot.

8

Being Male, Pale, Stale, and Straight

O NCE upon a time I went on a fishing expedition with two friends, one of whom happened to be a professional fisherman. He took us to a secluded spot on a small river in West Texas, and even then, we had to take our little fishing boat down a river of murky water for a couple of hours to get to a spot that was rarely frequented by the human species. While there we set a trotline and waited until the next day to run it. As we roughly approached the middle of the trotline, we noticed that something huge was lingering about, not putting up much of a fight, probably due to exhaustion. Much to the fright of the other friend, the fish we pulled into the boat from the trotline was a forty-five-pound yellow catfish. In the years since, I often refer to this fish, rather uncreatively, as "the Big One." And it did not get away.

If we could put out a trotline that would catch an ethical issue that would be so large as to frighten most of us as we haul it into our moral and ethical debates, it would be the issue of *identity*. Often referred to as "identity politics," the various issues associated with this innocent sound-ing label presently overshadow almost every other issue that consumes our moral energy. Like that forty-five-pound yellow-cat, identity politics is too vast to "eat" at one setting. It brings us to the table time and again. And until we evolve to a point in our moral discourse when identity poli-tics is no longer so political, no longer so contentious, and no longer an issue that keeps us in our own separate ethical bubbles (or rivers), we must overcome our fears, grab it by the fins, and haul it into our boats. If we sink trying to do so, then we should hope that the river is not too deep.

In this chapter, I will approach the issue of identity politics in the only way I know how: from my personal bubble as a white, straight male, hoping that I do not write anything that will cause my boat to capsize.[1]

Should We Play Favorites?

One of the most interesting, if not asinine, questions in theological circles is whether God shows partiality. Like a parent with multiple children, does God play favorites? From a biblical perspective, the answer is largely "yes." The prophet Isaiah seems to believe that God shows partiality toward the nation of Israel when he writes, "Here is my servant, whom I uphold, my *chosen*, in whom my soul delights" (Isaiah 42:1). The word "servant" here is likely a reference to the nation of Israel, so, at least in the mind of the prophet Isaiah, God favors the nation of Israel.

The same is true in the popular 29th Psalm. This is a "royal psalm," in that God is depicted as a king who sits on a throne. A king, of course, rules over "his" people, so the psalm ends by saying, "May the Lord give strength to *his* people! May the Lord bless *his* people with peace!" Again, that sounds like favoritism.

In the New Testament, God's favor expands beyond the nation of Israel, the Jews, to include gentiles. In a post-resurrection speech to a crowd in Jerusalem, the Apostle Peter says, "I truly understand that God shows *no partiality*, but in every nation anyone who fears him and does what is right is acceptable to him" (Acts 10:34–35). Peter seems to have had an "Oh, I get it!" moment by drawing the circle of God's favoritism wider than his people had previously imagined, and yet, to be clear, the circle still has boundaries. Although Peter claims "God shows no partiality," he (dis)qualifies this by suggesting God's partiality has only extended to people who fear God and do what is right. Presumably, that still leaves many people off the list of God's favorites.[2]

Finally, in the Gospels we see God's favoritism toward a specific individual, namely Jesus. The occasion of Jesus' baptism comes to mind. As he comes up from the water, the heavens open, the Spirit of God descends from the sky, and a voice from heaven suggests that God really does have a favorite child: "This is *my Son, the Beloved, with whom I am well pleased*" (Matthew 3:17).

---

1. Just wading into the waters of identity politics is dangerous enough.
2. Especially people who are no damn good.

Another way to describe what we see in these writings is to say that God engages in *identity politics*. Identity politics occurs when we prioritize or favor the concerns of one group of people over others. Typically, we are talking about favoring the concerns of a *marginalized* group—a group with relatively little power.

Whether we are aware of it or not, all of us engage in identity politics. It is human nature that we are partial to those who belong to our group or "tribe." We tend to promote our group's interests over the interests of other groups. God may not show partiality, but we sure do. All of us belong to multiple groups or tribes based on a variety of categories, such as age, religion, social class, profession or occupation, culture, language, ability, education, race or ethnicity, gender identity, sexual orientation, urban or rural habitation, and veteran status (just to name some of the more obvious categories). The study of how these categories collide and mingle is called "intersectionality." My congregation recently adopted a non-discriminatory policy that includes most, if not all, of these categories because we want to be as impartial as possible. We are trying *not* to play favorites, although we do, and we will.[3]

The goal of identity politics is to help relatively powerless people gain more power, self-determination, and political freedom. Classic examples of this are the Civil Rights, feminist, and LGBTQ+ movements, all of which have the expressed goal of strengthening previously marginalized groups. Of course, this sort of thing does not occur without a little push back from groups that fear the loss of all the perks that come with a more privileged identity. The classic example of this is the tribe to which I belong, the stereotypical "straight white male," a group that has historically enjoyed immense power and privilege.

Just as the Apostle Peter's contemporaries were uncomfortable with his (and Paul's) efforts to widen the circle of God's favor, the identity politics of twenty-first century America is making many of *us* uncomfortable. I would be lying if I said that it did not make *me* uncomfortable at times because as a straight white male, I can see the handwriting on the wall. My Waterloo is on the horizon. The apocalypse is upon me. My tribe has had to move over and make room, so to speak, and although I support this intellectually, my instincts and emotions are still human. I want to be one of God's favorite children, or at least belong to God's favorite tribe.

---

3. Because, you guessed it, some of us are no damn good.

The pulpit I inhabit on Sunday mornings is, in fact, a symbol of the privileged position of my tribe throughout history. There are twelve pictures of all our former pastors hanging neatly and sturdily on the wall in the narthex. All are faces of white men (mostly of German descent). That would be true in many of our congregations. Women have only been accepted in this pulpit in relatively recent times. And yet now, because of the growing power of identity politics within the church (especially the United Church of Christ), women occupy some of the most prestigious pulpits in the country. The worm has turned, as they say.

With all this in mind, I will revisit my earlier question: Does God play favorites? Does God prefer certain categories of people over others? Liberation theologians such as Pope Francis argue that God has a "preference for the poor" and oppressed. Think about what that says about God's view of relatively prosperous Americans. Whether God plays favorites or not is God's prerogative. As for us, we need to treat everyone with as much respect as possible because God's house has a very large roof. "In my Father's House are many rooms (or mansions)," says Jesus in John 14, an inclusive statement ironically utilizing exclusive, patriarchal language.

Because identity politics is a very real thing, I want to offer some advice on how to live faithfully in the context of this complex tapestry of humanity. Jonathan Haidt, the social psychologist I mentioned earlier, co-authored a book called *The Coddling of the American Mind* with Greg Lukianoff, the president of the Foundation for Individual Rights in Education.[4] They argue that the human mind evolved within the context of living in tribes that engage in frequent and often violent conflict. Even today we readily divide the world into "us" versus "them." "Them" might include enemies from a foreign country, fellow citizens who belong to another political party, or someone who belongs to another church down the street.[5] This is who we are, and always will be. Identity politics is inevitable. The question is how best to engage in identity politics. According to Haidt and Lukianoff, there are two ways.

The first way is called "common-*enemy* identity politics." Rather than appeal to our common humanity, these are the groups that believe the only way they can win is if other groups lose—what we call a zero-sum game. Any ideology that lifts one group up by tearing other groups

4. Lukianoff and Haidt, *The Coddling of the American Mind: How Good Intentions and Bad Ideas Are Setting Up a Generation for Failure,* Penguin Books, 2018.

5. For me, "them" also includes people who listen to contemporary country music. But I digress.

down is engaging in common-enemy identity politics. We should avoid that when we can.

The other option is called "common-*humanity* identity politics." Martin Luther King, Jr. is a good example of this. His movement tried to appeal to our common humanity while at the same time applying political pressure to gain more self-determination and political freedom for African Americans. King did not believe there had to be winners and losers. He believed everyone can be a winner. No one needs to give up their own self-determination and political freedom—we just need to widen the circle to include others.

We need to be aware and informed about identity politics, especially since we all engage in it, knowingly or unknowingly. All of us belong to multiple tribes that are struggling either to gain or maintain our power, self-determination, and freedom. Even as we play favorites, we need to remind ourselves that we all belong to one human family, that we are all God's children, and that we all have equal value and worth in God's eyes . . . that we can be better than no damn good.

On Being a Straight White Male (and Old)

If memory serves me correctly, I invented the phrase "male, pale, and stale" to refer to the fact that I am an oldish white man. Perhaps I heard it somewhere else and subconsciously began using it as if I heard it first in my own head. Regardless, when I googled the phrase "male pale stale" I read that it was used by the British press when Prime Minister David Cameron reshuffled his cabinet by disposing of ministers who were white, male, middle-aged, middle-class, and hence perceived boring, in favor of more young, female, and non-white people.[6] In the eyes of many of my contemporaries, especially those who do not share these particular demographic categories with me—including my "straight" sexuality—I and my ilk are largely responsible for most of the world's ills. We are at the front of the line for almost everything, including the designation "no damn good."

I have long since believed that to elevate my moral status from no damn good to damn good I need to find ways to work through my historically privileged demographic categories in ways that benefit other people.

6. https://english.stackexchange.com/questions/185731/what-is-the-origin-of-pale-male-and-stale

Admittedly, this is not always easy. Sometimes, in fact, my efforts to minimize the importance of my identity is met with suspicion and distrust. I have learned, for example, not to say out loud that it is becoming more and more difficult to be "male, pale, stale, and straight" as a pastor in the most liberal denomination in the country, the United Church of Christ. It *is* becoming more difficult in terms of having a voice at the table, relatively speaking, and yet saying it out loud sounds *very* disingenuous. It is the crème de la crème of First World Problems and Privilege.

There are only two strategic responses to this albatross, yet privileged, identity. First, I can simply ignore it and disappear into the shadows of my profession, occasionally grabbing the limelight like the groundhog on, well, Groundhog Day. Or, two, I can defend my honor with every ounce of genuine and disingenuous power I can muster so that the readers of this book might think, "He's not such a bad fella, for an old white guy." That's about as good as it can get for me.

On Being Male

I begin with the first of the four characteristics that define my specific demographic category: *maleness.* Because I grew up in a very male-centric patriarchal, often misogynistic, culture and religion, I will likely never shed the inner turmoil I feel when my wife asks me to do domestic chores or watch a Rom-Com on television. One reason for my inner turmoil is the fact that I never saw my own father busy with domestic chores, such as cooking, cleaning, laundry, etc., and I never ever saw him willingly or voluntarily use the television remote control in search of a "chick flick." And yet, while the inner turmoil is instilled in me in a way that will never ever exit my mind and body—short of an exorcism—I do make a conscious effort to shed any personal expressions of male chauvinism.[7]

I would be lying if I said that I have not felt an occasional sense of jealousy when I learn about a female pastor called to a celebrated pulpit or a cushy Conference or National position in my denomination. I have applied for many of these jobs over the years with nary a nibble. Apparently, my PhD would go much further if I were anything other than male, pale, stale, or straight. I tell myself not to begrudge anyone their success as I recommit myself to my current calling. I have learned to be content

---

7. The fact that there are so many words and phrases used to describe male privilege suggests one unequivocal truth: men are no damn good to the core.

with the cards dealt to me, words that sound disingenuous coming from the keyboard of a white straight male.

As I make my way through a relatively non-distinct preaching career, however, I can boast of a very telling claim to fame (although no one is likely to see it if I do not point it out). Other than my short-lived or interim pastoral positions over the years, a female has followed me in the pulpit after I moved on to my next calling. Every single time. In five congregations. And in every case the new pastor was the first female pastor in their history. Every single time. In five congregations. This suggests that either a) my preaching has moved the progressive dial on their views about female pastors, or b) I suck as a pastor and therefore ruined it for any male pastor that might have followed in my footsteps. I'll go with "a" unless I hear otherwise.

Perhaps my inner feminism reveals itself in my preaching in a way that gradually helps my parishioners "see the light." Where this came from is anyone's guess, but it came early. In my book, *Big Jesus*, I share an episode in my life that occurred as an undergraduate at Hardin-Simmons University in the late 1980s. I was dining one day in the cafeteria when a young lady approached me and asked if I am a feminist. I said, "Can a guy be a feminist?" After all these years, I believe the best answer is, "Yes, if one makes a conscious effort." If not, then one will need to make some apologies on occasion.

Her-Story

Speaking of men needing to apologize, the following story comes to mind from 2 Samuel 11:2–15:

> It happened, late one afternoon, when David rose from his couch and was walking about on the roof of the king's house, that he saw from the roof a woman bathing; the woman was very beautiful. David sent someone to inquire about the woman. It was reported, "This is Bathsheba daughter of Eliam, the wife of Uriah the Hittite." So David sent messengers to get her, and she came to him, and he lay with her. (Now she was purifying herself after her period.) Then she returned to her house. The woman conceived; and she sent and told David, "I am pregnant." So David sent word to Joab, "Send me Uriah the Hittite." And Joab sent Uriah to David. When Uriah came to him, David asked how Joab and the people fared, and how the war was

going. Then David said to Uriah, "Go down to your house, and wash your feet." Uriah went out of the king's house, and there followed him a present from the king. But Uriah slept at the entrance of the king's house with all the servants of his lord, and did not go down to his house. When they told David, "Uriah did not go down to his house," David said to Uriah, "You have just come from a journey. Why did you not go down to your house?" Uriah said to David, "The ark and Israel and Judah remain in booths; and my lord Joab and the servants of my lord are camping in the open field; shall I then go to my house, to eat and to drink, and to lie with my wife? As you live, and as your soul lives, I will not do such a thing." Then David said to Uriah, "Remain here today also, and tomorrow I will send you back." So Uriah remained in Jerusalem that day. On the next day, David invited him to eat and drink in his presence and made him drunk; and in the evening he went out to lie on his couch with the servants of his lord, but he did not go down to his house. In the morning David wrote a letter to Joab, and sent it by the hand of Uriah. In the letter he wrote, "Set Uriah in the forefront of the hardest fighting, and then draw back from him, so that he may be struck down and die."

I hope this does not come across as "mansplaining," but here goes . . . What do you think Bathsheba thought about all this? We really do not get her side of the story, do we? This is an R-rated story from 2 Samuel chapter 11—which is an appropriate chapter number because it shows how morally *bankrupt* King David was. *His*-story tells us that David was a man after God's own heart. And maybe he was. No one is perfect, right? He is certainly one of the "great" characters in the Bible— whatever "great" means. The word "great" is a morally neutral word. It does not always mean "good." The "Great Depression" comes to mind, as does, "Make America Great Again."[8]

I will say something now that is very uncomfortable to say yet needs to be said: The Bible was written by men, about men, and for men. Yes, a few ladies are mentioned here and there. And on occasion they are even cast in a good light. Usually, however, the writers of the biblical stories make sure that the female personalities in the Bible do not look so good. Eve comes readily to mind: "It's all her fault!" Even the first witness to the Resurrection of Jesus, Mary Magdalene, has mistakenly gone down in

---

8. MAGA compels me to ask when America was great *before*. I am sure that most historically underrepresented and oppressed minorities, many of whom were enslaved, would beg to differ.

his-story as a demon-possessed prostitute. A good woman in the scriptures just cannot catch a break. And then there are the supposedly "bad" women, such as Jezebel, although she does not seem to be any worse than the men in the story. Certainly, there are bad *men* in the Bible as well. You need to have a few culprits, such as Pharaoh and Judas Iscariot, and yet, on balance, the Bible is pro-male. Most of the good guys are guys, not gals. God is even our "Father," because in that place and time calling God "Mother" would have sullied God's reputation.

The Bible is not a history book, per se, although there are countless historical references in it. Some of it is historically accurate and some of it is not. Some of the storytelling in the Bible is just that: storytelling. Thus, while I would argue that, broadly speaking, there is some history in the Bible, I think it is evident that there is little *her-story*. There is very little (if any) that was written by women, about women (in a positive light), and for women. The Bible was written in a patriarchal, male dominated, even misogynist context. Them's just the facts, ma'am.

So, what do we do with these facts? Well, I think we do what women (and some men) have been trying to do for a while now: Give women a voice. Give women a place at the table. Give women a role from the pulpit. Give women power in the public arena. While we are certainly making progress, we have a long way to go.[9] By the way, did you notice how sexist it was for me to say "give women" etc. as if women cannot just take what they deserve? This is a good example of *microaggressions*.[10]

Again, what did Bathsheba think about all this? In the story from 2 Samuel 11, Bathsheba seems to have no voice, no will, no feelings, and no say in the matter. David, the main character, just does what he wants. He is like the Harvey Weinstein of the tenth century BCE. And what he did not "accomplish" in that department, his son, Solomon certainly did. Do you remember how many wives and concubines he had?

David may have earned a better reputation in other stories in the Bible, and yet here he truly is morally bankrupt. First, he is a coward. "In the spring of the year, the time *when kings go out to battle*," David

---

9. I know you are probably thinking about an old *Virginia Slims* commercial tagline: "You've come a *long way*, baby." That is just wrong on so many levels although, ironically, it was known as a feminist-minded advertising campaign at the time.

10. "Microaggression" is a term used for commonplace daily verbal, behavioral or environmental slights, whether intentional or unintentional, that communicate hostile, derogatory, or negative attitudes toward stigmatized or culturally marginalized groups. Happens all the time.

stays home in Jerusalem. What is he afraid of? His men are at war with the Ammonites, and he is a seasoned warrior. What is the deal here? Is he afraid the Israelites are outgunned? After all, their opponents are the *Ammo*nites.[11] Or maybe he is just trying to start a new tradition, one where kings are too important to risk their lives in battle.

Regardless of why he does not go into battle, it is not long before his Harvey Weinstein side is revealed. He is walking around on the roof of his house, no doubt cleaning out the gutters, when he sees a woman bathing and decides he wants her, so he sends a servant to go get her and bring her to him and the rest is his-story.

Apparently quite a bit of time passes in the story because she discovers she is pregnant. Since her husband, Uriah, is at war, David must be the father. We might assume that Bathsheba holds David's feet to the fire, yet the writer only has her say to David, "I'm pregnant." David then does what every "honorable" man in history has ever done—he tries to wriggle out of his responsibility. He sends for Bathsheba's husband to come home and be with his wife so that no one will be suspicious that Bathsheba is pregnant, and her husband is away.

Notice at this point that no one in the story is asking what Bathsheba wants to do—but that is really the point I am trying to make.

Uriah dutifully comes back from the war but does not go home to be with his wife because he does not think this is fair to all the other men who are away fighting King David's war. David even wines and dines Uriah, hoping to loosen him up enough to go home to be with his wife, but no dice. So, David goes to Plan B (which is not a reference to the "morning after pill") and sends Uriah to the frontline in the war against the Ammonites so that he will likely be killed and then he can just have Bathsheba all to himself. It works.

Here we have a story where one of the greatest men of the Bible is a coward, an adulterer, a conniver, and a murderer. And yet, history says David was a good guy. Bathsheba, well, at best she is just David's love interest and Solomon's mother. At worst, she is a loose woman who easily gave in to the desires of a powerful man. (Where have we seen that narrative before?)

His-story verses her-story. There really is no contest in the Bible or in Christian history. The stories have been written by men, about men, and for men (generally speaking). And yes, men are no damn good. At

---

11. I bet you did not see that coming.

the very least, they are afraid of something, but what is that something? A storm is brewing . . .

The Waves of Feminism

> When evening came, his disciples went down to the sea, got into a boat, and started across the sea to Capernaum. It was now dark, and Jesus had not yet come to them. The sea became rough because a strong wind was blowing. When they had rowed about three or four miles, they saw Jesus walking on the sea and coming near the boat, and they were terrified. But he said to them, "It is I; do not be afraid." Then they wanted to take him into the boat, and immediately the boat reached the land toward which they were going. (John 6:16–21)

In this incredible story, Jesus walks on the water in the middle of a storm because the disciples are on a boat, and they are afraid. The male disciples are afraid. Go figure. Do you think on some level this is what has been happening in the church in American society? Men are afraid that women will create a storm and the *waves* of change will capsize the boat. Using the word "waves" is appropriate here because scholars talk about the "waves of feminism." Depending on who is counting, there have been three or four waves in recent history. Let me give you a history lesson . . . I mean her-story lesson.

The first wave of feminism began with the Seneca Falls Convention in 1848, when hundreds of men and women met to advocate for women's equality—specifically, for their right to vote. It also challenged the notion that women should be "domesticated," stay at home, and not participate in politics.

The second wave of feminism began with women protesting the 1968 Miss America Pageant. In this wave, women fought for workplace equality and fought against workplace sexism. Rape and abortion became important topics, and this wave obviously led to the passage of Roe v. Wade in 1973.

The third wave of feminism occurred in the 1990s and 2000s. In this wave, other voices were included such as minority and lesbian women. There was a critique of ideal body types, and a rejection of the notion of women being sex objects.

Feminist scholars now claim we are in a fourth wave, which includes many of the topics of the past. However, the main topic today is sexual aggression against women and girls. There is more awareness of "human trafficking." Some of the major milestones of this wave of feminism are the Women's March on Washington, the #MeToo movement, and the Time's Up initiative.

These waves were all primarily created in secular society; and yet the waves have certainly splashed over into the Christian church and other religious institutions. (Actually, the waves go both ways. Sometimes the church *creates* the biggest splash and sometimes the church is drenched with a secular wave.) "Feminist theology" is the name we give to the religiously motivated waves of feminism. The purpose of feminist theology is to reconsider the traditions, practices, scriptures, and theologies of these religions from a female perspective. There is also "Womanist theology," which focuses on the experiences and perspectives of Black women.

Because of this ever flowing and heightening wave, we have seen an increased role of women in the ranks of the clergy and teaching professions. We have witnessed a reinterpretation of male-dominated imagery and language about God (what we often call "inclusive language"), and we have paid more attention to the women who have played a crucial role in the history of religion. In other words, we are now learning her-story as well as his-story.

As a man, I want to go on the record and say that I am not afraid of this. Like David, I might be afraid of going to war. Like Jesus' disciples, I might be afraid of being in a boat in the middle of a storm. But I am not afraid of the emerging march of women and the energetic wave of feminism that is spreading through church and society. And if I ever need to step aside to allow a woman's voice to be heard, I hope I do so willingly and with enthusiasm, and without the sexist need for mansplaining.

On Being Pale

And then there is my whiteness, i.e., paleness. Recently, I took two home DNA tests, the second one to confirm the startling results of my first one, that claims I am almost one hundred percent northern European (Scottish, British, Irish, etc.) without an ounce of Native American blood trickling through my veins. This was startling because, like many other Scots Irish Americans, I had been told my entire life that I am partially of Native American descent. For years, I was told that one of my great-grandmothers was Cherokee, and then more recently, according to a now-deceased uncle, that she was Apache.[12] Sadly, it turns out that I am nothing more than a pasty white guy from the British Isles.

This makes my arrival in Ferguson, Missouri as Senior Pastor of Immanuel United Church of Christ a year after Mike Brown's death in 2014 at the hands of a Ferguson police officer, well, uneventful. Because of this church's geographical location in the heart of Ferguson, two doors down from City Hall and just a few blocks from the police station and primary protest spot, my denomination's new President and General Minister at the time, John Dorhauer, used our sanctuary to spread the word about "white privilege" just weeks before I arrived. I missed that speech, but my largely white congregation of German heritage was quick to inform me that some of our members did not appreciate the concept of white privilege, even as they worship near the epicenter of the rebirth of the Black Lives Matter movement.[13] Traci Blackmon, a UCC clergy-woman from neighboring Florissant, Missouri, had a prominent role in the aftermath of Brown's death, enough to elevate her to national status in the struggle for black equality and justice.

While there was much local clergy participation in the protests of 2014–2015, the reality is that white male clergy participation, especially in the Protestant ranks, was less visible than their colleagues. This is partly due to white male privilege and the reluctance to "make waves," and yet I would also include the fear of being distrusted or rejected as another reason why they were largely absent. Personally, I am almost glad I came after most of the action, because if I had chosen to participate in the numerous protests to the same extent as my female interim predecessor, I may have fallen on the double-edged sword of a) the anger of a few of my white parishioners, and b) a nagging feeling that the local black community would see me as "in the way" and not appreciate my sincere efforts to help the cause.

Fortunately, in the ensuing years I have been able to become part of the solution rather than the problem through such actions as hosting and participating in the development of a mediation program between

12. Of this latter claim I was told by said uncle that I should never tell anyone because, as he saw it, people with Apache heritage are the most oppressed among all Americans. Personally, I thought it would be cool to be Apache.

13. The birth of BLM originated in the aftermath of the death of Trayvon Martin at the hands of racist George Zimmerman in 2012.

local residents and the police department, guiding my congregation to officially join a local ecumenical group that aims for racial justice and harmony in North St. Louis County, using our facilities for a summer day camp for local children, most of whom are children of color, and using our facilities as a warming site for the homeless during the winter months. Still, despite my sincere efforts to be someone that is more than a descendent of northern Europeans, skin color is an unalterable characteristic, save for a few sun rays. Like maleness, the historical privilege that comes with paleness has become something I am encouraged to recognize and not allow to "color" my worldview in ways that oppress others. One visible way to do this is to support the slogan, if not the organization, known as Black Lives Matter.

BLM and the Analogy of the Forest

One helpful way to understand the Black Lives Matter response to such things as police brutality, white supremacy, and systemic racism is by thinking about the analogy of a forest. Forests are often populated with a multitude of different kinds of trees. Each kind has its own unique "skin," (i.e., bark) which can be red, green, gray, white, orange, or even striped. The texture of each tree's skin can be thorny, smooth, rough, or deeply furrowed. Trees have a variety of "hair" color as well (i.e., leaves), with green being the most common color. The fall adds more variety to the color of their hair: yellow, orange, or red being the most common of the fall "styles." In the winter, some trees shed their hair after their experimentation with bright colors in the fall. Trees provide oxygen, shade, and shelter for animals. Without trees, life could not continue. Without tees, all of Creation would be heard saying, "I can't breathe." Trees also provide aesthetic pleasure to a species that also occupies the world in huge numbers: human beings.

Like trees, human beings come in various shapes, sizes, skin tones and textures, and hairdos. Most of these humans come in some shade of brown, from light to dark, with a slight hue of red or yellow for some. Humans often dwell in places where a majority, like trees in a forest, look much like they do, called mono or single-dominance systems, and yet some dwell in places that are as diverse as the Amazon rainforest. Regardless of where they live, both trees and humans, along with other species of flora and fauna, are Children of God and therefore deserve to be respected and cherished. Yes, they *all matter*.

Like the diversity of trees in a forest, in this country there is a great variety of people of different ethnicities. For the most part, people get along with one another like trees in a forest, often living side by side, drinking from the same undergrown streams, water ways, and drops of rain from the sky. The snow collects on their leaves or hair indiscriminately. They fight the winds that blow through their limbs or arms, they offer shade and protection to their younger saplings or siblings, and they mourn when one of their own has fallen. Yes, all lives matter.

And yet, sometimes it is appropriate to focus on one kind of tree or ethnic expression of humanity, perhaps an endangered species, one that is either near extinction or devalued. Sometimes we need to focus our attention on *their* worth and value. One can imagine a parallel universe, for example, where a variety of trees have yard signs that read "Dogwood Tree Lives Matter," which is not meant to exclude other trees. No other plant or animal is devalued simply because a specific plant or animal is intentionally valued.

That is the landscape for what is happening in America today. So, when we reflect on the reasons why there is such a vibrant modern-day Civil Rights movement called "Black Lives Matter," we can refer to two truisms and one question, all using the analogy of a forest.

The first truism is this: *We can't see the forest for the trees.*

We all suffer at times from an inability to see clearly what is important. We lack the ability to see the big picture because we are too narrowly focused on one or two specific trees. We cannot see the background, setting, or context because we tend to focus on the trees directly in front of us. Because of confirmation bias, we extrapolate from the "truth" we discern about these one or two trees while ignoring the plight of other trees, trees that are failing or falling.

If we want to believe that few or no trees are in distress, that few or no trees are being burned in wildfires or cut down by the lumberjack's axe, then we will focus on one or two trees that are *not* burning up or falling, even if there is ample evidence that many other trees *are* burning up or falling down. In terms of the plight of people of color, "we can't see the forest for the trees" refers to the fact that many white Americans choose to focus on a relatively small number of events that confirm their suspicions that black America is crying wolf about such things as police brutality, white supremacy, and systemic racism.

Obviously, some of the events that have been reported in the news and spread all over social media are more egregious than others. Yes, there have been a few examples where an act of constraint or even violence may have been "justified" according to existing laws. However, most incidents that have led to public outrage were *not* justified and thus were rightly protested. In the forest/world, people of color *do* suffer from police brutality, white supremacy, and systemic racism. That is the forest. And it is an old forest. So long as white America cannot see the forest for the trees—trees that conveniently confirm their biases—there will continue to be trouble in the forest.

Truism #2: *Where There's Smoke There's Fire*

According to *Science* magazine, the summer of 2020 witnessed the worst wildfire season on the West Coast in at least seventy years. The blazes killed dozens of people, destroyed hundreds of structures, and caused extreme air pollution that threatened the health of millions of residents. Ecologists fear the wildfires inflicted lasting damage on species and ecosystems. Even if one could not see the fires, almost everyone in the Western part of the United States and beyond could see or smell the smoke. Any reasonable person will conclude that the smoke proves there is fire. Where there's that much smoke there's always fire.

Because of the ubiquity of smart phone cameras, there is more than enough evidence of fire (i.e., police brutality, white supremacy, and systemic racism) than is needed to support the Black Lives Matter movement. And yet, even if we did not have all that physical evidence—the George Floyd murder being the most obvious and egregious recent example—even if all we had was eyewitness testimony from victims or bystanders, there is still enough smoke to claim that the fire is real.

Both truisms serve as appropriate analogies for the plight of black America in the twenty-first century, as they have for the last four centuries. Both truisms can help us overcome our natural prejudices and our confirmation biases to become part of the solution rather than the problem. Both truisms can help us open our eyes, followed by our hearts.

But now I would like to bring a question into this conversation, one that has been asked on many occasions, often for the sake of intellectual frivolity. It is a fun question, but in the context of the analogy between the plight of forests and people of color, it is one that is worth pondering. Here it is:

If a tree falls in the forest, and there's no one there to hear it, does it make a sound?

The Canadian songwriter, social activist, and environmentalist, Bruce Cockburn posed that question in the chorus of his 1989 song, "If a Tree Falls" and frames it within the context of deforestation. I suggest that the plight of people of color in America today is analogous to deforestation. Trees are being "cut down," too often, and for unnecessary reasons. In this analogy, law enforcement officers, a justice system that applies the law unequally, and white supremacists are the lumberjacks.

"If a tree falls in the forest, and there's no one there to hear it, does it make a sound?" is a thought experiment that raises questions about observation and perception. Like the two truisms, this is a question that uses one of our five senses in an analogous way. If we can't *see* the forest for the trees, does that mean we can't see what is happening to people of color? If we can't *smell* the smoke, does that mean there is no police brutality, white supremacy, and systemic racism? And if we can't *hear* falling trees, does that mean people of color aren't really falling?

Although, *I can't breathe* seems clear to me.

This is the dilemma for those who support, even indirectly with their inaction, such things as police brutality, white supremacy, and systemic racism: *We can see it, we can smell it, and we can hear it.* Once we wake up and conclude that everyone in the forest matters, then, and only then, can we say, unequivocally, *All Life Matters.* Until then, we need to lend our voices to and for those that do not feel as if they matter.

On Being Stale

And then there is my age to consider, i.e., staleness. I need to admit that I do not feel all that stale. In fact, I feel as creative as I have ever been, and yet it is true that chasing my dog across the yard is not as easy as it was thirty years ago. There is such a thing as "ageism," something I am beginning to see and experience in my early 60s, and yet I understand that my age and generation has as much to do with who I am as my maleness or whiteness. Although I am perturbed on occasion listening to millennials and their "OK Boomer" condescending remarks, I get why they do it. We sort of screwed up. Yes, the Boomers are responsible for the greatest cultural shift in the history of the planet—anyone remember the late 1960s?[14]—but on our watch we failed to finish the revolution in terms of

---

14. If you smoked too much grass in the 60s, you get a pass.

civil rights for minorities and women and gays and saving the freaking planet. If I were a millennial, I would be condescending as well.[15]

Although I consider myself to be progressive and cutting-edge, I had an awakening a few years ago when my wife and I attended an Emergent Christian conference in Memphis, Tennessee. Other than Brian McLaren and Phyllis Tickle, two of their presenters, my wife and I were older than most of the young clergy types in their 30s and 40s. After a couple of days of the conference I noticed that there was scant little said about such things as women in ministry, racism, or LGBTQ+ concerns. I asked someone why these were not important topics for them and the response I received was something like: "Why are you guys still talking about those things?"[16] I learned at that moment that sometimes we simply cannot escape our generational fights no matter how many conferences we attend that are dominated by younger people. At this point in my life, I am still struggling with the fact that I had to leave the 40–50-year-old clergy Facebook page in the not-too-distant past. At the same time, I need to struggle with the fact that my sense of ethics and morality will always be that of a "late boomer."

On Being Straight

Yes, I am male, pale, and stale. I am also a *straight* cisgender old white dude. That is worse than the trifecta of historical oppressors. A "quadfecta"? If I had to give myself a grade, I think it would be a "C" on maleness, a "C" on paleness (whiteness), a "C" on staleness (on being a boomer), but perhaps a "B" on the sexual orientation scorecard. No, I am not talking about the Kinsey Report. I am talking about my belief, self-delusional or not, that I have done my small part in this world to move the progressive dial forward on public attitudes toward the LGBTQ+ community. Yes, I have gay friends, but that is not what I'm talking about either.

My wife is constantly telling me to "toot my own horn," to let people know what I have done, to utilize my bragging rights. Getting to a place where I might have something to brag about, however, was not easy. I grew up in a culture that was most certainly not gay friendly. If anyone had a

15. Generation X'ers must feel like sitting at midcourt at a tennis match, watching the volleys back and forth between self-righteous boomers and condescending millennials.

16. On the other hand, the Emergent movement has been criticized for being too male, too white, and too straight. So, there's that.

"gaydar," they used it to punish people for exhibiting any characteristics that were considered "sissy."[17] I am sure I shared many of those same attitudes back in the day, although in West Texas the issue of one's sexual orientation was never seriously discussed. When my attitude may have shifted, I do not recall. All I know is that by the time I decided to turn in my keys to my mom and pop's mom and pop store in 1985 to go back to college, I must have been "woke" in at least a groggy sense of the word.

The topic of human sexuality became front and center for me in the late 1980s when I decided to focus on the field of Christian Ethics. I had written a paper in my Intro to Ethics class at Hardin-Simmons University titled, "Homosexuality and Ordination." It was only a progressive, cutting-edge paper because of the context in which it was written: A Southern Baptist University in West Texas. My thesis was that congregations and/or denominations should have the right to ordain anyone they choose. This, of course, lets conservative anti-gay churches off the hook, but they are not ordaining folks from the LGBTQ+ community anytime soon anyway. On the other hand, I was sending a subtle, yet strong, message to my Baptist peers that if a congregation or denomination does not harbor homophobic attitudes and adhere to a literalist (and faulty) understanding of scripture, they have every right to call lesbians and gays to ordained ministry.[18]

In 1989, while applying for the PhD program at Baylor University, another Southern Baptist institution of higher learning, I included my paper, "Homosexuality and Ordination" in my application packet. According to my future mentor, Dr. Dan McGee, this paper was the key to opening the door to my entrance to Baylor. While at Baylor, almost every semester someone presented a paper on the topic of human sexuality to the Ethics Seminar, a course that Ethics majors took repeatedly. I have probably explored this topic from every angle possible—please do not read into that—and have easily concluded that, well, yes, gay people are people, too.

---

17. Funny, I do not remember any aggressive attitudes toward girls who were tomboyish. We were more than willing to turn a blind eye to the possibility that the two girls that always wanted to sit in the back of the bus on those long ride homes from basketball tournaments in the dark of night might have been doing something other than "experimenting."

18. Back in those days, our conversation was generally limited to lesbians and gays or the "L" and "G" of the now-tortuous string of letters.

As I began my temporary journey at Baylor University, I also began my career-long journey with the United Church of Christ, perhaps the most progressive Christian denomination in America, especially in terms of its ethical and social justice stances. Many of our congregations have voted to become "Open and Affirming" in the past few decades, which is a public welcome to the LGBTQ+ community, allowing this community into full participation in the life of the church, including ordination. In 2005, I traveled to Atlanta, Georgia as a delegate to the UCC's biennial General Synod. There, in the shadow of the Centennial Olympic Park, nine years after the bombing at the Summer Olympics, we voted to become the first major Christian denomination to affirm same-gender marriage. I have voted in every presidential election since 1980, yet this was the most important vote in my life.[19]

In 2009 I successfully led my congregation at the time, St. Andrew UCC in Louisville, Kentucky, through the Open and Affirming (ONA) process. I delivered a sermon that morning, titled, "The Elephant in the Room," noting that there are people from the LGBTQ+ community sitting in the pews of virtually every congregation in the world. To vote against becoming ONA, I noted, is a personal affront against every human being who has sought sanctuary in the church of Jesus Christ because of their sexual orientation and gender identity. And now, as I write these words in early 2021, I am attempting to lead my second congregation through the ONA process.

Compared to many people in this land—especially colleagues serving progressive denominations—I might not exactly have bragging rights for my positions on the specific demographic categories of gender, ethnicity, and sexual orientation, but at least I consider myself to be on the right side of history. Yes, I am privileged in the sense that there are still many congregations that would call me to their pulpit before they call a woman, a person of color, a young pastor (with very little experience), or someone from the LGBTQ+ community. And yet, the Identity Politics dial is moving across this land, changing every day, and I sincerely hope that I have helped to nudge that dial in some small way. Identity Politics is the "the Big One," the issue (or series of issues) that has created a great stir in our ethical stew. The needles on our moral compasses are shaky at best, trying to point us in the right direction so that we will not have to apologize to our grandchildren for being on the wrong side of history.

19. This vote was a major "explosion" in the history of the UCC and I am glad I got to help detonate the bomb.

Identity Politics will never let us "off the hook," especially those of us who are male, pale, stale, and straight, because the world is trying to move past the murky waters we have created.

9

How to Become Damn Good People

As this book has made ambiguously clear, we are, for the most part, no damn good. I believe I have offered sufficient anecdotal, religious, philosophical, and sociological evidence to demonstrate this timeless truth. I have also attempted to answer the "Why?" question, producing a variety of largely unsatisfactory answers when offered separately, yet satisfactory when offered as a whole. Yes, there are those who want to continue with the misguided belief that we are inherently good, and who wonder why, then, God or evolution has created a world where bad things happen. People will be asking that question until the cows come home, i.e., the end of our species.[1]

In truth, I may have overplayed my hand about the depravity of humanity, which is why I highlighted the reality of moral ambiguity in Chapter Four. Our souls might be dark, yet that doesn't mean the candles can't be lit on occasion. I then turned to the "Greeks and Geeks" of ethical history, those who have largely mansplained to us what it is that makes us tick. The pursuit of "happiness" seems to be at the top of our dance card. I also gave a nod to my tribe, the "Christians," relaying to you, my dear readers, a little insight from the book we call the *Bible*.[2] Some Christians claim that our religion is the *only* source for moral and ethical knowledge, yet the Greeks and Geeks of history know better.

---

1. I suggest that in the future, cows will go back to the wild and hide from their human masters yet will come home once we are extinct or have lost our appetite for beef.

2. For the last time, please stop saying "Holy" Bible. That word is not in the Bible's original title, nor does it want to be.

I spent way too much time conveying to you what I think good-ness looks like. I think I'm right in my assertion that it doesn't look like pornography, but I will let you be the judge. Make sure your moral candles are lit before you create an opinion. Finally, I gave my opinion-ated answer to the question, "What is the most pressing ethical issue in the land?" Experience and evidence suggest to me that "Identity Politics" is the "Big One" that cannot get away from us. It is now, finally, after eons of evolution, on our moral hooks, and we need to reel it in.

In this final chapter, I want to answer another huge question, one that I should probably allow to get off my hook and dive back into the murky waters of philosophy and religion: "How can we become damn good people?" Whatever answers I offer here, please take with a grain of salt, but not too much salt, because salt causes high blood pressure.

I Love to Tell My Story

Because you can take the boy out of the Baptist, but you can't take the Baptist out of the boy, *I Love to Tell the Story* ranks high on my list of favorite hymns. Please don't judge. I love it, yet not because of the archaic theology. I love it because it has a nice melody, it has nostalgic value for me, and, ignoring the lyrics of the entire hymn for a moment, it reminds me of the first building block of an ethical and moral foundation: Tell-ing Our Stories. We need to start somewhere in our search to improve ourselves in this way. Also, we need to tell *specific* stories about *specific* issues. As I scanned my brain, asking what is one ethical issue (outside of Identity Politics) that I have struggled with the most over the years, it did not take long for the computer in my brain to spit out a word that is literally and figuratively a "trigger" for me: *guns*. The following is my "gun story." I hope you enjoy it. If not, do not shoot! Let us begin this story with the ambiguous Second Amendment.

Sometimes rules are cut and dry and cannot be bent or broken. Other rules, however, are not so cut and dry and require some interpreta-tion. Because of that, people will disagree about how to interpret the rule. A good example of this is the Second Amendment in our Bill of Rights, which was adopted on December 15, 1791 (you know, when everyone was walking around with AK-47s and other semi-automatic weapons). The Second Amendment reads:

"A well-regulated Militia, being necessary to the security of a free State, the right of the people to keep and bear Arms, shall not be infringed."

Unless you are so anti-gun that you think we should go door to door and confiscate every single weapon in America (even hunting rifles and shotguns), or you are so in love with guns that you think everyone, regardless of age, mental capacity, or criminal tendencies should own an arsenal of weapons, you probably understand that the Second Amendment is very much open to interpretation.

Years ago, while attending grad school at Baylor University, I wrote a paper on the ethical issues surrounding gun ownership and the Second Amendment, and my research led me to realize that many people interpret the Second Amendment based on feelings, not facts. This is true about most controversial ethical issues, so I was not surprised.

Like many Americans I am overwhelmed by the gun debate. Other cultures endure their fair share of gun violence, although I know of no other country where the debate about guns has reached our level of cacophony. As I see it, we are not making much progress in this debate. Perhaps the reason we are largely spinning our wheels like a teenager in a school parking lot can be blamed on that one seemingly benign exercise that occupies a prodigious chunk of our spare time: *debating*. America is divided not as much by red and blue-hued voters as it is by those who are in the daily practice of trying to convince others to see the world from their same pop-free bubble zone, and those who are capable of escaping said cacophony.

The *debaters*, most of whom are sincere in their efforts and are convinced of their righteousness, have, unfortunately, enabled us to kick the can down the road in only small, almost useless, increments. Their arguments stick in my head like a needle in my skull making claims such as, "guns don't kill people; people kill people," and "the Second Amendment applies only to a 'well-regulated militia.'" I am pretty sure I have heard every single cotton-picking argument ever made, and guess what, I ain't changing my mind. And neither are you.

We do not need any more debate points. Our cup already runneth over. The best thing we can all do in the middle of this endless cycle of debates about guns (or any other hot topic of the day) is *to tell our stories*. Our stories have more firepower (pun intended) than the seemingly endless trail of debate points. Therefore, in the spirit of transparency I will now tell the story of my relationship with guns in the briefest possible form, with bullet points (yes, puns are too easy):

- When I was about fifteen, my dad bought me a 22-rifle. For a couple of years, we hunted for deer and turkey. After I graduated from high school, I left the rifle at home. I preferred to wield golf clubs and softball bats.

- One night I was hanging out with some high school friends at a local motel. Apparently one of the occupants did not appreciate our noisy parking lot activities. He came outside and pointed a gun to my head. I put the car in reverse and got the hell out of Dodge.

- As a college student I worked as a cashier in a convenience store. One night a man held up the store at gunpoint. Yes, he pointed the gun at my head. (Looking back on those years, I am lucky I still have a head.) He finally left after I gave him some money out of the cash register, and he told me and my female friend to lock ourselves in the restroom for five minutes.

- As a young pastor with small children, we lived out in the country in a parsonage. A man who lived across the street would get drunk on weekend afternoons and randomly fire his weapons. The local sheriff's office said this was his "Second Amendment right," even as my family and I were forced to stay away from windows and inside the house on many occasions.

- My children spent time with some relatives for a holiday one year. I was able to come a day later and discovered that they were playing with their cousins in bedrooms where guns were sitting on beds and hanging on doorknobs, fully loaded. The owner of the house said her boys had been out hunting that morning and not to worry. Me and the kiddos quickly left.

- When my children were in their adolescent years, we got them a puppy. The puppy escaped the yard one morning before school. A few minutes later we heard a gunshot. The puppy ran home missing a leg. Yes, we lived in the country, and the shooter did not get punished.

- After we moved to Ferguson, I visited the site of the Mike Brown shooting one day with a couple of colleagues. While standing there near the sidewalk memorial, three local men walked up and surrounded us, flashing their pistols at us. After a brief conversation, we left.

- After my dad died, I was visiting my mom and discovered that my dad had kept my 22-rifle all these years. I took it home for nostalgic reasons. There are no bullets in my house.

This is my story. Everyone has a story. You might be able to guess what I think and feel about guns from my story, but that is not the point. The point is that our stories are real and need to be respected and heard. Only then will we be able to lower the level of cacophony.

The benefit of telling our stories, sharing our experiences, is that it gives us a better footing with the issue at hand. We have more authority if indeed we are the "author" of and own up to our experiences. Obviously, we can learn from our stories, so it is good to put pen to paper and write them out.

Sometimes, however, our stories are rather, well, embarrassing . . .

Precious, er, Embarrassing Moments

I put the word out one day asking people to relate an embarrassing moment, one that can be shared in public. Here are several examples:

- A friend of mine said her most embarrassing moment was the day she went to school as a teacher and the students noticed she was wearing two different shoes.

- A pastor who replaced me in a congregation I had previously served wrote to me about the time she did pulpit supply when she was twenty-three years old. She found out later that the church president mistook her for an acolyte when he saw her in her white robe.

- A member of my current congregation wrote to me about the time his cell phone went off during a photography club meeting after he—the leader of the club—just a few seconds earlier had told everyone else to be sure and turn off their cell phones.

- Another parishioner wrote about getting sick "all over the nurses" while donating blood at her university and later hearing someone on campus say, "Oh, there's that girl."

- Another lady told me about walking out of a public restroom with toilet paper stuck to the bottom of her shoe . . . while on a date![3]

- Finally, a friend said she accidentally set off an alarm system on the second day of a new job.

I have had a few embarrassing moments over the years as well:

- As a twenty-year-old I started a new job and met with my boss and new coworkers for breakfast in a restaurant on my first day. The boss ordered coffee for me, and I decided to add some cream, which I had never done before. As I was opening one of those little coffee creams, I squeezed too hard, and it shot all over my new boss's Hawaiian shirt.

- My children caught me "adjusting my pants" from the backside. One of my daughters asked, "Are you going to the movies?" I said, "No, why?" And all three of them chimed in and said, "Because you're picking your seat!"

Being embarrassed can be a good thing. It can be a teachable moment. Perhaps our embarrassment is the universe or God's way of saying, "See how stupid that was? Now, do not do that ever again!" Perhaps we should all pause at times in our lives and ask ourselves, "Am I embarrassed about anything I have ever said or done?" If the answer is yes, then perhaps lessons have been learned.

The most embarrassment I feel today is related to some views I harbored about people when I was younger. I grew up in a very socially isolated, ultra-conservative, culture. Looking back, I acknowledge I made some rather disparaging remarks about individuals and groups of people purely out of ignorance (and the fact that I am no damn good). I used to exhibit a little prejudicial behavior toward Hispanics, the largest minority ethnic group in West Texas. Yes, I was a product of my environment, but my racism toward Hispanics in my youth was inexcusable. It might be *explainable* in terms of my upbringing, yet it was also inexcusable. Similarly, my views about African Americans and the LGBTQ+ community in my younger years was based on misinformation and ignorance and rooted in prejudice and bigotry. And peer pressure. Don't forget peer pressure.

---

3. The same thing happened to me once in a movie theater. To this day, I habitually check the bottom of my shoes when I walk out of a public restroom.

Until I had lived a few years away from the cultural isolation of West Texas I was at least mildly exclusive in my understanding of people who were not like me. I was never as radical as the young white supremacists who gathered in Charlottesville, Virginia in 2018 or those who stormed the U.S. Capitol on January 6, 2021, but I did hang a rebel flag on my bedroom wall as a teenager and thought nothing of it. Even today I am a little embarrassed with who I was as a younger person. Again, it might be explainable, yet it is also inexcusable. I feel blessed (privileged?) that I have been able to evolve in my thinking about other people who do not walk in my moccasins because I realize not everyone has had the same opportunities I have had—coming out of culturally isolated West Texas—to see and experience other folks in different settings.

A few years ago, I heard the radio and television sportscaster, Colin Cowherd, talk about social issues. Something like domestic violence or gays in sports was the hot topic of the week. Before I share with you what he said that made such a big impression on me, I will share with you my theory about the world of sports, especially on a collegiate and professional level. Because sporting events gather people together from various communities, cultures, and countries, athletes and sportscasters tend to have a broader and more inclusive understanding of humanity than the general population. Although the world of sports is rooted in competition, which can bring out the worst in people at times, it is also acted out in the context of cultural diversity. Therefore, people in the sports world often "get it." They are "woke."[4]

Cowherd was talking about an important social issue one day when he claimed that being economically conservative was a viable option, yet unless we want to have to apologize to our grandchildren, we should not be *socially* conservative.[5] He understood that some of us will wake up one morning in the future and feel embarrassed or ashamed about our words or actions today. Therefore, it behooves us to look for those teachable moments. If we feel even slightly embarrassed about something we have said or done today, chances are the universe is offering us a teachable moment. We might be no damn good today, yet that does not mean we have to be *as* no damn good tomorrow.

4. This is true in some athletic circles more than others. Basketball players are on average more "woke" than baseball players. You can guess why.

5. He was likely referring to "trickle-down" theory, which might be a viable theory, but I'm still waiting to get wet.

We should give Jesus a lot of credit. He learned from his embarrass-ing moments quickly. In a story related to us from Matthew 15, a woman embarrasses Jesus, yet it does not take Jesus long to turn his embarrass-ment into a grace-filled teachable moment. The embarrassment is itself proof positive that this incident likely happened. After all, why else would such an embarrassing story about Jesus be included in Matthew and Mark's Gospels? Here is the story from Matthew 15:21–28:

> Jesus left that place and went away to the district of Tyre and Sidon. Just then a Canaanite woman from that region came out and started shouting, "Have mercy on me, Lord, Son of David; my daughter is tormented by a demon." But he did not answer her at all. And his disciples came and urged him, saying, "Send her away, for she keeps shouting after us." He answered, "I was sent only to the lost sheep of the house of Israel." But she came and knelt before him, saying, "Lord, help me." He answered, "It is not fair to take the children's food and throw it to the dogs." She said, "Yes, Lord, yet even the dogs eat the crumbs that fall from their masters' table." Then Jesus answered her, "Woman, great is your faith! Let it be done for you as you wish." And her daughter was healed instantly.

This might be the most revealing story about Jesus in the gospels. A woman of Syro-Phoenician or Canaanite origin approaches him about giving her daughter an exorcism. His disciples attempt to act as a buffer between Jesus and the woman, which Jesus accepts, and then makes a comment that sounds like an insensitive microaggression: "I was sent only to the lost sheep of the house of Israel." The woman breaks through the disciples' buffer zone and enters Jesus' personal space, saying, "Lord, help me." He then addresses her directly with an even more insensitive remark: "It is not fair to take the children's food and throw it to the dogs." He just called this super stressed out mother of a demon-possessed, i.e., psychologically tormented daughter, a "dog." In our culture, when we call a woman a dog, we mean she is "ugly," which is bad enough. In that day to call someone a dog was even more derogatory. It was an absolute insult. It was like using the "n" word.

Yet she persists, using one of the cleverest lines in all of scripture: "Yes, Lord, yet even the dogs eat the crumbs that fall from their masters' table." Do you see what she is doing here? She is using a derogatory word to refer to herself to diffuse the power of that word, and the power of the one who used that word in an insulting manner. People do that today as well. African Americans sometimes use the "n" word to take the power away from those who use that word as an insult. Gay and lesbian people often use the word "queer" for a similar purpose—to take away the power of the bigot's use of that word. By using the word "dog" to refer to herself, the Canaanite woman is cutting through Jesus' explainable, yet inexcusable, culturally isolated view of people who had never walked in his shoes. *And it embarrassed him.* Consequently, this became a teachable moment for Jesus and us as well.

You and I will continue to be embarrassed about silly things like squirting coffee cream on someone's shirt, getting caught adjusting our pants, or walking out of a public restroom with toilet paper stuck to the bottom of our shoes. There is very little we can learn from those things. These are incidents that prove we are fallible, but not necessarily faulty. At the same time, embarrassing moments of an ethical and moral nature have the power to teach us profound lessons and help us become better than no damn good. Still, at the end of the day, we just want to hear someone say to us, "This too shall pass."

This Too Shall Pass

Speaking of embarrassing moments . . . the actor and comedian Paul Rudd once said, "Embarrassment and awkward situations are not foreign things to me." He is not alone. I do not think we can get through life without a few faux pas now and then. By my count I have been publicly embarrassed no less than three times in my life.

My first memory of being embarrassed or humiliated occurred in high school. Truthfully, my entire high school experience was one long regrettable nightmarish saga. I graduated with only nineteen other hucksters from the small West Texas town of Sterling City, so when one made a mistake, everyone knew about it. My big mistake (which seems so small now) was showing up late to a carwash fundraiser. The funds were to be used for our senior trip, which consisted of a few parents "chaperoning" our small class as we descended upon New Orleans' French Quarter in the summer of '78. Showing up late for the fundraiser would not have been such a big deal except for the fact that I was the class treasurer. I was supposed to handle the money received from our customers. When I finally arrived, I learned that my classmates had voted me out of office.

Yes, they allowed me to go on our senior trip. Yet until my classmates had had a few Hurricanes under their belts, I was persona non grata.

I had to wait many years for my next great embarrassing moment. It was the summer of 2012. By virtue of winning a Putt-Putt tour stop in Louisville, Kentucky, I was invited to the national championship in the senior division. I was fifty-two years old at the time, and you know, one's putt-putt skills begin to diminish past the age of fifty. Bending over every few minutes to retrieve one's golf ball is very strenuous. Other than occasionally telling folks that I was invited to a national Putt-Putt championship, which is about as uncomfortable as wearing unmatched socks in public, the most embarrassing moment at the tournament was not all the putts I missed. It was the time I mindlessly walked past the tenth tee box just a few feet away from a fellow competitor's attempt to strike a good putt. He looked up at me after he missed his putt with the most scornful expression I had ever seen and yelled, "What are you doing?" I meekly said, "Sorry," and ducked into the clubhouse hoping to not be recognized the rest of the day. And yes, putt-putt putters take putting seriously.

My third most embarrassing moment occurred on a Sunday morning. This is my most embarrassing moment ever, bar none. I was sitting in the pastor's chair and was about to climb up into the pulpit to deliver my sermon. As fate would have it (and trust me, I will give fate a piece of my mind someday), I decided to find a "joke" to go with my sermon. I found one; however, I did not think it through. I misunderstood its meaning. Therefore, I opened my sermon with a brief joke, followed by a huge congregational gasp, and spent the rest of the morning looking for a place to hide. I learned that there is no place for a pastor to hide in worship. One does one's best to just ride the tidal wave of embarrassment until the last song is sung and the last prayer is uttered, walk briskly to the door, greet the parishioners as if nothing happened, and then run to one's car as fast as a professional putter/former class treasurer is able to run.[6]

There is an old Persian adage that says, "This too shall pass." I hope those Persians were smart people.

---

6. People who were not there that day often ask me what my inappropriate joke was about. All I can say is that I honestly forgot what "sanitary napkins" are. Believe me, holding up the chalice during communion a few minutes later and exclaiming, "This is the blood of Christ," was not my finest moment.

Hindsight is 20/20

To become better than no damn good, we must learn from our past mistakes, so let me do my best Jesus impression from his Sermon on the Mount: "You have heard it said, 'Hindsight is 20/20,' but I say unto you, 'Hindsight may not be 20/20, but it is certainly more accurate than foresight.'" The phrase "Hindsight is 20/20" was probably heard in the year 2020 more than any other time in human history. We were exasperated hearing it so much, and yet there will be one positive consequence of lavishing so much attention on this phrase: We might think more seriously about what it means and how it might apply to our lives.

Pardon my mansplaining . . . "Hindsight is 20/20" is a saying that means it is much easier to know what the right thing to do is *after* an action or event has taken place and we can now see the consequences more clearly. My favorite form of 20/20 hindsight, tongue-in-cheek, is that which happens the day after a full slate of professional football games, called "Monday morning quarterbacking." This phrase does not apply just to the next day assessment of coaching, quarterbacking, and refereeing decisions. It applies to anyone who judges and criticizes someone else's decision-making skills in any forum after the fact.[7]

Certainly, we humans would occasionally change our decisions and actions if only we knew how they would come to fruition. Human activity is handicapped in that we cannot always predict a future outcome, and so it behooves us to be attentive to the actual outcome of our decisions and actions so that we can be better suited to make decisions the next time a similar scenario arises. The lesson we can learn from all this ogling over the phrase "Hindsight is 20/20" is exactly that: Let us learn from our mistakes so that we do not have to keep repeating them. (Translation: Next time, Mr. Quarterback, throw the ball away rather than take a sack.) As a preacher this applies to me as well: I should take notice as to how people react to my preaching style, content, length, etc., so that *next Sunday* I can do better. (See? I am no different than a professional quarterback. We both do our thing on Sundays.)

By the way, in 2020 I predicted that ophthalmologists would be *Time* magazine's 2020 "Person(s) of the Year." I was certain that a few

---

7. Note: this differs slightly from the more confident species of man cave dwellers called the "armchair quarterback," who sits back and judges and criticizes *while* the action is taking place. They do not need to wait for Monday morning to share their obvious expertise.

of the more creative types in the ophthalmology business had already started licking their chops in anticipation of their profession's upcoming fortuitous windfall. People who had until then stubbornly refused to believe their eyesight is failing would storm the eye doctors' little storefront clinics like Santa Anna's army overwhelmed the outmanned Alamo. We preacher-types certainly made much hay out of all the "seeing" metaphors in scripture, hoping that 2020 would be the year when our parishioners would finally get our corny jokes, innuendos, and subtle points because mansplaining is bad form. Instead, we got a pandemic and people canceled their ophthalmology appointments. Go figure. But hey, if a pandemic does not teach us how to be better than no damn good, nothing will.

Me Thinks Thou Protesteth Not Enough

Another way to improve our ethical and moral lot is to learn to speak out for others. The art of protesting is one way to accomplish that, and some of us are becoming quite adept at it. I suggest American historians will look back to 2017, for example, as "The Year of Protests." At the time, a television reporter said we are now a "protest culture." The protests began almost as soon as the election was over in November of 2016, including the Women's March, which took place in every major city in the country. Meanwhile, an NFL player named Colin Kaepernick inspired dozens of other players to take a knee during the playing of the national anthem in response to racial injustices. My current city, St. Louis, is no stranger to protests related to racial issues. From the acquittal of Officer Darren Wilson in Ferguson to the acquittal of Officer Jason Stockley, St. Louis has almost perfected the art of protest.

The one thing the historians might forget, however, is that in 2017 we commemorated the five-hundredth anniversary of the beginning of a protest movement that, for good or bad, changed the world. I am talking about the Protestant Reformation. I hope it is not lost on you that the word "Protestant" stems from the word "protest."[8] Almost every mainline Protestant church and denomination in the western world owes its existence to the courageous act of a German monk named Martin Luther. You know the story: Allegedly, Luther nailed a document of ninety-five

8. If it is lost on you, then I fear the possibility of you becoming a lexicographer is nil.

theses to a church door in Wittenberg on October 31, 1517, criticizing the Roman church, among other things, of the sale of indulgences.

At the core of our being we are protesters. This is part of our religious DNA. Jesus himself felt the need on at least one occasion to walk into the corridors of power, the Temple in Jerusalem, and kick over the tables of those who were profiting from the sale of sacrificial animals. As Christians—not just Protestants—we cannot get through this life without feeling the need to kick a table or two ourselves. That does not mean you and I are likely to have a bundle of homemade protest signs in the trunks of our cars ready to join a march at the spur of a moment. It does not mean we are always mad about something, even if we are aware of life's injustices. Most of us, in fact, are like the Canadian man who joined a protest one day holding up a sign that read, "I'm a little upset." You gotta love Canadians.

In 2017 more people participated in a protest activity of some kind than at any other time in our history.[9] There is clearly some discontent out there and protests are likely to continue, so therefore what we need is *a Protest Reformation*. I am not as prolific a writer as Martin Luther, so I am only going to offer two points—rather than ninety-five. Whether we have the youthful energy to take it to the streets, the discipline of writing to our government representatives, the flair of writing letters to the editor, or the quiet determination to use our resources in ways that create a better world, we need a Protest Reformation. So here is my two-point proposal:

First, we should protest perceived *injustices*. Duh, right? Of course, people disagree about what injustices exist in our world and in our communities, and yet I do not think anyone would argue that none exist whatsoever. None of us live in a cave so deep and dark that we cannot see how others often experience unfairness if not complete and total oppression.

Unless you are Phil Robertson of Duck Dynasty fame. One day, I heard him say that he has never felt the need to protest anything. Phil apparently spends too much time making duck calls. If the Christian doctrine of original sin has any truth at all, if my assertion that people are no damn good is correct on any level, then we know that injustices are simply a fact of human existence. There are always wrongs that need to be made right. The holocaust survivor, Elie Wiesel, wrote, "There may be

9. If this is not true, it should be true.

times when we are powerless to prevent injustice, but there must never be a time when we fail to protest."[10] So, point number one: Protest injustices, especially if the injustices have nothing to do with us, which makes our acts of protestation more authentic.

Second, we should protest *disunity*. We are a divided nation. The fact that I have referred to the fall of 2016 to the fall of 2017 as the Year of Protests suggests that we as Americans are simply not on the same page, nor will we ever be. And yet we do not have to be on the same *page* so long as we are in the same *book*. That is, we need to open our eyes to the fact that we are part of the same story, the same history, and that despite our differences we need to learn empathy if not sympathy for others.

Ironically, the Protestant Reformation, a series of events that began to correct perceived injustices within the church, also led to disunity within the church. In 1995, one of the most prolific American theologians of our time, Stanley Hauerwas, said this: "On this Reformation Sunday long for, pray for, our ability to remember the Reformation—not as a celebratory moment, not as a blow for freedom, but as the sin of the church. Pray for God to heal our disunity, not the disunity simply between Protestant and Catholic, but the disunity in our midst between classes, between races, between nations. Pray that on Reformation Sunday we may . . . confess our sin and ask God to make us a new people joined together in one mighty prayer that the world may be saved from its divisions."[11]

One of the places the Christian church experiences disunity most acutely is at the communion table. For the five hundredth anniversary of the Reformation, I seriously considered kicking over a table (Jesus-style) in worship to symbolize protesting the "closed table," because, in my opinion, the greatest division in Christianity is between those that practice an open table and those that practice a closed table. Eventually I decided against kicking over my church's communion table. Every pastor will know why. (It's called "job security.") Nevertheless, we should not be afraid to be a Protestant—a protester. One can never protesteth too much.

---

10. Wiesel, Nobel Lecture, December 11, 1986.

11. Hauerwas, *Called to Communion: Reformation Meets Rome.* October 29, 1995.

Isn't that Ironic?

It is Martin Luther King, Jr. Sunday in January 1990. I preach my first
sermon ever as the called pastor of two UCC congregations north of
Waco, Texas. Although I was in my first year of PhD work at Baylor
University, I had emerged from Southern Baptist life to be part of what
I considered to be the most cutting-edge denomination in the country:
The United Church of Christ. I was very excited to be standing in that
pulpit. I felt like I had all the freedom in the world to say what I wanted
to say, especially on this specific Sunday. I knew that if I just mentioned
Dr. King's name from a Southern Baptist pulpit in Central Texas people
might get up and walk out of the room. Yet here I was in a UCC pulpit.
Surely no one would get angry if I mentioned Dr. King's name or talked
about racial justice or quoted Amos 5:24: ". . . let justice roll down like
waters, and righteousness like an ever-flowing stream" . . . which I did.

After all, this is the denomination that cut its teeth on racial justice.
The Civil Rights movement was just heating up in the late 1950s when the
United Church of Christ was born. They knew that theological differences
could tear apart this fragile union of four previous denominations. They
also knew that if they could find a common purpose, they would create
a greater sense of unity. That common purpose became the Civil Rights
movement. The UCC, a predominately white denomination, played no
small role in this movement. We were the primary ecclesiastical force
that helped open the television airwaves so that the rest of America could
see what was happening in the South.

So, here I was standing in a UCC pulpit, saying whatever I wanted
to say, not fearing the consequences. The next evening, I received a knock
on the front door of the parsonage. I opened the door to a member of my
new congregation who was standing there, alcohol on his breath. Without even saying "hello," he asked me, "Are you a nigger lover?" Welcome
to the United Church of Christ, I thought to myself.

I am a big fan of the song, "Ironic," by the Canadian pop-rock musi-
cian, Alanis Morrissette. "Isn't it ironic?" she asks throughout the song.
Well, isn't it ironic that my ministry began in 1990 with that disturbingly
racist knock on my door, and now I am pastoring a congregation in a
place that has become a focal point for America's conversation on race?[12]
Actually, I do not know if that meets the definition of irony or not, but it

12. Ferguson, Missouri. Yes, *that* Ferguson.

sure feels like it. Like pornography and goodness, you just know it when you see it.

I am no longer that naïve young man who thinks he can say whatever he wants to say from a United Church of Christ pulpit without possible unwanted consequences. I have my fair share of scars from previous attempts at speaking my mind. Sometimes, silence is golden. And yet, like the prophet Isaiah I also know that there are times when we can no longer keep silent for the sake of others. That phrase, "for the sake of others," is important. Isaiah 62:1 reflects this when the prophet writes, "For Zion's sake I will not keep silent." Speaking up, speaking our minds, hitting the streets in protest, forsaking our polite tendency toward silence *for the sake of others* is part of what it means to be followers of the Christ and people of the book (i.e., the Bible). The question is, for whom do we forsake silence? For whom are we called to speak our minds?

The context for Isaiah's words is the aftermath of the Babylonian Exile. Many of the previously exiled Jews have returned to their homeland. They are in the first stage of the restoration of Judah. But things are dire. The Temple has been destroyed. They have come home to a desolate and seemingly forsaken land. They are a humiliated people, so Isaiah promises not to keep silent until they have returned to their former glory.

It seems to me that people have been trying to do something very similar in the town of Ferguson. For the sake of Ferguson, people are unwilling to keep silent until Ferguson is somehow restored, not to its former glory, which is not admirable, but to a future glory. One attempt was the "I Love Ferguson" campaign instigated by the former mayor and city councilman, Brian Fletcher. For Ferguson's sake, the now deceased Ferguson VIP could not keep silent. A greater attempt was the reinvigoration of the Black Lives Matter movement, which began after George Zimmerman shot Trayvon Martin in Florida, but really picked up steam after Michael Brown was shot and killed by a Ferguson police officer.

Again, that naïve thirty-year-old man in 1990 no longer exists. I recognize that people have different opinions about what happened in Florida and Ferguson and other cases like it. But that does not take away from my point, reflected in the prophet Isaiah's words, that we are called to forsake silence for the sake of others. But for whom, or for what cause, should we forsake our silence?

Speaking up for our *own* sake is fine and dandy. It is necessary to do so on occasion. Yet as followers of the Christ and people of the book, our role in the world is to speak up for others, which, by the way, is exactly what a predominately white denomination called the United Church of Christ was doing back in the late 1950s and 60s. And as it was doing so there were many people who were knocking on the door of that new denomination—many people who even belonged to the denomination—asking, "Are you a nigger lover?"[13]

The UCC's support of the LGBTQ+ community in more recent years has unfortunately elicited the same kind of response. The consequences are often unwanted, and yet for the sake of others many people have chosen to forsake their silence. Again, for whom, or for what cause, should we forsake our silence? Honesty compels me to say that I have not always had the courage to speak out or forsake my silence for the sake of others. It is a difficult thing to do. Like many of you, I fear the consequences. I fear disagreements and opposition. I fear the occasional knock on my door, and I am not, by nature, a confrontational person. And yet I call myself a follower of the Christ and a person of the book. To be true to my calling I need to forsake my silence for the sake of others. I have no choice, and neither do you. So, where do we begin?

The first thing we need to do is get control of our narcissism, which is the mental illness most of us have that sees ourselves as the center of the universe. We need to learn to see the world through the eyes of others. We need to walk in someone else's shoes for a while, and I am not just talking about bowling shoes.

Second, we need to convince ourselves that people other than our own families and friends have value. Social scientists tell us that the further we get from ourselves and our families, the more difficult it is to feel and show love. The Christian faith compels us to fight against human nature and expand our circle of love and compassion.

Third, we need to tell ourselves that we do not have to agree with or like everything about people who do not belong to our social circle and who do not look like us or think like us. In fact, speaking up for the sake of those who are different than us and with whom we disagree is a more powerful testimony to our Christian discipleship than just speaking up for those whom we naturally love, like our family and friends.

Fourth, we need to ask ourselves, "For whom should we forsake our silence *that makes us uncomfortable the most*?" Now we are getting at the heart of Christian discipleship, compassion, love, and the Christian version of God's justice on earth.

13. I apologize for the use of that word, but I want the reader to feel the force of that statement as I once did.

Finally, we should note that to other people *we* might be the ones that would make them uncomfortable if they felt compelled to forsake their silence on our behalf. We might be the ones that would make others uncomfortable if they felt compelled to walk with us hand in hand or work with us side by side. And to once again quote the great Alannis Morrissette: "Isn't *that* ironic?

Stay Woke!

The world is divided into morning people and night people. Morning people, of course, like to rise early in the morning, while night people (a.k.a. "night owls") like to stay up late at night and sleep in. Here are a couple of quotes from night people: The first comes from science fiction writer, Glen Cook, who said, "Morning is wonderful. Its only drawback is that it comes at such an inconvenient time of the day." Similarly, Melchor Lim, an inspirational writer, said, "I believe there should be a better way to start each day . . . instead of waking up every morning." We humans did not evolve to become hibernators. I saw a cartoon picture one day depicting several bears hibernating in a cave. One bear, however, is wide awake. He says to his self, "Man, I really shouldn't have had that cup of coffee back in June."

All of that segues into this earnest command: Stay woke!

I am not suggesting that we get less sleep. "Stay woke" is urban slang for being aware of your surroundings and things that are going on, particularly in terms of social injustices, although the phrase is used in other contexts as well. "Stay woke" first came into public usage in a 2009 song by Erykah Badu called "Master Teachers." After that only a handful of Twitter users began using the phrase #StayWoke. In about 2013, a year before the Ferguson shooting, the phrase began to be used more frequently in response to police brutality and systemic racism throughout the United States.

#StayWoke is often used alongside #BlackLivesMatter. The latter, of course, became a staple during the Ferguson protests in 2014. After that #StayWoke began to be used in other contexts where perceived injustices were occurring. It has gained such widespread usage, in fact, that some people in the Black Lives Matter movement believe the phrase "stay woke" has been diluted and has lost its original purpose and meaning.[14]

14. Other people, such as James Carville, believe we have gone too far with the

I will let the social debaters tackle that one. I do admit, however, that I am drawn to the phrase in a more general sense. It seems to me that there are many perceived wrongs or injustices in our world and in our communities that require a higher level of attention because we are often distracted by other, less important, things. For example, a social activist once said, "While you are obsessing with the Kardashians, there are millions of homeless in the world. STAY WOKE."

So yes, I am drawn to the phrase "stay woke" although I recognize it is grammatically incorrect. But that's part of its attraction for me. Just by being grammatically incorrect it is, by sound and definition, rebellious against the status quo. As a baby boomer, I admit that there is a part of me that loves to rebel against the status quo.[15] While people in the mid-twentieth century Civil Rights movement did not use the phrase "stay woke" (to my knowledge), it does remind us of the "awakening" that took place in that era in American history. It also reminds us that the struggle continues. Only a person who is intellectually or ethically "asleep" would suggest that race is no longer an issue in our country and in many places around the world.[16] And it is not going away easily. We can say the same about many other "isms" in our society that stubbornly persist.

I agree with the so-called social prophets of our day who believe there are times when someone needs to grab a bullhorn or hold up a sign in protest for whatever perceived social ills are vexing us. And yet, I do not agree with the use of violence to make a social statement. I believe the use of violence diminishes one's moral high ground.[17] Nevertheless, when I observe what is happening in the world, I am generally supportive of those who feel the need to speak more loudly, write more boldly, walk more frequently, and protest more profusely. As Dr. King said, "Our lives begin to end the day we become silent about things that matter." Dr. King would be the first to say, "stay woke!"

"stay woke" movement. Some might argue that if our wokeness puts others to sleep (from too much emphasis on it), we may have gone too far. Perhaps they want us to be woke to our excessive wokeness. Nah.

15. As a teenager growing up in a small, rural community in West Texas, I tacked up a "Rebel flag" in my bedroom, thinking it was just that: a flag representing my teenaged rebellion. I should have known at that time that living thirty-five miles from a small town named Robert Lee, Texas suggests that my Rebel flag had other motives for hanging on my wall.

16. The recent pushback against "critical race theory" is evidence of this moral laziness.

17. I fully expect some pushback for this comment!

So, yes, one way to be good (or at least better than no damn good) is to listen to the voices that are crying out for justice in our world today. We should stay woke to the plight of the poor, the downtrodden, the sexually harassed, the bullied, the oppressed, and all those things that contribute to every ounce of human misery that occurs in every corner of the globe.

And yet sometimes, our desire to be good requires a little more nuanced approach . . .

Learn to Mediate

Get up, shower, and go somewhere. If you rub elbows with the masses long enough you will experience first-hand the antics of someone who, on the surface at least, seems to be an undesirable companion. There are people that are difficult to be around. We are surrounded by difficult people like we are surrounded by the proverbial and biblical "great cloud of witnesses." The word "difficult" means "not easy to do," but in terms of people it means "hard to please." No matter how we describe them, these people are no damn good.

We all have stories to tell about encounters with difficult people. Yet, what we often fail to realize is that sometimes *we* are the difficult person. We all have the potential to be no damn good.[18] How would we know if we are a difficult person? In the spirit of Jeff Foxworthy, let me give you a list. You might be a difficult person if . . .

- You must stand on your head to smile
- Your parrot only knows swear words
- Your parents or your children move and "forget" to tell you where
- Your spouse changes your home phone number while you're away on a trip
- You often walk into businesses when they are coincidentally closing
- Tele-marketers hang up on you
- Someone keeps sending in your obituary to the paper
- The radio station plays songs just to annoy you

18. This reminds me of the time I told my son to stop hanging around with the wrong crowd and he said to me, "Dad, I *am* the wrong crowd.

- There is a collective groan when you walk into a room at work or at home

- The devil tells you to take it easy on people[19]

Ever since there have been people in the world, there have been difficult people in the world.[20] Difficult people even had their own television sitcom called, appropriately, *Difficult People*, starring Julie Klausner and Billy Eichner, who play the roles of two struggling and jaded comedians living in New York City. The two comedians seemingly hate everyone but each other.[21]

Sometimes difficult people can be so difficult that mediation is required. A few years ago, I was asked to participate in a program in Ferguson, Missouri dealing with relations between police officers and citizens. The U.S. Justice Department, in response to the Mike Brown shooting, issued a consent decree for Ferguson. One of the points of the decree is that a mediation program would be developed to help mitigate some of the distrust between the police department and the community. I was asked by the head of St. Louis Mediation Services to be a "listener" and write down themes that I heard in the conversations between about a dozen people from Ferguson, people who came from all walks of life.[22] The goal was to produce a mediation program that would become a model for the entire country.

As a pastor, I am occasionally called upon to mediate between parishioners who have disagreements or gripes with one another. Most of the time, one or both of the parties involved could be categorized as a difficult hard-to-please person. Sometimes, the flow of the anger is directed at the clergy. We have a name for those who aim their hostility in the direction of a pastor: "clergy killer."[23] I realize that sounds a little harsh but remember, the problem with the church is that its full of people, and the problem with people is that they are no damn good, and some folks—even church folks—are *really* no damn good.

19. From watching the Netflix series, *Lucifer*, we know that the devil is not so bad. He just likes to punish bad people.

20. I'm looking at you, Grunt-man, who lived about 250,000 years ago.

21. *Difficult People* aired on Hulu from August 5, 2015 – September 26, 2017.

22. My wife remains perplexed that I would be tapped as a "listener."

23. For a good description of these particularly difficult parishioners, and strategies to deal with them, see Rediger, *Clergy Killers: Guidance for Pastors and Congregations Under Attack*, Westminster John Knox Press, 1997.

Luckily for me and my colleagues, there is a scriptural model for dealing with difficult people. One might argue that it is not the most practical approach to this problem, but that does not mean we cannot pick up a few pointers. In Matthew 18:15–17, Jesus offers a step-by-step approach to mediation between people who are at odds with one another:

> If another member of the church sins against you, go and point out the fault when the two of you are alone. If the member listens to you, you have regained that one. But if you are not listened to, take one or two others along with you, so that every word may be confirmed by the evidence of two or three witnesses. If the member refuses to listen to them, tell it to the church; and if the offender refuses to listen even to the church, let such a one be to you as a Gentile and a tax collector.

I try to imagine what the situation was that inspired this strategical approach. Did the Hatfield's and McCoy's have first century Palestinian ancestors? Given the Jewish aversion to pigs, it is rather unlikely that an ancestor of the Hatfield clan stole a hog from the pigsty that belonged to an ancient McCoy.[24] But you gotta wonder.

I was about to write, "Here is Jesus's step-by-step approach to conflict resolution," and then I realized that due to the fact Matthew 18:15–17 mentions the church three times Jesus could not have said such words. Unless his divinity implies more than I realize, the future church was likely not even on his radar. Nevertheless, we can overlook such a minor detail, slick back our hair like a stage-stompin' televangelist, open our floppy Bibles, and exclaim, "Jesus said . . . " Whether this is Matthew's voice reflecting a conflictual situation in the late first century church, or Jesus' voice as he tries to break up a feud between two disciples that are hellbent on stealing one another's prized hogs, the truth is that a long time ago in a galaxy far, far away, there were difficult people. After all, it is not possible to have a community of people of any size or structure without a few rascals and bad apples.

"If another member of the church sins against you . . . " Actually, "if" is not accurate. It should have read: "*When* another member of the church sins against you . . . " So, what do we do with these ornery folks?

24. Apparently, this is what started the Hatfield-McCoy squabble back in the day. FYI, in our Kentucky days, my wife lived for a while just down the street from a descendent of the Hatfield clan and I once had a parishioner that descended from the McCoy clan. They might be "no damn good," but they seem as good as anyone else I know.

Step one: Go and talk to them alone and point out their "fault" and see how they respond. I guess that is always a good place to start. You need to stand up for yourself, right? And yet, how often are we able to successfully change someone's behavior by pointing out their faults?[25] When I try, I only make things worse. People tend to get defensive when their faults are pointed out. In fact, they often double-down on their faults. Out of sheer stubbornness, if not meanness, they will get worse.

If that does not work—and it is unlikely to work—then step two is to take one or two witnesses with you so at least you will have some backup support when the difficult person decides to express their version of the conflict to other people. That is actually very good advice, and I have used it on several occasions in a church setting, especially in my role as a pastor. I never want to get into a mediation situation alone with another church member because it can too easily become a situation where two different versions of the conflict emerge. Witnesses are imperative.

If the presence of witnesses does not work, step three is to take the matter to the entire church. Here is where I tend to disagree with Jesus (and/or Matthew). I do not believe in airing one's dirty laundry for everyone to see. Apparently, confidentiality was not highly valued in the first century. Can you imagine the potential lawsuits if we were in the habit of tattle-telling or publicly humiliating one another in front of an entire congregation on Sunday mornings?

Finally, if public shaming does not work, then the fourth step in Jesus' mediation program is to shun the difficult person as if they are gentiles or tax-collectors (although this does not sound like Jesus to me). Ironically, most of our congregations are overrun with gentiles, so that strategy would not work in our setting. And the last thing I would do is shun an IRS agent, i.e., tax collector. Trust me, I do not need to draw unnecessary attention to my finances.

I conclude, therefore, that we should not accept Jesus/Matthew's mediation program as an acceptable model for us today. Things have changed. However, we still need to think hard about what to do with difficult people in our midst. Of course, we should not live under the illusion that if all the difficult people left the church, everything would be hunky dory. There will always be conflicts that stem from the presence of difficult people in a congregation. Statistics relayed to me anecdotally claim that roughly 20% of the people in a congregation support the

25. Unless your marriage is super strong, do not try this at home.

pastor, 20% are against the pastor, and the other 60% could not care less one way or another. Because of that, there are always difficult people lurking in the shadows ready to strike like a rattlesnake with very little warning, and there is always the ironic possibility that the pastor him/ herself is a difficult, hard to please person. My same sources suggest that any given person at any given time is only happy with about 75% of what is going on in a church.[26]

Obviously, everyone has the potential for being a no damn good person. Even in the healthiest of congregations there are always a few people who are, at any given time, hard to please. Yes, there are people out there who are truly toxic, can never be pleased, and will always cause a certain amount of trouble. And yet, the reality is that any one of us can be a difficult person today, if not tomorrow. It is easy to focus on others as difficult people and, like Jesus or Matthew, try to determine how to handle them. It is more difficult, however, to understand our own role as either a difficult person or as someone who makes difficult people worse than they really are.

Before we come up with a church-wide mediation program to deal with difficult people, let us look at ourselves first. Maybe we need to shun our own negative, hard to please, curmudgeon-like ways. Maybe we need to mediate between the better nature of our angels and the darkness of our own souls before we start pointing out the faults of others. Until we learn to smile standing on our feet rather than our heads, we should work on ourselves first.

Learn to Negotiate

I did not see this coming. As a young man I would have never envisioned the career path that has chosen me as much as I have chosen it. After I had been a minister for about ten years, I asked a friend of mine why *he* thought I was a minister and he wisely said, "Because this is the most radical thing *you* could have done." Despite the ongoing scientific explanations for human behavior, I will take his words as gospel.

On the twenty-fifth anniversary of my ordination, I chose to speak rather than have a friend fly in to speak because I do not have any friends. I am kidding. I have a friend. One, I think. The other reason I wanted to speak is because no one knows my ordination story better than I do. I

---

26. With anonymous sources like this, who needs friends?

had a front row seat. To have someone else speak at my ordination anniversary would be like having a preacher who did not know me very well officiate at my funeral. That is not ideal.

My ordination took place in a very specific context which has had a great deal of influence on the kind of ordained minister I have become. Specifically, my ordination took place in the context of the Branch Davidian-Waco tragedy of 1993. I remember the events as if they were yesterday. I was attending Baylor University for grad school and was the licensed pastor of two small congregations outside of Waco, Texas. The parsonage in which my family and I resided at the time was located about five miles as the crow flies from Mt. Carmel, the home of the Branch Davidian compound. Even so, I was not familiar with their community. However, on Saturday, February 27, 1993, I woke up to read the headline from the *Waco Tribune-Herald*: "The Sinful Messiah." It was a damning story about a young man who was just a few months older than me, Vernon Wayne Howell, aka "David Koresh," the leader of the little community that lived at Mt. Carmel.

The next day, Sunday, February 28, I left after the last hymn was sung at St. Paul United Church of Christ in Gerald, Texas to drive to First Congregational Church in Ft. Worth where I would endure a three-hour long Ecclesiastical Council. This is the event where I answered grueling questions and sweated out a vote for the approval of my ordination by the North Texas Association of the South-Central Conference of the United Church of Christ. While driving to Ft. Worth I heard on the radio that the Bureau of Alcohol, Tobacco, Firearms and Explosives (ATF) had invaded the Branch Davidian compound. Four ATF officers and six Davidians were killed in the raid.

In the ensuing weeks, I learned more about Koresh and his followers through a couple of Baylor professors who had known them personally. I used binoculars to watch the actions of the feds from a bridge a mile away from the compound, and went for a joyride in Koresh's black Camaro, thanks to the owner of the wrecking yard who was "babysitting" all the vehicles the feds had hauled away from the compound.

The next several weeks had everyone on edge wondering how it would end. On April 19, I was playing golf at a local course. When I came back to the clubhouse after my round, the golf pro said to me, "Something is happening at the compound." At that point, no one needed to explain the word "compound." I hurried home, walked through my backdoor, and turned on the television at precisely the moment the feds stuck the nose of their tanks through the windows of the compound to smoke them out with tear gas. Fire erupted immediately. Because of the fierce winds that day and the cheap plywood used to construct the compound, the fire spread quickly. I looked out my backdoor and saw the black smoke billowing up into the sky. We later learned that seventy-six of the residents died that day. Coincidentally, I was preparing for my ordination service the entire time the siege was happening, and it overshadowed everything that was happening to us.

As the years went by, I learned one very important thing about that event. Philosophically, it was a struggle between two different mindsets or approaches to conflict. First, there were the *tacticians*, the federal agents who were always ready to take aggressive action, just as they had done a year earlier at Ruby Ridge. By definition, a tactician is a person who is adept at the art of disposing and maneuvering forces *in combat*. Tacticians are trained to solve problems through force. I think it is safe to say that the tactical approach to Waco did not end well.

Second, there were the *negotiators*. A negotiator is someone that is trained to deal or bargain. They seek to find peaceful solutions to problems. From what I have read about both the Ruby Ridge and Waco incidents, the tacticians won the battle, but the negotiators have won the war. Since 1993, the ATF and FBI have reassessed their approach and have concluded that there should be a greater emphasis on and utilization of negotiation.

What does this have to do with my ordination and ministry? Simply put, my approach to preaching, evangelism, and moral guidance is much more in the negotiator vein than in the tactician vein. I am not out to *win* souls or *conquer* the world for Christ. I am not a prayer *warrior*, a social justice *warrior*, or a culture *warrior*. I am not a Crusader nor Jihadist. I do not preach "hellfire and brimstone," which is pure spiritual manipulation. I do not "love the sinner but hate the sin," because anytime the word "hate" enters the conversation, a tactician is talking, not a negotiator.

I am a negotiator. My desire is to influence, prod, persuade, shepherd, guide, and lure people into a healthy spiritual and moral life. I may want the same results as the tactician, yet I am not willing to concede that the end justifies the means. This is the context in which I was ordained, and it continues to be the foundational event that shapes who I am today. Ordained or laity, all of us need to decide about what kind of disciple we will be: a tactician or a negotiator. I think history tells us which is "good," and which is "no damn good."

Advice Column

I hope this chapter read like some sort of elongated advice column for people who want to try to become better at being human. If an elongated advice column is not your cup of tea, then here's a brief enough version to cut out and tape to your refrigerator door or steering wheel. If the latter, please do not read while driving . . .

To be damn good people we need to:

- Learn to tell our own stories, often expressed as "my truth," to ourselves and others. While telling our stories we gain more understanding about ourselves and the world that encircles us.

- Learn from the teachable moments that present themselves to us, no matter how embarrassing.

- Learn to speak out for others, especially when it makes us uncomfortable. The "comfort zone" is not where people grow as ethical human beings.

- Learn to mediate between ourselves and others and negotiate for peaceful solutions rather than prepare for conflict.

That's it. You may now collect your merit badge for "ethics and morality," after you build that campfire.

An Epic Log

N o matter how hard we work to be better than no damn good, we will fall short. When we draw our last breath, we will have fallen short. Because we are who and what we are, this is inevitable. And yet, that doesn't have to be the last word written about us. In this last section, which I have creatively titled "An Epic Log" (as opposed to an "epilogue," which I'm sure you noticed), I share with you two wonderful truths that no one, not even the Grinch, can steal from you. The two truths are: 1) We are a work in progress, and 2) There is always another chance to get it right.

A Work in Progress

People often ask me why I pursued a PhD in Ethics and I tell them with a straight face that I wanted to study something I was not very good at.[1] At the time, I was equally interested in Old Testament studies, but I would have had to study Hebrew to work on a PhD in Old Testament and I was already thirty years old at the time. So, I went with the *easier* choice: Christian Ethics.

Boy was I wrong. One might say I began with a Deuteronomy attitude, thinking that everything was pretty much black and white, yet I ended my program at Baylor University with a Jesus attitude, realizing that very little is black and white in terms of ethics and morality. And that is where I remain to this day. Like you, I am a "work in progress." In fact, every time I see a "work in progress" sign, usually in relation to road work, I think about stealing the sign and bringing it to my office to remind me that everything about me—my sense of morality, my

---

1. Well, truthfully no one ever asks me that because my conversations with people never get past the "small talk" stage.

theology, my spirituality—is a work in progress. But then I am reminded that stealing is morally and ethically wrong.[2]

But is it *always* wrong? I can make a case for "justified stealing," such as stealing food for someone who is starving to death, stealing medicine for someone who will die without it, stealing a pet that is being abused, etc., if you have no other recourse. And what about stealing, say, weapons of mass destruction from someone who is planning to use them on innocent people? You see, the field of ethics is not as easy as one might think it is. Someone once said, "If electricity comes from Electrons, then morality must come from Morons." Whoever said that was a moron.

There is only one thing more difficult than *understanding* morality and ethics, and that is trying to *create* moral and ethical people. Because we are a work in progress, there is no way to snap our fingers or wiggle our noses and instantaneously create moral people. There is one thing we know for certain: we cannot legislate morality.

India learned that lesson a few years ago. Apparently, the Sikh community in India, which is a minority religion in a nation dominated by Hindus, is constantly ridiculed in Indian society. So, the Sikhs appealed to the Indian Supreme Court to get them to regulate jokes about the Sikh community. The Court concluded that it cannot "lay down moral guidelines" for its citizens, and even if it could, it could not enforce such guidelines. In other words, they concluded that morality cannot be legislated. Well, we can, and we cannot. We can pass laws that outlaw bad behavior, as we have done. And while those laws sometimes help citizens progress in their morality, the truth is we cannot create moral people instantaneously. We are a work in progress.

Yet are we *making* progress? Are we becoming a more ethical and moral species? That is a good question, and not just because I asked it. Peter Singer, one of the premier ethicists in the world today, said, "After a century that saw two world wars, the Nazi Holocaust, Stalin's Gulag, the killing fields of Cambodia, and the atrocities in Rwanda and Darfur, the belief that we are progressing morally has become difficult to defend." He wrote that in 2008. I wonder what he would say after we put immigrant children in cages and separated them from their parents or after the storming of the U.S. Capitol on January 6, 2021. Singer goes on to

---

2. A parishioner made a sign for me, made from wire, spelling out the words "Work in Progress" in cursive (which means many people will not be able to read it). She was affirming my desire to be better than no damn good.

make the case that there has been progress worldwide in terms of human rights, although many problems remain. Still, we are making progress.

One of the more interesting things I learned while studying ethics in school is that the Bible itself reveals a work in progress in terms of theology and ethics. At first there was the ethical position that is highlighted in the book of Deuteronomy. Scholars refer to this as Deuteronomist theology. It is a very simple black and white theology. I will summarize it this way: If you obey God, you have chosen God's blessings and therefore life; if you disobey God, you have chosen God's curses and therefore death. Choose life, the writer says. None of us would disagree with that. The problem, however, is this: How do we always know when we are choosing life or choosing death?

During the Trump administration, the phrase "alternative facts" entered our public discourse. Unfortunately for them, there are no such things as alternative facts. Facts are facts. And yet, in terms of ethics and morality there often are alternative *possibilities*. Rational people of good faith disagree on a multitude of issues. For instance, the pro-life or anti-abortion movement uses terminology pulled straight out of the book of Deuteronomy when they say, "Choose Life." Pro-choice people, for their part, argue that we should value life beyond conception and birth. Each side uses a complex set of arguments to support their position. So long as our sense of morality is a work in progress we will continue to disagree about the issue of abortion, as well as other issues such as animal rights, euthanasia and end of life issues, health care as a right or a privilege, sexuality issues, economic issues, how we should understand religious freedom, racial issues, what to do with refugees, environmental issues, and even such seemingly minor issues as whether we should allow our children to play football.

The list of questions about what is right or wrong is endless. And so long as there are disagreements about them, we should consider ourselves a work in progress. I truly believe that, as a species, we are making progress. And yet we need to begin with the awareness that not everything is black and white. We are not usually given a simple choice of blessings versus curses, life versus death. We cannot criticize the writer of Deuteronomy, however. He was simply a product of his moment.[3]

---

3. I use the male pronouns because he was likely a "he," and if he were a "she," she would likely be more flexible in her sense of right and wrong. Only a dude would formulate a Deuteronomist view of theology and ethics.

Some people have suggested that the way to look at human history is by using the analogy of an individual human being. Just as a younger person is less mature than an older person (not counting those of us who never grow up), the further we go back in history the more *immature* people were. When we deal with children, we tend to lay things out in simple black and white terms, do we not? At the time in which the book of Deuteronomy was written, perhaps the people needed simpler choices. To use the language of the Apostle Paul they needed "milk." They were not ready for "solid food." They were not ready for complex nuanced choices of right and wrong. For their civilization to stabilize after their long journey in the wilderness, they needed some simple straight talk: Worship God and you will live; chase after other gods and you will die. Very simple, right?

Then we get to Jesus. This may sound biased, but I believe Jesus was way ahead of his time.[4] He must have believed his followers were ready for some "solid food," because he sure dishes it out! Referring to those earlier days when the Israelites were less mature, he says, "You have heard that it was said to those of ancient times (in other words, their less sophisticated simpleton ancestors), 'You shall not murder.'" For the most part, that is an easy law to follow. Most of us can dance through life without committing murder. Most of us will be able to approach the Pearly Gates or the Seat of Judgment some day and say, "Nope, I didn't murder anyone. I guess I'm good, right?"

Let us compare this level of ethics and morality to building a road. Thinking that not committing murder is all there is to morality is like building a one lane dirt road. We do not need much skill for that. Jesus, however, is trying to build a multi-lane freeway in terms of ethics and morality. "But I say to you," he says, "that if you are unnecessarily *angry* or insulting to others, you can't just say to yourself, 'Well, at least I am not a murderer.'" It is more sophisticated, nuanced, and complex than that, he is saying.

He uses the same kind of moral logic with other ethical issues throughout the rest of Matthew 5. None of us have reached the apex of moral superiority just because we have not murdered anyone, committed adultery, divorced his wife (because women really did not have the same option back then), or sworn falsely. We are *all* a work in progress.

---

4. He may have been a time traveler, which could explain his exit from the tomb after three days. Just saying.

To be clear, I do not recommend anyone enrolling at the local seminary for a post-graduate degree in ethics. I would not wish that on my worst enemy, which proves by the way, that, relatively speaking, I am a damn good moral person. Still, I recommend that the next time you pass a sign that says, "Work in Progress," say to yourself, "Yes, yes I am, by golly." But don't steal the sign.

Second Chances

As I reflect on folks who might epitomize the human no-damn-goodness in our contemporary context, I have decided to stay away from the folks Captain Obvious might select, such as Donald Trump or Bernie Madoff.[5] Instead, I have decided to go with a choice that fits the *Breaking Bad, Better Call Saul,* or *The Sopranos* morally ambiguous mold. I choose Tiger Woods.

As you may recall, Tiger Woods' morally suspect woes and domestic troubles began with his then-wife, Elin Nordegren, when she apparently discovered that Tiger had been playing around with something other than golf clubs. She discovered that he was having multiple affairs and then chased him out of the house with, obviously, a five-iron. In his haste to escape her wrath he crashed into a fire hydrant and a tree as he was backing out of his driveway and then she proceeded to smash his car with said golf club.[6] This was (probably) the low point of Tiger's life, that is, until he was pulled over for a DUI a few years later, allegedly on prescription pain medicine for his multiple back surgeries, and then was involved in a terrible car accident in 2021.[7] After the initial incident, a collection of jokes about Tiger were generated on the internet. I will share a few of the ones that can be appropriately shared in a morally enlightened book such as this one:

- The police asked Tiger's wife how many times she hit him. "I can't remember," Elin said, "just put me down for a 5."
- Ping (a golf club manufacturer) has a new set of irons called "Elins." They are clubs you can beat Tiger with.
- Did you hear Tiger changed his name to Cheetah?

5. I apologize if I have offended any Bernie Madoff fans.
6. Alanis Morissette would call this ironic.
7. Tiger needs to stay out of motorized vehicles, maybe even golf carts.

- Tiger crashed into a fire hydrant and a tree. He couldn't decide between an iron or a wood.

- Tiger Woods is so rich that he owns lots of expensive cars. Now he has a hole in one.

Everyone seemed to enjoy making fun of and criticizing Tiger Woods. After all, it seemed that after all his domestic troubles and multiple back surgeries, his career was over. But then there was the last tournament of 2018 and the 2019 Masters, which he won. Tiger has played sparingly after recovering from a lower lumbar spinal fusion, the only professional athlete ever to come back from such a serious surgery.[8]

If you are not a golf fan none of this means anything at all to you, and I understand that. However, just know that sports talk radio had a field day (or would that be a "course day"?) over the Tiger "comeback" story. Television ratings for any tournament in which he competes on the weekend goes through the roof. People who had not watched a minute of golf in the past few years were back to watching professional golf. Personally, I was moderately caught up in the Tiger comeback, and yet I did not think much about it until I was listening to sports talk radio one Monday night driving home from Bible study. The radio host told his co-host that what we were seeing is none other than the great American Myth of Redemption, otherwise known as the Myth of Second Chances. And we love it.

The American Myth of Redemption is rivaled only by the Myth of the American Dream, the rags-to-riches Horatio Alger story. A professor from the University of Tennessee, Dr. Wilfred McClay, has written extensively on the American Myth of Redemption. He defines redemption in both sacred and secular terms. In sacred terms, redemption means "deliverance from sin, atonement, expiation, absolution, regeneration, the debt forgiven, release from stigmatization, the ransom paid, the captive set free." In secular terms, redemption means "a new beginning, a fresh start, a transformation, a liberation from guilt, a new lease on life, even if not an entirely clean slate." McClay says that the Myth of Redemption touches upon one of the deepest moral and emotional foundations of American life: We love our heroes to fail or fall and then rise to the occasion. "Leaders," he says, "are more likely to be embraced fully and heartily when they have first been shown to stumble badly, to be flawed

---

8. If you do not know golf requires athleticism, I do not know what to do with you.

and human and vulnerable, and then allowed to rise again, scarred to be sure, but also contrite and humbled and seasoned."[9]

Using an image proposed by Isaiah Berlin, "crooked timber," I suggest Tiger Woods has been swinging with flawed "crooked sticks" in terms of his golf and his personal life, and now we shall see if he can consistently hit the ball straight—literally and figuratively. Only time will tell.[10]

America, of course, did not invent this myth or story of redemption or second chances. We inherited it from our Judeo-Christian tradition. As the Adam and Eve myth suggests, humanity *is* constructed out of crooked timber. Therefore, according to the biblical narrative, God entered into one covenant or agreement after another to try to get people to "straighten up."[11] If the mythology of scripture can be trusted, God has given humanity second, third, fourth chances—and more. There have been covenants made between God and Noah, Abraham, Moses, and King David—just to name the big ones. In Christian mythology, the final covenant is made with humanity through Jesus . . . who dies on a straight piece of timber.

The covenant God makes with Jeremiah is particularly interesting. The sixth-century Israelites are exiled in Babylon. They believe this is due to their unfaithfulness to God—their crooked timber-ness. They believe God is punishing them. The prophet Jeremiah, who is witnessing all of this, decides to instill a little hope in them by claiming that God will make a *new covenant* with them and give them another chance. It will be unlike the covenants of the past, especially the one with Moses that consisted of a written Law. This time, says Jeremiah, God will put the Law *within them* and will *write it on their hearts* (31:33). Jeremiah hopes that this time, because it will become part of our inner nature, God's covenant will stick and will lead to their redemption.

A second example of the Myth of Redemption is found in Psalm 51. According to tradition, Psalm 51 reflects King David's indiscretion with Bathsheba. Like Tiger Woods, David seems to have been a bit of a "player," if you know what I mean. He is certainly no damn good. This psalm reflects his—or an anonymous writer's—sincere contrite heart. He is seeking redemption through God's mercy and love. He wants to

9. McClay, "Still the Redeemer Nation," *Wilson Quarterly*, Spring 2013.

10. A question to ponder is, would we have made such a big deal out of a historically important athlete's indiscretions if he had not been a person of color?

11. And presumably hit the ball straighter.

be made "whiter than snow."[12] Using words that sound like Jeremiah's covenant with God, the psalmist wants a "clean heart." This is one of the clearest examples in the Bible of the Myth of Redemption, the Myth of Second Chances.

Jesus, of course, is the *embodiment* of the Myth of Redemption, the Myth of Second Chances. John's Gospel offers the perfect analogy of this myth: "Unless a grain of wheat falls in the earth and dies, it remains just a single grain; but if it dies, it bears much fruit" (John 12:24). This is a coded reference to the death and resurrection of Jesus, written decades after Jesus died on that piece of timber, yet it has much broader implications. It speaks very clearly to the Myth of Redemption and Second Chances. Something needs to die to bear fruit. Someone needs to fall from grace to be redeemed. I ask you: Isn't there something uniquely American about someone who was good, becomes no damn good, and then becomes good once again?[13]

The Struggle Continues

The title of this book, "People Are No Damn Good," is meant to be an exaggeration of sorts. It's almost a meaningless statement. It's almost like saying, "Dogs bark at strangers." Of course, they do. It's part of their nature. My Yorkie barks more than the average dog because that's part of what it means to be a Yorkie. It's not his personality, his upbringing, or the quality of the food he eats that makes him bark so much. It's his *breed*. To a large extent, the human "breed" is no damn good as well. No amount of therapy, medication, or high-brow training will make much of a difference. It matters very little how well we are raised, how well-balanced our diets are, or how much we enjoy our jobs, spouses, children, pets, weather, recreational opportunities, books, hobbies, sex, or vacations. We are a less hairy version of an insane Yorkie. We will "bark" (i.e., do bad things) given enough ability and opportunity. As I stated earlier, the biggest mystery is why some of us do *good* things on occasion.

The subtitle of this book, "A Pastor's Struggle with Ethics and Morality," is *not* an exaggeration of sorts. The reader may have struggled with an initial interpretation of this subtitle. Am I, the author, trying to say that

12. Sort of like Michael Jackson, but not really.

13. Isn't that the hope for America as a country, that we would become "good" (not great) once again?

some, many, or all pastors, priests, rabbis, imams, gurus, etc., struggle in a professional sense to understand the nature of humanity in terms of good and evil? Or am I trying to say that I, personally, have struggled, and continue to struggle with, being and doing good rather than bad? I suppose what I have accomplished in my subtitle is a double entendre of sorts. The first interpretation is obvious—all religious professionals, as well as other professionals in the social and mental sciences, struggle with the question of humanity's inherent goodness or badness. The second interpretation, that I, personally, struggle with a sense of right and wrong, is much more awkward to admit. Of course, with our inability to maintain absolute privacy in today's social media-driven climate, the most curious among you can find enough skeletons in my closet to start a lucrative bone marrow cottage industry from your garage. As you do so, however, remember that I am still a work in progress.

Bibliography

AJOT. Why Warren Buffett Doesn't Think Climate Change Is His Problem | AJOT. COM, February 19, 2016.

Brooks, David. "The Moral Bucket List," *The New York Times*, April 11, 2015.

Captain Obvious. https://uncyclopedia.ca/wiki/Captain_Obvious.

Freakonomics. https://en.wikipedia.org/wiki/Freakonomics.

Haidt, Jonathan. *The Righteous Mind: Why Good People are Divided by Politics and Religion*. Vintage, 2012.

Kosterman, Chuck. *But What If We're Wrong: Thinking about the Present as If it Were the Past*. Simon & Schuster, 92.

Hauerwas, Stanley. "Called to Communion: Reformation Meets Rome." October 29, 1995.

Ingraham, Christopher. *Washington Post* article, June 19, 2018.

Lampert, Vincent. https://en.wikipedia.org/wiki/Vincent_Lampert.

Lukianoff, Greg, and Haidt, Jonathan. *The Coddling of the American Mind: How Good Intentions and Bad Ideas Are Setting Up a Generation for Failure*. Penguin Books, 2018. https://english.stackexchange.com/questions/185731/what-is-the-origin-of-pale-male-and-stale.

Matthew Effect. https://en.wikipedia.org/wiki/Matthew_effect.

McClay, Wilfred M. "Still the Redeemer Nation." *Wilson Quarterly*, Spring 2013.

McFague, Sallie. *Models of God: Theology for an Ecological, Nuclear Age*. Philadelphia: Fortress Press, 1987.

National Center for Health Statistics (CDC), Jun 2018.

Pavlovitz, John. *Hope and other Superpowers: A Life-Affirming, Love-Defending, Butt-Kicking, World-Saving Manifesto*. New York: Simon & Schuster, 2018.

Putnam, Robert D. *The Upswing: How America Came Together a Century Ago and How We Can Do It Again*. Simon & Schuster, 2020.

Reading Rockets. https://www.readingrockets.org/articles/researchbytopic/4862.

Rediger, G. Lloyd. *Clergy Killers: Guidance for Pastors and Congregations Under Attack*. Westminster John Knox, 1997

Shelley, Marshall. *Well-Intentioned Dragons: Ministering to Problem People in the Church*. Baker, 1985.

Stout, Martha. *The Sociopath Next Door*, Broadway Books, 2005.

Theory of Everything. https://en.wikipedia.org/wiki/Theory_of_everything.

Turpin case. https://en.wikipedia.org/wiki/Turpin_case.

Vance, J. D. *Hillbilly Elegy: A Memoir of a Family and Culture in Crisis*. Harper, 2016.

Wiesel, Elie. Nobel Lecture, December 11, 1986.

Williams, Roy H., and Drew, Michael R. *Pendulum: How Past Generations Shape Our Present and Predict Our Future,* Vanguard Press, 2012.

Wrede, William. *The Messianic Secret.* 1901.